T0189377

Advances in Computer Vision and Pattern Recognition

Titles in this series now included in the Thomson Reuters Book Citation Index!

Advances in Computer Vision and Pattern Recognition is a series of books which brings together current developments in this multi-disciplinary area. It covers both theoretical and applied aspects of computer vision, and provides texts for students and senior researchers in topics including, but not limited to:

- Deep learning for vision applications
- Computational photography
- Biological vision
- Image and video processing
- Document analysis and character recognition
- Biometrics
- Multimedia
- Virtual and augmented reality
- Vision for graphics
- Vision and language
- Robotics

Ke Gu · Hongyan Liu · Chengxu Zhou

Quality Assessment of Visual Content

 Springer

Ke Gu ⓘ
Faculty of Information Technology
Beijing University of Technology
Beijing, China

Hongyan Liu ⓘ
Faculty of Information Technology
Beijing University of Technology
Beijing, China

Chengxu Zhou ⓘ
Faculty of Information Technology
Beijing University of Technology
Beijing, China

ISSN 2191-6586   ISSN 2191-6594 (electronic)
Advances in Computer Vision and Pattern Recognition
ISBN 978-981-19-3349-3   ISBN 978-981-19-3347-9 (eBook)
https://doi.org/10.1007/978-981-19-3347-9

This Springer imprint is published by the registered company Springer Nature Singapore Pte Ltd.
The registered company address is: 152 Beach Road, #21-01/04 Gateway East, Singapore 189721,
Singapore

Preface

Nowadays, the visual signals collected nationwide exceed 500,000 TB per day, accounting for 85% of the total Internet traffic. How to make full use of and deep mine the massive visual signals via advanced image processing techniques is the key to promote the rapid development of industries such as security surveillance, medical applications, distance education, social networking, and so on. During the past two decades, important image processing techniques, such as image quality assessment (QA) and enhancement, and object detection and recognition, have attracted extensive and in-depth studies from researchers in the fields of multimedia signal processing, computer image processing, pattern recognition and intelligent systems, automatic detection technology, etc., and have obtained a series of important research accomplishments. The acquisition equipment, storage media, transmission system, and processing algorithm inevitably have an impact on visual signals during the processes from collecting and generating to receiving visual signals, which causes the degradation of image quality and further inhibits the accuracy of subsequent object detection and recognition algorithms. Therefore, image QA is usually considered as the basis of the above-mentioned important image processing techniques, possessing two significant capabilities: One is that image QA can be used to monitor the whole procedure of visual signal processing and the other is that it can be employed to optimize the model structure and parameters of visual signal processing techniques. Based on the aforesaid analyses, this book mainly reviews the representative research on image QA during the past decade and analyzes their applications, performance, and prospects in various important fields, such as screen content images, 3D-synthesized images, sonar images, enhanced images, light-field images, virtual reality images, and super-resolution images, expecting to provide guidance and reference for engineering applications in various types of fields.

The main audiences of this book are graduate students, engineers, specialists, and scholars who are interested in image QA techniques in varied subject areas, e.g., optics, electronics, mathematics, photographic techniques, and computer technology. The authors anticipate that a systematic review of the current state of the technologies, key challenges, and future trends in QA of visual signals will enable the readers to obtain a deeper, more comprehensive, and more systematic understanding and appreciation of image QA and ideally will offer a positive impetus to the work and research.

In Chap. 1, the authors first outline the basic theories from the classification of image QA, namely subjective assessment and objective assessment, to the classification of objective image QA, namely full-reference assessment, reduced-reference assessment, and no-reference assessment according to the presence of distortion-free reference images or not. The authors then briefly analyze the research background, image characteristics, and cutting-edge technologies of different types of image QA in hot fields, such as screen content images, 3D-synthesized images, sonar images, enhanced images, light-field images, virtual reality images, and super-resolution images.

Screen content images are generated by computers, covering massive Internet information. Screen content images are composed of three kinds of complicated contents, namely texts, graphics, and illustrations, in each of which distortion causes various degrees of degradation. For the QA of screen content images, Chap. 2 first introduces the full-reference QA method based on structural similarity, in order to estimate structural changes and different statistical properties of regions. Second, it presents the reduced-reference QA method based on the fusion of macroscopic and microscopic features, in order to solve the problem of unsatisfactory prediction monotonicity. Third, it introduces the no-reference QA method based on adaptive multi-scale weighting and big data learning, in order to address the issues of monotonous color and simple shape in screen content images. Finally, the authors discuss the future research trend of QA of screen content image and point out that it is necessary to construct accurate and efficient objective QA models of screen content images.

3D-synthesized images possess the significant function of generating new viewpoints based on rendering technique, but tend to introduce specific geometric distortions that cause the quality degradation. For the QA of 3D-synthesized images, Chap. 3 first presents the no-reference QA method based on autoregressive modeling and multi-scale natural scene statistical analysis, in order to capture geometric distortion. Then, it introduces the no-reference QA method based on pixel-based changes in transform domains, in order to measure color and depth distortion. Finally, it presents the no-reference QA method on account of structural variations caused by geometric, sharpness, and color distortions, in order to assess the quality of blurred, discontinuous, and stretched 3D-synthesized images.

Sonar images contain important underwater information like submarine geomorphology, marine organism, and wreck remains in dim light and are prone to typical underwater distortion due to the poor underwater acoustic channel condition. For the QA of sonar images, Chap. 4 first introduces the sonar image quality database and the full-reference QA methods based on local entropy and statistical and structural information, in order to measure underwater distortion in sonar images. Second, it presents the task- and perception-oriented reduced-reference QA methods based on the human visual system, in order to assess the poor-quality sonar images in the complicated underwater environment. Finally, it describes the no-reference QA method based on contour degradation measurement, in order to overcome the difficulty of failure to acquire reference sonar images in the dynamic underwater environment.

Image enhancement has the function of changing the visual perceptual quality of images. How to optimize the model structures and parameters to achieve proper enhancement based on the QA of enhanced images has been a hot issue in recent years. For the QA of enhanced images, Chap. 5 first establishes the contrast-changed image QA database and presents the reduced-reference QA methods based on phase congruency and histogram statistics. Then, it introduces the no-reference QA methods that fuse non-structural information, sharpness, and naturalness and are based on feature extraction and regression. Finally, it shows evaluation criteria guidance-based automatic contrast enhancement technique.

Light-field images record the light intensity in different directions of the sensor, which is important for the research of next generation imaging technology. However, they tend to lose visual details in the processes of acquisition and transmission. For the QA of light-field images, Chap. 6 first introduces the full-reference QA method based on single- and multi-scale Gabor feature extraction, in order to address the problem of ignoring the perceived characteristic of the human visual system. Second, it illustrates the reduced-reference QA method based on depth map distortion measurement, in order to deal with different sizes of light-field images. Third, it presents the tensor-oriented no-reference QA methods based on spatial-angular measurement, in order to capture the high-dimensional characteristics of light-field images. In the end, the above-mentioned QA methods are validated on relevant databases, and the necessity of establishing efficient light-field image QA methods is pointed out.

Virtual reality images have attracted an amount of attention for providing an immersive experience. They have the characteristics of omnidirectional view, massive data, and so on, which are so vulnerable to external interference that their quality deteriorates. For the QA of virtual reality images, Chap. 7 first describes the databases that contain projection format, stitching, and double fisheye images, in order to fill the blank of lack of a virtual reality image database. Then, it presents the no-reference QA method based on the 3D convolutional neural network, in order to tackle the issue that the reference virtual reality images are inaccessible. Finally, it shows the no-reference QA method based on a multi-channel neural network, in order to overcome the problem of the full range of compression distortion in video coding technology.

It is important to generate a high-resolution image from a low-resolution image by super-resolution technique, but there often exist artifacts and blurring distortions during the process. For the QA of super-resolved images, Chap. 8 first introduces the super-resolution image database based on interpolation and image enhancement. Second, it presents the full-reference QA methods based on quality loss function and L_2 Norm. Finally, it introduces the QA approaches based on two-stage regression model, pixel similarity between image blocks, and natural scene statistical model.

This book collects the work programs of several research groups from all over the world. It introduces the image QA algorithms in various hot fields from different perspectives, which has scientific research value and engineering application value. This book is written by Ke Gu, Hongyan Liu, and Chengxu Zhou. We have received great help from Jing Liu, Shuang Shi, and Shuangyi Xie, so we would like to express our sincere thanks to the experts, authors, teachers, and friends who have guided and supported us.

Beijing, China   Ke Gu
                                                                                    Hongyan Liu
                                                                                   Chengxu Zhou

Contents

Acronyms

2D-CNN	2D convolutional neural network
3D-CNN	3D convolutional neural network
3DSWIM	3D-synthesized view image quality metric
ACR-HR	Absolute category rating-hidden reference
ADD-SSIM	Analysis of distortion distribution-based structural similarity
ADM	Accurate depth map
AGCWD	Adaptive gamma correction with weighting distribution
AGGD	Asymmetric generalized Gaussian distribution
APT	Autoregression-plus threshold
AR	Autoregression
ASIQE	Accelerated screen image quality evaluator
AVC	Advanced video coding
BER	Bit error rate
BIQME	Blind image quality measure of enhanced images
BL	Bi-lateral
BLL	Binarized low-frequency
BQMS	Blind quality measure for screen content images
BRISQUE	Blind/referenceless image spatial quality evaluator
CC	Contrast change
CCID2014	Contrast-changed image database
CC-NSIs	Camera-captured natural scene images
CCT	Cross-content-type
CDF	Cumulative normal distribution function
C-D-F 9/7	Cohen-Daubechies-Feauveau 9/7 wavelet transform
CGIs	Computer graphic images
CI-VSD	Color-involved view synthesis distortion
CNNs	Convolutional neural networks
C-PCQI	Colorfulness-based patch-based contrast quality index
CPP-PSNR	Craster parabolic projection-based peak signal-to-noise ratio
CP-PSNR	Content-based peak signal-to-noise ratio
CROSS	Cross-reference omnidirectional stitching dataset

CU	Coding unit
CVIQD	Compression virtual reality image quality database
DCT	Discrete cosine transform
DeepQA	Deep image quality assessment
DeepSim	Deep similarity
DIBR	Depth image-based rendering
DI-VSD	Depth-involved view synthesis distortion
DMOS	Differential mean opinion score
DWT	Discrete wave transform
EAP	Equal-area projection
EID	Enhanced image database
EOT	Existence of target
EOV	Variation of entropy
EPIs	Epi-polar images
ERP	Equirectangular projection
FES	Free energy excitation significance detection technology
FoV	Field of view
FR	Full-reference
FSIM	Feature similarity
FTQM	Fourier transform-based scalable image quality metric
FVV	Free viewpoint video
GB	Gaussian blur
GDD	Gradient direction distribution
GGD	General Gaussian distribution
GMSD	Gradient magnitude standard deviation
GN	Gaussian noise
GUI	Graphical user interface
HE	Histogram equalization
HEVC	High-efficiency video coding
HEVSQP	High-efficiency view synthesis quality prediction
HMD	Head-mounted display
HMF	Histogram modification framework
HOG	Histogram of oriented gradient
HR	High-resolution
HVS	Human visual system
IAM	Image activity measurement
IGM	Internal generative mechanism
ITU	International telecommunication union
IW-SSIM	Information weighted structural similarity
J2C	JPEG2000 compression
JC	JPEG compression
J-S	Jensen-Shannon
KRCC	Kendall rank correlation coefficient
LBP	Local binary pattern
LC	Layer segmentation backed coding

LCD	Liquid crystal display
LF	Light-field
LF IQM	Light-field image quality assessment metric
LFC	Light-field coherence
LFCIA	Light-field cyclopean image array
LGF-LFC	Log-Gabor feature-based light-field coherence
LL	Low-frequency
LOG	Laplacian of Gaussian
LOGS	Local geometric distortions and global sharpness
LPI	Laplace pyramid image
LR	Low-resolution
MAD	Most apparent distortion
MASM	Macrostructure measurement
MB	Motion blur
MC360IQA	Multi-channel neural network for blind 360-degree image quality assessment
MDID	Multiply distorted image database
MGGD	Multivariate generalized Gaussian distribution
MISM	Microstructure measurement
ML	Maximum likelihood
MLR	Multiple linear regression
MNSS	Multi-scale natural scene statistical analysis
MOSs	Mean opinion scores
MP-PSNR-RR	Morphological pyramid peak signal-to-noise ratio reduced reference
MRDM	Multi resolution depth map
MRF	Markov random field
MSCN	Mean subtracted and contrast normalized
MSE	Mean square error
MVD	Multi-view video plus depth
MW-PSNR	Morphological wavelet peak signal-to-noise ratio
NCP-PSNR	Non-content-based peak signal-to-noise ratio
NIQMC	No-reference image quality metric for contrast distortion
NQM	Noise quality measure
NR	No-reference
NRCDM	No-reference contour degradation measurement
NR-LFQA	No-reference light-field image quality assessment
NR-SRIQA	No-reference super-resolution image quality assessment
NSI	Natural scene image
NSIQM	No-reference sonar image quality metric
NSIs	Natural scene images
NSS	Natural scene statistics
OA	Opinion-aware
O-DMOS	Overall differential mean opinion score
OPT	Optical flow estimation

OR	Outlier ratio
OU	Opinion-unaware
OUT	Outliers in 3D-synthesized images
PC	Phase congruence
PCA	Principal component analysis
PCQI	Patch-based contrast quality index
PCS	Pair comparison sorting
PCSC	Principal component spatial characteristics
PDF	Probability density function
PLCC	Pearson linear correlation coefficient
PR	Partial-reference
PSIQP	Partial-reference sonar image quality predictor
PSNR	Peak signal-to-noise ratio
P-VQA	Perceptual video quality assessment
QA	Quality assessment
QACS	Quality assessment of compressed screen content image
QADS	Quality assessment database for super-resolution images
QMC	Quality assessment metric of contrast
QoE	Quality of experience
QP	Quantization parameter
RBF	Radial basis function
RD	Rate distortion
RDCT	Reconstructed discrete cosine transform
RDO	Rate distortion optimization
ReLU	Rectified linear unit
RICE	Robust image contrast enhancement
RIQMC	Reduced-reference image quality metric for contrast change
RMSE	Root mean square error
RR	Reduced-reference
RWQMS	Reduced-reference wavelet-domain quality measure of screen content pictures
SAIs	Sub-aperture images
SAS	Synthetic aperture sonar
SC	Screen content image compression
SCIs	Screen content images
SD	Standard deviation
SGD	Stochastic gradient descent
SI	Spatial information
SIFT	Scale-invariant feature transform
SIQA	Sonar image quality assessment
SIQAD	Screen image quality assessment database
SIQD	Sonar image quality database
SIQE	Screen image quality evaluator
SIQM	Structure-induced quality metric
SIQP	Sonar image quality predictor

SLTDM	Stereo-like taxonomy depth map
SPIHT	Set partitioning in hierarchical trees
SPQA	Screen content perceptual quality assessment
S-PSNR	Spherical peak signal-to-noise ratio
SQI	Screen content image quality index
SQMS	Saliency-guided quality measure of screen content
SR	Super-resolution
SRCC	Spearman rank correlation coefficient
SS	Single stimulus
SSD	Sum of squared difference
SSDC	System-sparse set and disparity coding
SSIM	Structural similarity
SSIQE	Simplified screen image quality evaluator
SSMR	Single stimulus with multiple repetitions
STD	Structure-texture decomposition
SVD	Singular value decomposition
SVQI	Structural variation-based quality index
SVR	Support vector regression
TAVI	Tensor angular variation index
Tensor-NLFQ	Tensor-oriented no-reference light-field image quality evaluator
TH	Transmission loss under high-efficiency video coding compression
TPSIQA	Task- and perception-oriented sonar image quality assessment
TS	Transmission loss under screen content image compression
UAC	Underwater acoustic channel
UCA	Unified content-type adaptive
ULBP	Uniform local binary pattern
V-DMOS	Vectored differential mean opinion score
VIFP	Visual information fidelity in pixel domain
VQEG	BZVideo quality experts group
VR	Virtual reality
VSD	View synthesis distortion
VSNR	Visual signal-to-noise ratio
VSQA	View synthesis quality assessment
VSQP	View synthesis quality prediction
WLBP	Weighted local binary pattern
WN	White noise
WS-PSNR	Weighted-to-spherically uniform peak signal-to-noise ratio

Chapter 1
Introduction

1.1 Quality Assessment of Traditional Images

Image quality assessment (QA) is one of the basic techniques of image processing. It can evaluate the degree of image distortion by analyzing and studying the characteristics of images. In an image processing system, image QA plays an important role in system performance evaluation, algorithm analysis, and comparison.

For many decades, there has been a lot of research on image QA. These image QA approaches can be classified as subjective image QA and objective image QA based on whether a human is involved in quality evaluation. Subjective QA is expensive and time-consuming. In contrast, objective image QA uses the computational model to automatically evaluate the perceived quality of images, which is convenient and fast. Because of its advantages of high precision and strong robustness, objective image QA has been favored by a wide range of researchers. Objective image QA can be further classified into three types according to the utilization of the reference image information. They are, respectively, full-reference (FR) image QA, reduced-reference (RR) image QA, and no-reference (NR) image QA. The FR image QA utilizes complete pristine image information in the processing. The RR image QA only adopts part of the pristine image information to assess image quality. The NR image QA is totally different from the two models above-mentioned, due to its implementation of quality inferring without using any reference information. Several QA methods of traditional images are listed below, such as noise quality measure (NQM) [1], visual information fidelity in pixel domain (VIFP) [2], visual signal-to-noise ratio (VSNR) [3], the structural similarity (SSIM)-based QA method [4], the natural scene statistics (NSS)-based QA method, the information weighted structural similarity (IW-SSIM)-based QA method [5], peak signal-to-noise ratio (PSNR) [6], spherical PSNR (S-PSNR) [7], Craster parabolic projection-based PSNR (CPP-PSNR) [8], the VSNR based on the near-threshold and supra-threshold properties of human vision [3], the most apparent distortion based on the Fourier transformation and the Log-Gabor filtering [9], and so on. Most of these methods fail to effectively evaluate the quality of new types of visual signals such as screen content images, 3D-synthesized images, sonar images, enhanced images, light-field images, virtual reality images, and super-resolution images, so it is urgent to establish efficient QA methods that are specific to particular images.

1.2   Quality Assessment of Screen Content Images

With the rapid development of computer technology and the popularity of electronic devices, screen content images (SCIs) have received much attention from researchers as the main computer-generated signals. The visual quality of SCIs, which is the basis for image processing techniques, is inevitably subject to external interference during image compression, transmission, display, and so on, further resulting in poor image quality. Therefore, it is necessary to first evaluate the quality of SCIs in order to ensure the efficiency and accuracy of image processing systems. Most of the existing image QA metrics were designed based on the assumption that the human visual system (HVS) is highly adapted to deriving the scene's structural information. Besides, various QA methods of natural scene images (NSIs) have been proposed recently, most of which can effectively evaluate the quality of NSIs rather than SCIs. There are few studies on SCIs which contain complicated content like texts, graphics, and illustrations, and the distortion causes varying degrees of degradation in different areas.

This book elaborately introduces two FR QA, a RR QA and two NR QA methods of SCIs proposed in recent years, and the details are illustrated in Chap. 2. One of the FR QA models of SCIs is named structural variation-based quality index (SVQI) on account of the association between the perceived quality and the structural variation [10]. The other FR QA model of SCIs incorporates both visual field adaptation and information content weighting into structural similarity-based local QA [11]. The RR QA method of SCIs extracts the macroscopic and microscopic structures in the original and distorted SCIs separately and compares the differences between them in order to obtain the overall quality score [12]. One of the NR QA models of SCIs named unified content-type adaptive (UCA) is applicable across content types [13]. The other NR QA model of SCIs is based on big data learning and uses four types of features including the picture complexity, the screen content statistics, the global brightness quality, and the sharpness of details to predict the perceived quality of SCIs [14]. In addition, there are some methods that can be learned by any interested readers, such as screen content perceptual quality assessment (SPQA) [15], reduced-reference wavelet-domain quality measure of screen content pictures (RWQMS) [16], blind quality measure for screen content images (BQMS) [17], and so on.

1.3 Quality Assessment of 3D-Synthesized Images

Technological advances in 3D visual signals continue to make 3D imaging and display techniques draw a large amount of attention in several different fields, such as remote education, security monitoring, entertainment, and so on. The depth image-based rendering (DIBR) technique is utilized to synthesize new viewpoint images of the same scene from a limited number of reference-free multiple views, solving the problems of high cost and complexity [18]. The introduction of DIBR causes geometric distortion in 3D-synthesized images, which results in a decrease in the perceived quality of 3D-synthesized images. With this concern, it is imperative to design efficient perceptual QA methods for 3D-synthesized images before processing these images to avoid operating on low-quality images and reducing the efficiency of the whole process. The DIBR technologies introduce particular distortions when utilizing depth information to transfer occluded regions on the outlines of foreground objects, which are more likely to destroy the semantic structure of images. Several image QA approaches are tailored to particular scenes or common distortions (i.e., blur and noise) and, thus, are not applicable to evaluate the perceived quality of 3D-synthesized images.

To solve the problems mentioned above, the researchers have been concerned about 3D-synthesized image QA approaches based on DIBR. This book elaborately introduces six NR 3D-synthesized image QA approaches, and the details are illustrated in Chap. 3. These methods are mainly classified into three categories, namely the models based on NSS, domain transformation, and structural transformation. The first type includes two blind image QA models based on the autoregression (AR) with local image description [19] and the multi-scale natural scene statistical analysis (MNSS) using two new NSS models [20]. One of the second-type methods is the high-efficiency view synthesis quality prediction (HEVSQP) QA model that quantifies the effects of color and depth distortion in 3D-synthesized images [21]. The other one is the new QA model which combines local and global models to evaluate geometric distortion and sharpness changes in wavelet domain [22]. The third type includes two image quality prediction models based on local changes in structure and color and global changes in brightness [23] as well as the image complexity [24]. In addition, there are some methods that can be learned by any interested readers. For example, the 3D-synthesized view image quality metric (3DSWIM) [25] measures local geometric distortion and global sharpness changes [26]. The view synthesis quality assessment (VSQA) modifies the distorted view or similarity view from the reference view and the composite view [27]. The reduced version of morphological pyramid peak signal-to-noise ratio (MP-PSNR-RR) image QA can evaluate the geometric distortion in 3D-synthesized images influence generated by DIBR [28].

1.4   Quality Assessment of Sonar Images

It is possible to obtain important information by observing sonar images, such as submarine geomorphology, marine organism, and wreck remains, so the sonar imaging technique is widely utilized in the field of ocean exploration, underwater rescue [29, 30], etc. The sonar imaging technique can acquire clearer images in a dim environment based on the temporal distribution of echo received by sonar equipment. However, the sonar images are inevitably distorted due to the influence of the complex underwater environment in the formation and propagation processes, resulting in poor sonar image quality. Therefore, the QA prior to the analysis of sonar images can exclude low-quality sonar images with information loss, further increasing the efficiency of performing underwater tasks. Generally speaking, images obtained in different scenes possess various characteristics. For example, NSIs have rich color changes, complex textures, and coarse lines. Sonar images are gray and simple due to the unavailability of natural light, which differ dramatically from NSIs [31]. In addition, more attention has been paid to the structural features of sonar images containing task information in underwater detection and scene rendering. Most of the previous QA studies focus on camera-captured natural scene images (CC-NSIs) and are not suitable for effectively assessing the visual quality of sonar images.

In order to fill the gap in the study of sonar image QA, this book introduces an FR image QA, two RR image QA, and an NR image QA methods of sonar images presented in recent years, and the details are illustrated in Chap. 4. The FR image QA approach named the sonar image quality predictor (SIQP) combines the statistical and structural information [32]. One of the RR image QA approaches is the task- and perception-oriented sonar image quality assessment (TPSIQA), which considers the underwater tasks and better estimates the perceptual quality of sonar images [33]. The other RR image QA approach is the partial-reference sonar image quality predictor (PSIQP) that can predict the image quality by using image information, comfort index, and SSIM index [34]. The NR image QA approach is the no-reference contour degradation measurement (NRCDM), which can evaluate the sonar image quality on the basis of the degree of contour degradation [35]. In addition, there are some classical QA methods of sonar images, namely the QA method of synthetic aperture sonar (SAS) based on navigation error degree [36]; the method based on sonar platform motion, navigation error level, and environmental characteristics [37]; and the method called no-reference sonar image quality metric (NSIQM) that measures the contour degradation degree of the test and the filtered images [38].

1.5   Quality Assessment of Enhanced Images

In many real-world applications, such as object detection and recognition, original images require to be enhanced appropriately to improve the perceptual quality [39]. Image enhancement is the frequently used technique for improving the visual quality of images. Among, contrast enhancement is a popular type of image enhancement method that can improve the perceived quality of most images. Its goal is to create more aesthetically beautiful or visually instructive images or both. The contrast of an image can be dramatically increased by reassigning pixel values. Due to its ease of use and speed, histogram equalization is commonly employed in many image post-processing systems. However, the problem in these methods such as over-enhancement still requires attention. Therefore, it has been a hot issue in recent years to optimize the model structures and parameters in order to realize appropriate enhancement using enhanced image QA. The classic image QA methods may be separated into subjective and objective evaluation. For current image enhancement studies, the quality of enhanced images is mostly determined by subjective tests, which are time-consuming and costly. To overcome the limitations of subjective assessment, researchers have turned their research priorities to the design of objective assessment. Despite the emergence of hundreds of objective image QA models, very few efforts have been made for the issue of contrast-changed image QA.

This book elaborately introduces two enhanced image databases, two NR QA approaches of enhanced images, and two contrast enhancement methods, and the details are illustrated in Chap. 5. One enhanced image database is based on five image enhancement algorithms and three image processing software [40]. The other database includes 655 images which are created by five categories of contrast-oriented transfer functions [41]. One of NR QA approaches of enhanced images is the first opinion-unaware (OU) blind image QA metric named blind image quality measure of enhanced images (BIQME), which can effectively obtain the prediction quality of enhanced image [39]. The other NR QA approach is based on the theory of information maximization to realize the judgment of images having better contrast and quality [42]. One of the contrast enhancement methods is an automatic robust image contrast enhancement (RICE) model based on saliency preservation [43]. The other image contrast enhancement framework is based on cloud images, solving the difficulty of multi-criteria optimization [44].

1.6 Quality Assessment of Light-Field Images

In recent years, the light-field (LF) imaging technology has attracted wide attention in many practical applications, such as underwater imaging, 3D object recognition, super-resolution (SR) imaging, and so on. Yet, the LF images will inevitably damage visual details in the acquisition, coding, denoising, transmission, rendering, and display, which will affect the perceived quality of low-frequency images.

In order to better assess the quality of LF images, a large number of researchers have done work to design different LF image QA approaches. This book elaborately introduces an FR LF image QA, a RR LF image QA, and two NR LF image QA methods proposed in recent years, and the details are illustrated in Chap. 6. The FR LF image QA methods measure the LF coherence between the pristine LF image and the corrupted LF image to evaluate the image quality [45]. The RR LF image QA methods investigate the association between the perceptual quality of LF images and the distortion of the estimated depth map [46]. One of the NR LF image QA methods named no-reference light-field image quality assessment (NR-LFQA) evaluates the quality degradation of LF images on the basis of the spatial information and the angular consistency [47]. The other NR LF image QA method is a novel tensor-oriented no-reference light-field image quality evaluator named Tensor-NLFQ that is based on tensor theory. In addition, there are some methods that can be learned by any interested readers. For example, [48] came up with an FR image QA model called the multi-order derivative feature-based model to explore the multi-order derivative features. Huang et al. [49] presented an FR LF image QA algorithm that is based on dense distortion curve analysis and scene information statistics.

1.7   Quality Assessment of Virtual Reality Images

With the development of multimedia techniques, virtual reality (VR) technologies, such as 3D real-time image display and 3D positioning tracking, have attracted a lot of attention. The images generated by VR technologies can provide observers with an immersive and realistic viewing experience and further improve the efficiency of human-machine interaction. However, the omnidirectional view characteristics lead to high resolution and massive data of 360-degree images, which in turn make images so sensitive to external interference that their quality deteriorates. Based on this consideration, it is significant to design efficient image QA methods for VR images to prevent low-quality images from causing undesirable user experience. Traditional image QA methods have poor performance due to the limitation of VR image databases and cannot effectively assess the perceptual quality of VR images with high-dimensional characteristics.

In order to fill the gap in the research of QA methods of VR images, this book elaborately introduces four different QA methods of VR images proposed in recent years, and the details are illustrated in Chap. 7. These VR image QA approaches are classified into four categories according to the different observing subjects, namely subjective QA, objective QA, subjective-objective QA, and cross-reference stitching QA, respectively. The subjective QA method is based on the database named compression VR image quality database (CVIQD) [50] that consists of raw images and images with JPEG compression to evaluate the VR image quality. The objective QA approach named weighted-to-spherically uniform peak signal-to-noise ratio (WS-PSNR) assesses the visual quality of VR images in terms of the reweighting of pixels according to their position in space [51]. For subjective-objective QA, deep learning is employed to assess the omnidirectional images quality. Two typical image QA methods named vectored differential mean opinion score (V-DMOS) and overall differential mean opinion score (O-DMOS) are presented to effectively assess the panoramic image quality [52]. For cross-reference stitching QA method, which focuses on evaluating the area of stitched omnidirectional images, [53] designed a typically used method. The method concentrates on the stitching regions by convolutional sparse coding and compound feature selection to quantify ghosting and structure.

1.8 Quality Assessment of Super-Resolution Images

With the increasing demand for image or video resolution, the SR technique is widely utilized in medical image processing, infrared imaging, security monitoring, and other fields. The high-resolution images can be generated from the given low-resolution images via the image SR techniques like bilinear interpolation, bicubic interpolation, and the Lanczos resampling. However, these pixel integration operations cause serious mixed artifacts and fuzzy distortion in the edge and high-frequency regions, resulting in poor image perception quality. Therefore, it is essential to effectively assess the SR image perceptual quality before further analysis of SR images, in order to improve the accuracy of processing systems. The commonly used image QA methods do not systematically consider the artifacts and distortions that appear in SR images, so they are not applicable to assess the SR image quality.

Deep learning, especially convolutional neural networks (CNNs), has been broadly applied to image processing tasks [54]. Therefore, this book elaborately introduces two QA methods based on deep learning and a QA method based on NSS of SR images presented recently, and the details are illustrated in Chap. 8. One of the deep learning-based QA methods of SR images is the method based on a cascade regression, which establishes the mapping relationship between multiple natural statistical features and visual perception scores by learning a two-layer regression model [55]. The other deep learning-based QA method of SR images is the method based on the combination of SR image QA loss function and L_2 Norm, which can effectively assess the visual perceptual quality of SR images [56]. The NSS-based QA method of SR images is the method that quantifies the degradation of image quality using deviations from statistical models of frequency energy falloff and spatial continuity of high-quality natural images [57]. In addition, there are also some approaches, such as the metric named the deep similarity (DeepSim) [58], the dual-stream siamese network used to assess the distorted image perceptual quality score [59], and the model called the deep image quality assessment (DeepQA) [60]. The interested readers can learn these above-mentioned methods on their own.

References

1. Damera-Venkata N, Kite TD, Geisler WS (2000) Image quality assessment based on a degradation model. IEEE Trans Image Process 9(4):636–650
2. Sheikh HR, Bovik AC (2006) Image information and visual quality. IEEE Trans Image Process 15(2):430–444
3. Chandler DM, Hemami SS (2007) VSNR: a wavelet-based visual signal-to-noise ratio for natural images. IEEE Trans Image Process 16(9):2284–2298
4. Wang Z, Bovik AC, Sheikh HR et al (2004) Image quality assessment: from error visibility to structural similarity. IEEE Trans Image Process 13(4):600–612
5. Wang Z, Li Q (2011) Information content weighting for perceptual image quality assessment. IEEE Trans Image Process 20(5):1185–1198
6. Saad MA, Bovik AC, Charrier C (2012) Blind image quality assessment: a natural scene statistics approach in the DCT domain. IEEE Trans Image Process 21(8):3339–3352

7. Yu M, Lakshman H, Girod B (2015) A frame work to evaluate omnidirectional video coding schemes. In: Paper presented at the IEEE international symposium on mixed and augmented reality, pp 31–36, Oct 2015
8. Zakharchenko V, Choi KP, Park JH (2016) Quality metric for spherical panoramic video. In: Paper presented at the optics and photonics for information processing X, San Diego CA
9. Larson EC, Chandler DM (2010) Most apparent distortion: full-reference image quality assessment and the role of strategy. J Electron Imaging 19(1):011006
10. Gu K, Qiao J, Min X et al (2017) Evaluating quality of screen content images via structural variation analysis. IEEE Trans Vis Comput Graph 24(10):2689–2701
11. Wang S, Gu K, Zeng K et al (2016) Objective quality assessment and perceptual compression of screen content images. IEEE Comput Graph Appl 38(1):47–58
12. Xia Z, Gu K, Wang S (2020) Towards accurate quality estimation of screen content pictures with very sparse reference information. IEEE Trans Ind Electron 67(3):2251–2261
13. Min X, Ma K, Gu K et al (2017) Unified blind quality assessment of compressed natural, graphic, and screen content images. IEEE Trans Image Process 26(11):5462–5474
14. Gu K, Zhou J, Qiao J et al (2017) No-reference quality assessment of screen content pictures. IEEE Trans Image Process 26(8):4005–4018
15. Yang H, Fang Y, Lin W (2015) Perceptual quality assessment of screen content images. IEEE Trans Image Process 24(11):4408–4421
16. Wang S, Gu K, Zhang X et al (2016) Subjective and objective quality assessment of compressed screen content images. IEEE J Emerg Sel Top Circuits Syst 6(4):532–543
17. Gu K, Zhai G, Lin W et al (2016) Learning a blind quality evaluation engine of screen content images. Neurocomputing 196:140–149
18. Battisti F, Callet PL (2016) Quality assessment in the context of FTV: challenges, first answers and open issues. IEEE ComSoc MMTC Commun Front 11(22):22–27
19. Gu K, Jakhetiya V, Qiao J et al (2018) Model-based referenceless quality metric of 3D synthesized images using local images description. IEEE Trans Image Process 27(1):394–405
20. Gu K, Qiao J, Lee S et al (2020) Multiscale natural scene statistical analysis for no-reference quality evaluation of DIBR-synthesized views. IEEE Trans Broadcast 66(1):127–139
21. Shao F, Yuan Q, Lin W et al (2018) No-reference view synthesis quality prediction for 3-D videos based on color-depth interactions. IEEE Trans Multimedia 20(3):659–674
22. Yue G, Hou C, Gu K et al (2019) Combining local and global measures for DIBR-synthesized image quality evaluation. IEEE Trans Image Process 28(4):2075–2088
23. Yan J, Fang Y, Du R et al (2020) No reference quality assessment for 3D synthesized views by local structure variation and global naturalness change. IEEE Trans Image Process 29:7443–7453
24. Wang G, Wang Z, Gu K et al (2020) Blind quality metric of DIBR-synthesized images in the discrete wavelet transform domain. IEEE Trans Image Process 29:1802–1814
25. Battisti F, Bosc E, Carli M et al (2015) Objective image quality assessment of 3D synthesized views. Signal Process Image Commun 30:78–88
26. Li L, Zhou Y, Gu K et al (2018) Quality assessment of DIBR-synthesized images by measuring local geometric distortions and global sharpness. IEEE Trans Multimedia 20(4):914–926
27. Conze PH, Robert P, Morin L (2012) Objective view synthesis quality assessment. Int Soc Opt Photonics 8288:53
28. Jakhetiya V, Gu K, Lin W et al (2018) A prediction backed model for quality assessment of screen content and 3-D synthesized images. IEEE Trans Ind Inf 14(2):652–660
29. Jeong TT (2007) Particle PHD filter multiple target tracking in sonar image. IEEE Trans Aerosp Electron Syst 43(1):409–416
30. Lo KW, Ferguson BG (2004) Automatic detection and tracking of a small surface watercraft in shallow water using a high-frequency active sonar. IEEE Trans Aerosp Electron Syst 40(4):1377–1388
31. Gu K, Wang S, Yang H (2016) Saliency-guided quality assessment of screen content images. IEEE Trans Multimedia 18(6):1098–1110

32. Chen W, Gu K, Lin W et al (2019) Statistical and structural information backed full-reference quality measure of compressed sonar images. IEEE Trans Circuits Syst Video Technol 30(2):334–348

33. Chen W, Gu K, Zhao T et al (2020) Semi-reference sonar image quality assessment based on task and visual perception. IEEE Trans Multimedia 23:1008–1020

34. Chen W, Gu K, Min X et al (2018) Partial-reference sonar image quality assessment for underwater transmission. IEEE Trans Aerosp Electron Syst 54(6):2776–2787

35. Chen W, Gu K, Lin W et al (2019) Reference-free quality assessment of sonar images via contour degradation measurement. IEEE Trans Image Process 28(11):5336–5351

36. Debes C, Engel R, Zoubir AM et al (2009) Quality assessment of synthetic aperture sonar images. In: Paper presented at oceans 2009-Europe, 1–4 May 2009

37. Williams DP (2010) Image-quality prediction of synthetic aperture sonar imagery. In: Paper presented at IEEE international conference on acoustics, speech and signal processing, pp 2114–2117, March 2010

38. Chen W, Yuan F, Cheng E et al (2018) Sonar image quality assessment based on degradation measurement. In: Paper presented at oceans - MTS/IEEE Kobe techno-oceans, 1–5 May 2018

39. Gu K, Tao D, Qiao J et al (2017) Learning a no-reference quality assessment model of enhanced images with big data. IEEE Trans Neural Netw Learn Syst 29(4):1301–1313

40. Li L, Shen W, Gu K et al (2016) No-reference quality assessment of enhanced images. China Commun 13(9):121–130

41. Gu K, Zhai G, Lin W et al (2015) The analysis of image contrast: from quality assessment to automatic enhancement. IEEE Trans Cybern 46(1):284–297

42. Gu K, Lin W, Zhai G et al (2016) No-reference quality metric of contrast-distorted images based on information maximization. IEEE Trans Cybern 47(12):4559–4565

43. Gu K, Zhai G, Yang X et al (2015) Automatic contrast enhancement technology with saliency preservation. IEEE Trans Circuits Syst Video Technol 25(9):1480–1494

44. Wang S, Gu K, Ma S et al (2015) Guided image contrast enhancement based on retrieved images in cloud. IEEE Trans Multimedia 18(2):219–232

45. Tian Y, Zeng H, Hou J (2020) Light field image quality assessment via the light field coherence. IEEE Trans Image Process 29:7945–7956

46. Paudyal P, Battisti F, Carli M (2019) Reduced reference quality assessment of light field images. IEEE Trans Broadcast 65(1):152–165

47. Shi L, Zhou W, Chen Z et al (2020) No-reference light field image quality assessment based on spatial-angular measurement. IEEE Trans Circuits Syst Video Technol 30(11):4114–4128

48. Tian Y, Zeng H, Xing L et al (2018) A multi-order derivative feature-based quality assessment model for light field image. J Vis Commun Image Represent 57:212–217

49. Huang Z, Yu M, Xu H et al (2018) New quality assessment method for dense light fields. In: Proceeding SPIE 10817: 1081717, Nov 2018

50. Sun W, Gu K, Zhai G et al (2017) CVIQD: subjective quality evaluation of compressed virtual reality images. In: Paper presented at the IEEE international conference on image processing, pp 3450–2454, Sept 2017

51. Sun Y, Lu A, Yu L (2017) Weighted-to-spherically-uniform quality evaluation for omnidirectional video. IEEE Signal Process Lett 24(9):1408–1412

52. Xu M, Li C, Liu Y et al (2017) A subjective visual quality assessment method of panoramic videos. In: Paper presented at the IEEE international conference on multimedia and expo, pp 517–522

53. Ling S, Cheung G, Callet PL (2018) No-reference quality assessment for stitched panoramic images using convolutional sparse coding and compound feature selection. In: Paper presented at the IEEE international conference on multimedia and expo, San Diego, 23–27 July 2018

54. Lecun Y, Boser B, Denker J et al (1989) Backpropagation applied to handwritten zip code recognition. Neural Comput 1(4):541–551

55. Zhang K, Zhu D, Jing J et al (2019) Learning a cascade regression for no-reference super-resolution image quality assessment. In: Paper presented at the IEEE international conference on image processing, pp 450–453, Sept 2019

56. Yan B, Bare B, Ma C et al (2019) Deep objective quality assessment driven single image super-resolution. IEEE Trans Multimedia 21(11):2957–2971

57. Yeganeh H, Rostami M, Wang Z (2012) Objective quality assessment for image super-resolution: a natural scene statistics approach. In: Paper presented at the IEEE international conference on image processing, pp 1481–1484, Sept 2012

58. Gao F, Wang Y, Li P et al (2017) Deepsim: deep similarity for image quality assessment. Neurocomputing 257:104–114

59. Liang Y, Wang J, Wan X et al (2016) Image quality assessment using similar scene as reference. In: Paper presented at the European conference on computer vision, 3–18 Oct 2016

60. Kim J, Lee S (2017) Deep learning of human visual sensitivity in image quality assessment framework. In: Proceedings of the IEEE conference on computer vision and pattern recognition 1969–1977

Chapter 2
Quality Assessment of Screen Content Images

2.1 Introduction

With the quick evolution of multimedia and social networks, computer-created signals, especially screen content images (SCIs), have turned pervasive in people's daily lives. Recently, applications based on images and videos have increasingly appeared on phones, vehicles, and cloud platforms, generating various digital SCIs, and thus, relevant image processing techniques have been gaining more and more attention. During SCI processing, digital images introduce a variety of distortions when acquired, processed, compressed, stored, transmitted, and reproduced, which can cause deterioration of the perceptual quality of images. The image quality assessment (QA) method can also be utilized to optimize image processing models, so it plays an essential role in the image processing domain, including subjective assessment and objective assessment. The objective image QA methods are often used in order to solve the issue of humans spending a lot of time judging the subjective quality of images. Therefore, it is extremely important to design accurate and effective QA methods for SCIs, which can contribute to reduce the inevitable distortions in various processes such as screen image acquisition, transmission, coding, and display.

Unlike the camera-generated natural scene images (NSIs) acquired from real-world scenes, SCIs are mostly generated by computers. There mainly are texts, tables, dialogs, and some content produced by computers in the SCIs. The main difference between SCIs and NSIs can be described from two perspectives. The first one is that computer-generated discontinuous-tone SCIs have the characteristics of pattern repetition, sharp edge, thin line, and less color, while NSIs usually have the characteristics of continuous-tone, smooth edge, thick line, and more color. The second one is that SCIs are mostly without the noise because they may be exclusively computer-produced, while the process of acquiring NSIs may introduce noise since the physical limitations of imaging sensors. With this concern, the image QA models of NSIs are ineffective in evaluating the visual quality of SCIs, so it is necessary to establish SCI QA models.

© The Author(s), under exclusive license to Springer Nature Singapore Pte Ltd. 2022   11
K. Gu et al., *Quality Assessment of Visual Content*, Advances in Computer Vision
and Pattern Recognition, https://doi.org/10.1007/978-981-19-3347-9_2

The basic ideas of image QA of SCIs are as follows. The first train of thought is that the structural similarity (SSIM) between the original and contaminated SCIs is calculated by some quality-related features. The above features are chrominance, chromaticity, contrast, and some edge features (e.g., edge contrast, edge width, edge direction, etc.). Then it carries out a weighted summation or regression operation on the obtained similarity feature map to further obtain the final score. The second way of thinking is that SCIs should be segmented according to the human visual system (HVS). Human eyes pay attention to different areas when looking at SCIs. The different regions (such as text region and image region) should be divided, analyzed separately, and finally integrated together to form a final score. For example, human eyes pay more attention to the readability of SCIs than the change of color and saturation for text, so the text is more important than image areas.

At present, the researches on SCIs are relatively new, especially in image QA. According to the accessibility of reference information, the SCI QA methods are divided into full-reference (FR) types, reduced-reference (RR) types, and no-reference (NR) types, separately. Some representative works of FR image QA have been published with good results. In [1], Gu et al. studied the association between the perceived quality and the structural variation and provided the structural variation-based quality index (SVQI) metric for evaluating quality. It was compared with traditional FR image QA approaches in [2–6]. In [7], Ni et al. used gradient direction in accordance with local information to assess the visual quality of SCIs. In [8], Gu et al. designed an FR metric that is mostly based on simple convolution operators to gauge prominent domains in order to assess the quality of SCIs. In [9], Fang et al. divided SCIs into text and graphic areas and combined the visual quality of text and graphic areas using a weighted method. In this work, gradient information and brightness resources based on structural features were selected for similarity calculation to derive the visual quality of SCIs. In [10], Ni et al. established an FR metric that relies on the local similarity extracted by the Gabor filter in LMN color space. In [11], Fu et al. proposed an FR model by applying different scales of Gaussian. All the above-mentioned QA models require the participation of reference images, but most of SCIs cannot obtain reference images, so NR image QA approaches for SCIs are urgently needed.

Conventional NR QA methods designed for SCIs can be divided into three categories. For the first dominant category, the perceptual quality of SCIs is predicted by utilizing the theory of free energy, which is suitable for NSI QA [12]. Inspired by this, in [13], Gu et al. constructed a superior NR SCI quality evaluation model called screen image quality evaluator (SIQE), which extracted 15 resources, including image complexity, screen content information, overall brightness, and detail clarity. It used effective support vector regression (SVR) to convert resources into overall quality scores and compared them with the excellent performance NR model in [14, 15]. The second category relies on texture and brightness characteristics. In [16], a valid NR QA method for evaluating the quality of SCIs was proposed. The method extracted texture and brightness features from texture and brightness histograms and trained these features based on SVR to derive the overall quality score. For the third category, sparse representation is considered. In [17], Shao et al. proposed a NR image quality predictor for SCIs to explore this problem from the angle of sparse representation. For evaluating the performance of those QA methods, we compared them with state-of-the-art competitors using four extensive employed standards, namely the Pearson linear correlation coefficient (PLCC), the Spearman rank correlation coefficient (SRCC), the Kendall rank correlation coefficient (KRCC), and root mean square error (RMSE).

The organization of this chapter is arranged as shown below. Section 2.2 introduces in detail the modeling process and comparison and analysis of three types of QA approaches of SCIs, namely the FR type, the RR type, and the NR type. Section 2.3 compares several advanced image QA approaches of SCIs with the proposed approaches. Section 2.4 finally draws the conclusion and provides future work.

2.2 Methodology

In this section, we give a detailed introduction to five advanced SCI QA methods. We divide these QA approaches into three categories, namely the FR image QA method, the RR image QA method, and the NR image QA method. More specifically, we first introduce two FR methods. One method is to systematically combine the measures of global and local structural variations to yield the final quality estimation of SCIs. The other method is to incorporate both visual field adaptation and information content weighting into local QA on the basis of SSIM. Second, we introduce a RR method that compares the differences in macroscopic and microscopic features between original SCIs and the corresponding distortion version to deduce the overall quality rating. Third, we introduce two NR methods. One method is a unified content-type adaptive (UCA) NR image QA approach, which is suitable for different content types. The other method evaluates image quality by extracting four categories of features that represent the complexity of the picture, screen content statistics, global brightness quality, and detail sharpness. Finally, we analyze the performance of these methods with the typically used indices of PLCC, SRCC, KRCC, and RMSE.

2.2.1 Full-Reference QA of Screen Content Images

Structural information is one of the main bases for FR image objective QA. Extracting structural information from the background is the main function of HVS, and it can be implemented adaptively by this system. Hence, using structural information to measure the distortion of images is a more effective QA method in accordance with the HVS. Here, we will introduce two FR image QA methods founded on structural variation and SSIM.

Evaluating Quality of SCIs via Structural Variation Analysis

Recently, the free energy theory [18, 19] was proposed by Friston's team. The theory assumes that cognitive processes in the human brain are based on internal generative mechanisms. On this basis, we can learn that the input visual signals can be obtained according to the free energy theory. The cognitive process can be represented by a probabilistic model consisting of a prior component and a likelihood component. Although the current level of knowledge does not fully reconstruct the cognitive process of the human brain, it is reasonable to suppose that there are differences between the input visual signals and the internal generative mechanism. This difference is intimately associated with human perception of visual quality [12].

We hypothesize the internal generative mechanism can explain the external input visual signal by altering the model parameters ω vector. t represents an input visual signal. Its "surprise" is calculated by integrating the joint distribution $\mathcal{P}_{(t,\omega)}$ on the space of model parameters:

$$- \log \mathcal{S}_{(t)} = - \log \int \mathcal{Q}_{(\omega|t)} \frac{\mathcal{P}_{(t,\omega)}}{\mathcal{Q}_{(\omega|t)}} \, d\omega, \tag{2.1}$$

where the $\mathcal{Q}_{(\omega|t)}$ denotes the assistant posterior distribution of the t, which is regarded as an approximate posterior to the true posterior $\mathcal{P}_{(\omega|t)}$. The human brain tries to decrease the difference between the assistant posterior and the true posterior by changing the $\rightarrow$ in $\mathcal{Q}_{(\omega|t)}$ to describe the perceptual visual signal t accurately. We apply Jensen's inequality to Eq. (2.1) and yield the following:

$$- \log \mathcal{S}_{(t)} \leq - \int \mathcal{Q}_{(\omega|t)} \log \frac{\mathcal{P}_{(t,\omega)}}{\mathcal{Q}_{(\omega|t)}} \, d\omega = \mathcal{F}_{(\omega)}. \tag{2.2}$$

On the basis of the definition in statistical thermodynamics and physics [20], the free energy $\mathcal{F}_{(\omega)}$ can be calculated from the right part of Eq. (2.2). According to Bayes' theorem, we know that $\mathcal{P}_{(t,\omega)} = \mathcal{P}_{(\omega|t)} \mathcal{S}_{(t)}$. Then Eq. (2.2) can be demonstrated as follows:

$$\begin{aligned} \mathcal{F}_{(\omega)} &= \int \mathcal{Q}_{(\omega|t)} \log \frac{\mathcal{Q}_{(t,\omega)}}{\mathcal{S}_{(t)} \mathcal{P}_{(\omega|t)}} \, d\omega \\ &= -\log \mathcal{S}_{(t)} + KL(\mathcal{Q}_{(\omega|t)} \parallel \mathcal{P}_{(\omega|t)}), \end{aligned} \tag{2.3}$$

where $KL(\mathcal{Q}_{(\omega|t)} \parallel \mathcal{P}_{(\omega|t)})$ represents a Kullback-Leibler (KL) divergence between $\mathcal{Q}_{(\omega|t)}$ and $\mathcal{P}_{(\omega|t)}$. We find that the free energy changed with $KL(\mathcal{Q}_{(\omega|t)} \parallel \mathcal{P}_{(\omega|t)})$, and $\mathcal{F}_{(\omega)}$ have a strict upper bound since $KL(\mathcal{Q}_{(\omega|t)} \parallel \mathcal{P}_{(\omega|t)})$ is a non-negative component. Only when the $\mathcal{Q}_{(\omega|t)}$ equals to $\mathcal{S}_{(t)}$, $\mathcal{F}_{(\omega)}$ can achieve the minimum value $-\log \mathcal{S}_{(t)}$. Equation (2.3) reveals that the $\mathcal{F}_{(\omega)}$ is inhibited by minimizing the KL divergence of the approximate posterior against the true posterior. This situation reflects the brain will decrease the KL divergence as explaining input visual signal.

The corrupted image $\mathcal{D}$ can be represented as follows:

$$\mathcal{D} = \mathcal{R} + \Delta, \tag{2.4}$$

where $\mathcal{R}$ stands for the original image, and Δ is the error difference. Relying on the free energy theory, we are aware that the human brain actively recovers the corrupted image $\mathcal{D}$ by decreasing the error difference. In this way, the human brain can achieve a satisfactory visual perception or semantic understanding. We assume that the true posterior corresponds to $\mathcal{R}$, and the deduced approximate posterior corresponds to $\mathcal{R}'$ that is recovered by the human brain. The implementation of the recovering process is closely associated with the image QA. In particular, since certain characteristics of the HVS, the brain does not need to recover.

Measurement of Structural Variation

According to all the content mentioned above, the human brain is a long-term well-trained organ, and thus, it works in an extremely efficient manner. In the process of evaluating the perceived quality of SCIs, the human brain first makes a basic perception about the overall structure of a given image. Especially, for the low contrast images (i.e., too light or too dark images), the brain will ignore the details. After completing basic perception, the human brain will target local structures, selectively perceiving changes in detail. At last, the human brain systematically combines basic and detailed perception to achieve the ultimate image QA.

Variations in Global Structures In the process of basic perception to global structures, we focus on two significant features, which are the contrast and complexity of images. The contrast is closely related to the perceptual quality of images. Too low contrast will seriously degrade the image quality, making it difficult for the human brain to capture the details and make sense of semantic information. We suppose that the pristine image $\mathcal{R}$ has the baseline brightness and contrast, and the information entropy changes as they deviate. Next, we utilize the variation of entropy (EOV) to represent the feature as follows:

$$\mathcal{F}_1 = \frac{\mu_{(\mathcal{D})} + \nu_{(1)}}{\mu_{(\mathcal{R})} + \nu_{(1)}}, \tag{2.5}$$

where $\nu_{(1)}$ is a minor fixed value to prevent the feature value from being too large. $\mathcal{D}$ and $\mathcal{R}$ represent the original and distorted images, respectively. The entropy value μ can be calculated by

$$\mu = -\int \mathcal{H}_{(\beta)} log \mathcal{H}_{(\beta)} \, d\beta, \tag{2.6}$$

where $\mathcal{H}_{(\beta)}$ represents the probability density of grayscale β. To find the EGM's impact, we compare eleven categories of distortions from three databases, consisting of screen image quality assessment database (SIQAD) [6], quality assessment of compressed screen content image (QACS) database [21], and SCTL database [22]. From the SIQAD database, we select seven types of distortions, including contrast change (CC), motion blur (MB), Gaussian blur (GB), JPEG2000 compression

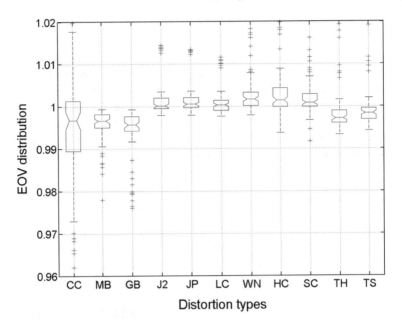

Fig. 2.1 Box plot of EOV distribution across 11 categories of distortions from three SCI databases (©[2021] IEEE. Reprinted, with permission, from [1].)

(J2C), JPEG compression (JC), layer segmentation backed coding (LC) [23], and white noise (WN). From the QACS database, three types of distortions are picked out, namely high-efficiency video coding (HEVC), high efficiency video coding compression (HC) [1], and screen content image compression (SC). From the SCTL database, transmission loss under HEVC compression (TH) and transmission loss under screen content image compression (TS) are selected. Figure 2.1 shows that only changing the image contrast can largely reshape the histogram, while other distortion categories sightly impact the EOV distribution.

The other feature we considered is the image complexity, which is an abstract concept. The images with high complexity consist of edge, texture, and other high-frequency information, which generally have stronger noise masking effects. Compared with smooth areas, these edge and texture regions are poor at self-expression. Based on this, we utilize the classical linear autoregressive (AR) model, which can be established in each local patch:

$$r_i = \mathcal{V}_\psi(r_i) \cdot \mathbf{a} + d_i, \tag{2.7}$$

where r_i is the pixel value at i; $\mathbf{V}_\psi(r_i)$ composes a vector of ψ member neighborhood; $\mathbf{a}$ is the vector containing ψ AR parameters; d_i denotes the difference error term between the given pixel and the corresponding output estimation. For obtaining the best AR parameter vector $\mathbf{a}$, we design the following linear equation:

$$\mathbf{a}_{opt} = \arg\min_{\mathbf{a}} ||\mathbf{r} - \mathbf{R} \cdot \mathbf{a}||_n, \tag{2.8}$$

where $\mathbf{r} = (r_1, r_2, ..., r_\delta)^T$ contains pixels around δ in a $\sqrt{\delta} \times \sqrt{\delta}$ patch; $\mathbf{R}(i, :)$ equals $\mathcal{V}_\psi(r_i)$; n is the standard order assigned as 2. We find the linear equation's solution to be $\mathbf{a}_{opt} = (\mathbf{R}^T\mathbf{R})^{-1} \mathbf{R}^T \mathbf{r}$ by adopting the least square method. We observe that the AR model has a good performance on texture area, but poorly at the edge area. To solve this problem, we propose a tradeoff better filter by integrating bi-lateral (BL) filter with the AR model. We replace $\mathbf{a}$ and d_i with $\tilde{\mathbf{a}}$ and $\tilde{d}_i$. $\tilde{\mathbf{a}}$ represents a collection of BL filter's parameters, which is determined by two distances. One is the spatial distance between i and j (j is the index of the adjacent pixel of i). The other is photometric distance of r_i and r_j. Based on this, Eq. (2.7) can be rewritten to express the BL filter as follows:

$$BL_j = e^{\{\frac{-||i-j||^2}{2\sigma_1^2} + \frac{-(r_i-r_j)^2}{2\sigma_2^2}\}}, \tag{2.9}$$

where σ_1 and σ_2 are two constant variances adopted to make tradeoff in the density between the spatial distance and photometric distance. $\tilde{d}_i$ is also the difference term. To inherit the advantages of AR and BL models, a linear fusion is employed to obtain the filtered image:

$$r'_i = \frac{1}{1 + \phi_i}[\mathcal{V}_\psi(r_i)\hat{\mathbf{a}} + \phi_i \cdot \mathcal{V}_\psi(r_i)\tilde{\mathbf{a}}], \tag{2.10}$$

where ϕ_i is a non-negative weight of a space variant, which can be utilized to manipulate the correlated contribution of AR and BL models. We set ϕ_i as 9 to stress the significance of edges, and the image complexity feature can be predicted by

$$\mathcal{F}_2 = - \int \mathcal{H}'_{(\theta)} log \mathcal{H}'_{(\theta)} d\theta, \tag{2.11}$$

where $\mathcal{H}'_{(\theta)}$ represents the feasibility density of grayscale θ in the error map between the input image and the related filter version.

Variations in Local Structures Edge variation is the primary feature that can be perceived to reflect local structural details. Among many edge variation measurement methods, the Scharr operator [24] has better performance. Therefore, we convolve the reference image $\mathcal{R}$ by utilizing the Scharr operator and obtain the following:

$$\mathcal{I}_{(\mathcal{R})} = \sqrt{\mathcal{I}_{(\mathcal{R},x)}^2 + \mathcal{I}_{(\mathcal{R},y)}^2}, \tag{2.12}$$

where $\mathcal{I}_{(\mathcal{R},x)} = \mathcal{M} \otimes \mathcal{R}$ and $\mathcal{I}_{(\mathcal{R},y)} = \mathcal{M}^T \otimes \mathcal{R}$. $\mathcal{M} = \frac{1}{16}[3, 0, -3; 10, 0, -10; 3, 0, -3]$. $\otimes$ is the convolution operation. Also, the $\mathcal{I}_{(\mathcal{D})}$ can be derived by applying the Scharr operator to the distorted image $\mathcal{D}$. We measure the edge variations of original and distorted images as follows:

$$A_{(R,D)} = \frac{2\mathcal{I}_{(R)}\mathcal{I}_{(D)} + \nu_2}{\mathcal{I}^2_{(R)} + \mathcal{I}^2_{(D)} + \nu_2}, \tag{2.13}$$

where ν_2 is a minor constant positive value similar to ν_1. Different from the previous studies, we present two inherent attributes of human perception. One of them is the HVS, which is more susceptible to sudden local window alters in a series of signals [25, 26]. For original image R, its corresponding filter version can be obtained by $R^* = \mathbf{h} \otimes R = (1 - \mathbf{g}) \otimes R = R - \mathbf{g} \otimes R = R - R^+$, where $\mathbf{g}$ represents the low-pass Gaussian function. R^+ is a parameter corresponding to the R^*. We compare the original image and the corresponding filtered image:

$$\begin{aligned}
B'_{(R,R^*)} &= A_{(R,R)} - A_{(R,R^+)} \\
&= 1 - \frac{2\mathcal{I}_{(R)}\mathcal{I}_{(R^+)} + \nu_2}{\mathcal{I}^2_{(R)} + \mathcal{I}^2_{(R^+)} + \nu_2}.
\end{aligned} \tag{2.14}$$

The other attribute is the movement tendency of the human eye, which is accustomed to moving from left to right when reading text content. Thus, the local window should contain the present fixation point and its adjacent right pixels. We apply an associated high-pass filter to pre-enhance the visual input signal to avoid the effect of motion blur. Similarly, we define its filtered version as $R^\dagger$, which corresponds to the parameter R^-. We generate the filtered images as $R^\dagger = \mathbf{h}' \otimes R = (1-\mathbf{g}') \otimes R = R - \mathbf{g}' \otimes R = R - R^-$, where $\mathbf{g}'$ is a motion blur function. We make a comparison between the original image and the corresponding filtered image by

$$\begin{aligned}
B''_{(R,R^\dagger)} &= A_{(R,R)} - A_{(R,R^-)} \\
&= 1 - \frac{2\mathcal{I}_{(R)}\mathcal{I}_{(R^-)} + \nu_2}{\mathcal{I}^2_{(R)} + \mathcal{I}^2_{(R^-)} + \nu_2}.
\end{aligned} \tag{2.15}$$

We then propose a linear weighting function by integrating the two perceptual attributes:

$$B_{(R)} = \frac{1}{1 + \alpha_i}[B'_{(R,R^*)} + \alpha_i \cdot B''_{(R,R^\dagger)}]. \tag{2.16}$$

We roughly assume the space-variant positive number α_i is the unit. It reflects that the image and text parts are almost equal in size. The linear weighting function can be rewritten as follows:

$$B_{(R)} = 1 - \frac{\mathcal{I}_{(R)}\mathcal{I}_{(\mathbf{g} \otimes R)} + \frac{1}{2}\epsilon_2}{\mathcal{I}^2_{(R)} + \mathcal{I}^2_{(\mathbf{g} \otimes R)} + \epsilon_2} - \frac{\mathcal{I}_{(R)}\mathcal{I}_{(\mathbf{g}' \otimes R)} + \frac{1}{2}\epsilon_2}{\mathcal{I}^2_{(R)} + \mathcal{I}^2_{(\mathbf{g}' \otimes R)} + \epsilon_2}, \tag{2.17}$$

where $\mathbf{g}$ and $\mathbf{g}'$ are fixed parameters. We measure the edge variations by modifying $A_{(R,D)}$ with the weighting map $B_{(R)}$:

$$\mathcal{F}_3 = \frac{\sum_i \mathcal{A}_{(\mathcal{R}_i, \mathcal{D}_i)} \cdot \mathcal{B}_{(\mathcal{R}_i)}}{\sum_i \mathcal{B}_{(\mathcal{R}_i)}}. \tag{2.18}$$

The other feature denotes the variations in corners. The introduction of different distortions will change the corners of the original image correspondingly, which proves that corners can be effectively adopted to evaluate image quality [27]. The uncontaminated image can be rewritten in a matrix format $\mathcal{R} = [r_{ij}]$. The high-efficiency Shi-Tomasi detector [28] are adopted to detect corners. The corner map $\mathcal{C}_{(\mathcal{R})}$ can be defined as follows:

$$c_{ij} = \begin{cases} 1 & if \ r_{ij} \in \mathcal{C}_{(\mathcal{R})} \\ 0 & otherwise \end{cases}, \tag{2.19}$$

where $r_{ij} \in \mathcal{C}_{(\mathcal{R})}$ indicates a corner with coordinates (i, j). We define distorted image's corner map as $\mathcal{C}_{(\mathcal{D})}$. Note that $\mathcal{C}_{(R_i)}$ and $\mathcal{C}_{(D_i)}$ are binary maps, $\mathcal{C}_{(R_i)}\mathcal{C}_{(D_i)} \equiv \mathcal{C}_{(R_i)} \cap \mathcal{C}_{(D_i)}$, $\mathcal{C}_{(R_i)}^2 \equiv \mathcal{C}_{(R_i)}$, $\mathcal{C}_{(D_i)}^2 \equiv \mathcal{C}_{(D_i)}$. Similar to Eq. (2.13), we calculate the corner's variations between the pristine and contaminated images by

$$\mathcal{F}_4 = 2 \sum_i \frac{\mathcal{C}_{(R_i)} \cap \mathcal{C}_{(D_i)} + \frac{1}{2}\varepsilon_3}{\mathcal{C}_{(R_i)} + \mathcal{C}_{(D_i)} + \varepsilon_3}. \tag{2.20}$$

Proposed SCI QA Metric

We extract four features associated with global and local structures from basic and detailed perceptions. To integrate these features reliably, three reference SCIs are elaborately picked from the SIQAD database, exhibited in Fig. 2.2. In Fig. 2.2, each column corresponds to $\mathcal{F}_1$, $\mathcal{F}_3$, and $\mathcal{F}_4$ from left to right. Notice that we ignore $\mathcal{F}_2$, since it is only determined by the reference image.

In the second column, the distribution of sample points is irregular. We use blue and red dots to stand for contrast alter and other distortion categories, respectively. Although differential mean opinion score (DMOS) is discrepant, blue points have an approximate linear relationship and red dots are almost equal. In the third and fourth columns, it can be obviously found that each plot has a near-linear relationship and consistent ordering. In other words, they are all negatively correlated with subjective DMOS values. For the image complexity characteristic, it can be utilized to normalize for clearing the interference of different image contents. Furthermore, the brain first perceives the global structures of images. In the case of a normal image (the image is not over-bright or over-dark), the brain perceives global structure and local structure in turn. Then the brain systematically integrates these two structural variations to predict the image's perceptual quality. Based on the above analysis, the final quality is calculated by

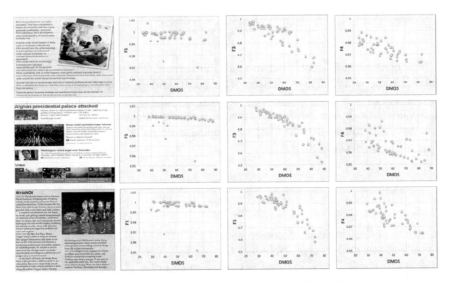

Fig. 2.2 Comparison of the global and local features derived from three original SCIs chosen from the SIQAD database. From left to right, four columns are related to pristine images, scatter plots of DMOS, and three features $\mathcal{F}_1$, $\mathcal{F}_3$, and $\mathcal{F}_4$ (©[2021] IEEE. Reprinted, with permission, from [1].)

$$Q(\mathcal{R}, \mathcal{D}) = \begin{cases} 0 & if \ \frac{\mathcal{F}_2}{\mathcal{F}_1} \geq \mathcal{T}_r \\ \frac{1}{\mathcal{F}_2^{\alpha}} \prod_{i=1,3,4} \mathcal{F}_i & otherwise \end{cases}, \tag{2.21}$$

where Q_r is a fixed threshold that is designed to distinguish whether the global contrast of the image is extremely low or the complexity is extremely high. α is a constant manipulating operator to reduce the $\mathcal{F}_2$ value for making four features have comparable magnitudes.

Objective QA and Perceptual Compression of SCIs

In [29], an objective SCI QA algorithm was proposed and used to optimize the coding procedure of SCI compression. Specifically, the proposed model takes into account field adaptation and information content and uses a weighted strategy based on local SSIM to evaluate the quality of images. In addition, it proposes a new perceptual SCI compression scheme based on the concept of divisive normalization transform to boost the coding efficiency of SCIs. Compared with traditional methods, this algorithm has a better performance.

Objective QA of SCIs

SCIs usually contain pictorial regions and textual or graphical content produced by computers. These regions often show different statistical characteristics. Here, we introduce two statistical features that can help distinguish graphic regions from text regions and assist in the development of QA methods of SCIs compression.

It can be found in the relevant literature of NSS that the amplitude spectrum of natural images decreases as the spatial frequency decreases in proportion to $1/f_s^p$ [32]. f_s represents spatial frequency and p represents image correlation frequency. And the typical textual images computer-generated seem a little "unnatural". This inspires people to further study this characteristic on SCIs. As shown in Fig. 2.3, the Fourier transform is used to decompose natural and textual images. The same result can be observed in [32]. In other words, it can be seen that the energy of the natural image decreases as the spatial frequency decreases, and the relationship between them is approximately a straight line on a log-log scale. The peak appears at the middle and high frequency of the textual image. We can also find that larger characters lead to peak frequency to lower frequency. This shows the connection between peak values and stroke width and spacing. Though these features are not explicitly used in the design of the image QA methods, it is obviously learned from these examples that the statistical characteristics of textual images are different from

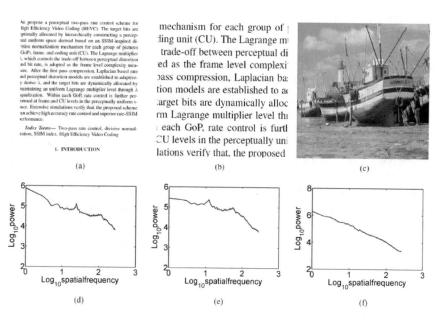

Fig. 2.3 An exemplified frequency energy falloff curve of textual and natural images in log-log scale. **a** and **b**: Different scales' textual images; **c**: A natural image; **d** and **e**: Frequency energy falloff curve of textual images in (**a**) and (**b**); **f**: Frequency energy falloff curve of the natural image (**c**) (©[2021] IEEE. Reprinted, with permission, from [29].)

(a)	(b)	(c)	(d)

Fig. 2.4 An exemplified SCIs and its corresponding local information content maps (brighter means higher information content). **a, c** SCIs; **b, d** Corresponding information content maps (©[2021] IEEE. Reprinted, with permission, from [29].)

those of natural images. Based on this, we need to separate them when designing QA metrics.

The valid information content model [30] is established by using the Gaussian source transmitted to the receiving end through the Gaussian noise (GN) channel to locally model the input signal [31]. The mutual information between the input signal and the output signal is the number of perceived information content, which can be quantified in the following equation:

$$\omega = log_2 \left(1 + \frac{\sigma_p^2}{\sigma_n^2} \right), \tag{2.22}$$

where σ_p^2 represents the variance in the local window x. σ_n^2 refers to the constant parameter used to describe the noise degree of the visual channel.

Figure 2.4 shows the local information maps processed by Eq. (2.22) and their corresponding original images. This example illustrates the distribution of perceptual information in space and the difference between textual and graphical areas. Because the local variances surrounding high-contrast edges are usually significant, text regions containing rich high-contrast edges usually have a high content of local information. They are easier to observe than image regions.

The SSIM index is an effective quality measure [2], which can be used to estimate the local quality of SCIs. Two local image blocks x and y with size $l \times l$ are extracted from the pristine image and the contaminated image separately. The SSIM between them is expressed as follows:

$$SSIM(x, y) = \frac{(2\eta_x \eta_y + B_1)(2\sigma_{xy} + B_2)}{(\eta_x^2 + \eta_y^2 + B_1)(\sigma_x^2 + \sigma_y^2 + B_2)}, \tag{2.23}$$

where η_x, σ_x, and σ_{xy} separately denote the mean, standard deviation, and cross-correlation of the local window. B_1 and B_2 are positive numbers set to prevent the instability generated as mean value and variance value are 0. The specific settings are as follows:

$$B_1 = (K_1 L)^2, \tag{2.24}$$

$$B_2 = (K_2 L)^2, \tag{2.25}$$

where L is the dynamic domain of pixel values. The K_1 and K_2 are separately two constants, where $K_1 = 0.01$ and $K_2 = 0.03$.

It is necessary to distinguish between image and text content in order to assess their perceptual distortions in different and more appropriate methods. In terms of visual field, the perceptual span involved in scanning text content when we view SCIs is significantly less than the perceptual or visual search range when reading NSIs. Hence, we will consider adjusting the window size when processing the content in the textual and pictorial areas.

Here, we use the block classification method of information content map to process the image. It can be observed from Fig. 2.4 that the text domain in the SCIs has a higher salience and contains more information than the pictorial area. We set the threshold T_f for the sum of the information contained in each 4×4 block to achieve the classification of blocks. The mass of each image block region ω_T and ω_P can be described by S_T and S_P. Specifically, they are calculated by spatial adaptive weighted pooling to obtain correlative weights of local content in text or image:

$$Q_T = \frac{\sum_{i \in \omega_T} SSIM_i \cdot \omega_i^\alpha}{\sum_{i \in \omega_T} \omega_i^\alpha}, \tag{2.26}$$

$$Q_P = \frac{\sum_{j \in \omega_P} SSIM_j \cdot \omega_j^\alpha}{\sum_{j \in \omega_P} \omega_j^\alpha}, \tag{2.27}$$

where α is the parameter used to adjust the weighted strength. Based on experience, we set the thresholds T_f and α as 30 and 0.3. Since the field of view of the text area is smaller than that of the image area, we use Gaussian windows of different sizes and different standard deviations to calculate local SSIM values, which are represented by k_t and k_p separately. The ω_i and ω_j are local information, which can be calculated through their respective windows. And the SSIM values are also calculated in these windows. It is worth noting that text content is not the only difference between NSIs and SCIs, but it is the most important feature of SCIs.

The final SCI quality index (SQI) is achieved by calculating the weighted averages of Q_T and Q_P of the correlative weights of text and image regions:

$$SQI = \frac{Q_T \cdot \mu_T + Q_P \cdot \mu_P}{\mu_T + \mu_P}, \tag{2.28}$$

where $\mu_T = \frac{1}{|\Omega_T|} \sum_{j \in \Omega_T} \omega_{u,j}^\alpha$ and $\mu_P = \frac{1}{|\Omega_P|} \sum_{j \in \Omega_P} \omega_{u,j}^\alpha$. The windows are utilized to calculate weights and need to be the same size.

Perceptual SCI Compression

In addition to an objective QA method of SCIs, we will introduce a scheme for screen content coding on the basis of the recently designed QA method. It improves the performance of SCI compression. In this method, we use video coding based on segmentation normalized transformation [32]. The coding scheme normalizes the discrete cosine transform (DCT) coefficients of the residual block B_k by using the positive perceptual normalization parameter f to change the DCT coefficients into the range of perceptual consistency:

$$B(k)' = \frac{B(x)}{f}. \tag{2.29}$$

Then, we use A_s to denote the predefined quantization step. The quantization process of normalized residuals can be described as the following:

$$
\begin{aligned}
A(k) &= sign\{B(k)\}round\left\{\frac{|B(k)'|}{A_s} + \xi\right\} \\
&= sign\{B(k)\}round\left\{\frac{|B(k)|}{A_s \cdot f} + \xi\right\},
\end{aligned} \tag{2.30}
$$

where ξ is the rounding offset in quantification. Accordingly, inverse quantization and $B(k)$ reconstruction are performed at the decoder:

$$
\begin{aligned}
R(k) &= R(x)' \cdot f = A(k) \cdot A_s \cdot f \\
&= sign\{B(k)\}round\left\{\frac{|B(k)'|}{A_s \cdot f} + \xi\right\} \cdot A_s \cdot f.
\end{aligned} \tag{2.31}
$$

We make an adaptive adjustment to the quantization parameters of each coding unit (CU), and the transform coefficients can be converted to a perceptually uniform space. Given the reference block x and the reconstructed block y, the SSIM in the DCT domain can be computed as follows:

$$
\begin{aligned}
SSIM(x, y) = {}& \left(1 - \frac{(X(0) - Y(0))^2}{X(0)^2 + Y(0)^2 + N \cdot B_1}\right) \\
& \times \left(1 - \frac{\frac{\sum_{k=1}^{N-1}(X(k)-Y(k))^2}{N-1}}{\frac{\sum_{k=1}^{N-1}X(k)^2-Y(k)^2}{N-1} + B_2}\right),
\end{aligned} \tag{2.32}
$$

where X and Y are the DCT coefficients separately that correspond to x and y. N represents the block size. C_1 and C_2 defined as fixed values are determined by the SSIM index. Assuming that each CU consists of l DCT blocks, the normalization factor of AC coefficient is as follows:

$$f_{ac} = \frac{\frac{1}{l}\sum\limits_{i=1}^{l}\sqrt{\dfrac{\sum\limits_{k=1}^{N-1}(X_i(k)^2-Y_i(k)^2)}{N-1}+B_2}}{E\left(\sqrt{\dfrac{\sum\limits_{k=1}^{N-1}(X(k)^2-Y(k)^2)}{N-1}}+B_2\right)}. \tag{2.33}$$

Since the distortion blocks cannot be obtained before actual encoding, we can only use the original blocks and apply f_{ac} to obtain the quantization parameter (QP) offset for each CU.

After finishing the division normalization, the rate distortion optimization (RDO) is carried out via the minimizing process of the perceived distortion D under the condition that the rate R obeys a constraint R_c. The above step can be translated into an unconstrained optimization problem:

$$\min\{RD\} \ where \ J = D + \gamma \cdot R, \tag{2.34}$$

where RD represents the rate distortion (RD) cost. γ denotes the Lagrangian multiplier that can be used to control the tradeoff between rate and perceived distortion. D is defined by calculating the sum of the squared difference (SSD) between the normalized pristine coefficient and the distortion coefficient:

$$D = \sum_{i=1}^{l}\sum_{k=0}^{N-1}(B_i(k)' - R_i(k)')^2 = \sum_{i=1}^{l}\sum_{k=0}^{N-1}\frac{(B_i(k) - R_i(k))^2}{f_{ac}^2}. \tag{2.35}$$

Since the DCT coefficients are split and normalized to a space with uniform perception, the Lagrange multiplier γ in the optimizing process of rate distortion is not touched in the encoder.

Window adaptation and information content weight process may well explain the major difference between SSIM and SQI. Specifically, in the case of situation to the SQI method, we first classify the block types by assessing the local information content in each block. Next, we make a comparison with the predefined threshold. Relying on the idea of SQI, the text block's normalization factor is given:

$$f_t = f_{ac}/g_t, \tag{2.36}$$

where the g_t is relatively important to local blocks in information content, defined as follows:

Fig. 2.5 Spatial adaptive divisive normalized parameters visualization for classical SCI (darker pixels denote higher normalization parameters). **a** Pristine SCI; **b** Normalization parameters obtained from SSIM; **c** Normalization parameters accessed from SQI (©[2021] IEEE. Reprinted, with permission, from [29].)

$$
g_t = \sqrt{\frac{2\left(\frac{1}{l}\frac{1}{N}\sum_{i=1}^{l}\sum_{k=1}^{N}\omega_{i,k}^{\alpha}\right)\cdot\mu_T}{\left(\frac{1}{|\Omega_T|}\sum_{j\in\Omega_T}\omega_j^{\alpha}\right)\cdot(\mu_T+\mu_P)}},
\tag{2.37}
$$

where N represents the size of the block, k is the spatial location index in the block, and i denotes the block index in each CU.

In a similar way, the normalization factor of an image block is given by

$$
f_p = f_{ac}/g_p,
\tag{2.38}
$$

where

$$
g_P = \sqrt{\frac{2\left(\frac{1}{l}\frac{1}{N}\sum_{i=1}^{l}\sum_{k=1}^{N}\omega_{i,k}^{\alpha}\right)\cdot\eta_P}{\left(\frac{1}{|\Omega_P|}\sum_{j\in\Omega_P}\omega_j^{\alpha}\right)\cdot(\eta_T+\eta_P)}}.
\tag{2.39}
$$

Figure 2.5 shows the splitting normalization factors obtained from SSIM and SQI for classical SCIs. For better visualization, the splitting normalization factor is calculated within each 4×4 block. The results show that compared with pictorial regions, this method is more responsive to the HVS, and it can allot tiny normalization factors to text regions with high-contrast edges. Therefore, through the split normalization method that is proposed for SCI compression, we can adapt to the process of bit allocation for improving the whole SCI quality.

2.2.2 Reduced-Reference QA of Screen Content Images

In general, the main works of this research are displayed as follows. First of all, this research designs a new and effective SCI QA model, which appropriately combines the measurement of macroscopic and microstructure changes. Based on this framework, this part deploys appropriate measurements to get the changes in macro and microstructure and merges these two measured values to deduce the whole quality estimation of the input SCIs. Secondly, compared with the latest quality inspection indicators currently used for SCI QA, the introduced QA method in this section has achieved superior performance. Finally, we find the designed QA model only uses very sparse reference information and accurately conveys a small amount of information in header files.

Toward Accurate Quality Estimation of SCIs with Very Sparse Reference Information

The design principle of the model in this part is to combine the macrostructure and microstructure to deduce the quality of SCIs. Specifically, extracting the macrostructure and microstructure of the established histogram can greatly reduce the dimensionality of the reference information to only two features. In this way, these two features can be used to compare the discrepancy between distortion and the original SCI. The designed quality model is shown in Fig. 2.6.

Macroscopic Structure Measurement

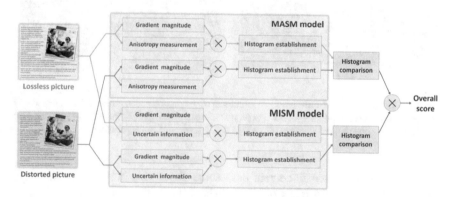

Fig. 2.6 Statement of the working process of the designed QA method (©[2021] IEEE. Reprinted, with permission, from [39].)

Fig. 2.7 Comparisons of the macroscopic structures of the natural scene and screen images. **a** and **b** Original natural scene and screen content pictures, separately. **c** and **d** The maps of macroscopic structures of (**a**) and (**b**), respectively (©[2021] IEEE. Reprinted, with permission, from [39].)

Natural scenario and screen content have some differences in macrostructure. By comparison, the macrostructure of NSIs can be considered as the outline of images. The SCIs are concentrated in the text area, which contains a lot of semantic information, as exhibited in Fig. 2.7.

The macrostructure measurement (MASM) model plays an important role in this method, and the model is proposed to select the important structure of SCIs. Based on anisotropy, the MASM model can be considered as a directional metric, deployed by combining gradient and anisotropy measured value.

Gradient Magnitude As mentioned earlier, the change of structure tends to appeal to the perception of the HVS [33]. The gradient magnitude is usually utilized in the application of computer vision and image processing algorithms. Specifically, this article calculates the gradient by using the Scharr operator, which can be computed by the following two convolutions masks:

$$G(s) = \sqrt{G_h^2 + G_v^2}, \tag{2.40}$$

where

$$G_h = H_h \otimes S = \frac{1}{16} \begin{bmatrix} +3 & 0 & -3 \\ +10 & 0 & -10 \\ +3 & 0 & -3 \end{bmatrix} \otimes S, \tag{2.41}$$

$$G_v = H_v \otimes S = \frac{1}{16} \begin{bmatrix} +3 & +10 & +3 \\ 0 & 0 & 0 \\ -3 & -10 & -3 \end{bmatrix} \otimes S, \tag{2.42}$$

where S denotes a SCI signal, and H_h and H_v represent the Scharr convolution masks with the horizontal and vertical directions, respectively. The gradient magnitude can be underlined as the structural information of textual region and graphical region by the above convolution operation.

Anisotropy Measurement It is easy to arise strong visual perception through a macrostructure with intensity changes and preferred directions. This macrostructure is considered to be large anisotropy. In contrast, structures with uniform scattering are generally considered to have less anisotropy, which usually results in less perception of structural changes. It can be inferred that the macroscopic structure can be directly extracted by anisotropy measurement. In practice, anisotropy measurement has been extensively studied in many pioneering research to obtain the local heterogeneity of intensity changes [34–36]. In this study, the anisotropy measurement means the pixel intensity distribution of the SCI. It also implies the fundamental direction change near the local pixel [6, 9, 37].

From the perspective of the structure tensor, the anisotropy measurement as a matrix is produced according to the gradient magnitude of the SCI. Particularly, the structure tensor can be expressed by

$$T(i) = \begin{pmatrix} \Sigma_j \langle \nabla_h S_j, \nabla_h S_j \rangle & \Sigma_j \langle \nabla_v S_j, \nabla_h S_j \rangle \\ \Sigma_j \langle \nabla_h S_j, \nabla_v S_j \rangle & \Sigma_j \langle \nabla_v S_j, \nabla_v S_j \rangle \end{pmatrix}, \tag{2.43}$$

where pixel $j \in R(i)$ near pixel i with a predefined radius; ∇_h and ∇_v represent the partial differential operators in the directions of horizontal and vertical, respectively; and $\langle \cdot, \cdot \rangle$ is the inner product of two vectors. In terms of mathematics, $T(i)$ is a semi positive-definite symmetric. As a 2×2 matrix, $T(i)$ has two eigenvectors η_i^* and η_i^* and the two corresponding non-negative eigenvalues λ_i^* and λ_i^*. From this, we define the anisotropy measurement as the correlative distance between $\lambda_i^\star$ and λ_i^*, expressed as follows:

$$A(i) = \frac{\lambda_i^\star - \lambda_i^* + \epsilon}{\lambda_i^\star + \lambda_i^* + \epsilon},$$

(2.44)

where ϵ is a minor constant used to prevent division by zero. Equation (2.44) denotes the value of anisotropy measurement A between 0 and 1. A equals or approximates the maximum value 1 when there is a vital alter in the pixel intensity of the structure, i.e., 1) $\lambda_i^\star \gg \lambda_i^*$ and 2) $\lambda_i^\star > 0$ and $\lambda_i^* = 0$. When the structures have the same direction ($\lambda_i^\star \approx \lambda_i^*$), the anisotropy measurement converges to 0. The inner product $\langle \eta_i^\star, \eta_i^* \rangle$, with values ranging from 0 and 1, is used to assess the difference in direction between two vectors. In most cases, the pixels of SCIs with fine anisotropy are easily perceptible, so anisotropy measurement provides a better method to find the main direction of the SCI. Given the above considerations, the MASM model in this research can be defined as follows:

$$MASM(S) = G \cdot A,$$

(2.45)

where G and A are obtained from Eq. (2.40) and Eq. (2.44), respectively.

Microscopic Structure Measurement

The microstructure measurement (MISM) model is also critical in this method, which is defined by measuring the main visual information and uncertain information.

Gradient Magnitude The calculation of gradient magnitude can be found above.

Uncertain Information The input visual signal passes through the HVS channel before entering the brain when image is perceived. In this process, the lens represents low-pass filters, and it can decrease specific high-frequency information [7, 8]. In essence, the procedure of human visual perception can be approximately denoted as a low-pass filter [33]. By sufficiently considering the special functions of HVS and SCIs, the Gaussian and motion low-pass filters merged to derive the uncertain information [38]. The text content of viewing behavior is explained, and the uncertainty information generated during the "fixation" and "saccade" stages of the eye is measured effectively [10, 39]. Especially, a Gaussian filter can be denoted as follows:

$$H_g(p, q) = \frac{1}{2\pi\delta^2} \exp(-\frac{p^2 + q^2}{2\delta^2}),$$

(2.46)

where δ denotes the criterion deviation of the control smoothing intensity. Subsequently, the research generates the Gaussian smoothed image by convoluting it with the input SCI S:

$$S_g = S \otimes H_g.$$

(2.47)

In this way, the uncertain information is derived by quantifying the discrepancy between S and S_g. Due to the maximum value, boundedness, and symmetry, we use the normalized form of gradient similarity [31]:

$$GS_g = f(S, S_g) = \frac{(G(s) - G(S_g))^2}{G^2(S) + G^2(S_g)}.$$ (2.48)

The motion filter is expressed by

$$H_m(p, q) = \begin{cases} 1/t & if \ \Gamma(p, q, \phi), \Upsilon(p, q) \leq t^2/4 \\ 0 & otherwise \end{cases},$$ (2.49)

where $\Gamma(p, q, \phi) = p \sin\phi + q \cos\phi$ and ϕ denotes motion filter's special direction. $\Upsilon(p, q) = p^2 + q^2$; t indicates the quantity of motion in pixels considered in the convolution step. The motion filtered image can be derived by convoluting it with the input SCI S:

$$S_m = S \otimes H_m.$$ (2.50)

Like the Gaussian filter, the uncertain information obtained from the motion blur is expressed by

$$GS_m = f(S, S_m) = \frac{(G(s) - G(S_m))^2}{G^2(S) + G^2(S_m)}.$$ (2.51)

In summary, as for the SCI S, we calculate the number of uncertain information through a simple direct average [40], which can be expressed by

$$U = \frac{1}{2}(GS_m + GS_g).$$ (2.52)

The proposed MISM model is denoted as follows:

$$MISM(S) = G \cdot U.$$ (2.53)

The MISM model is utilized to generate maps, and the result is exhibited in Fig. 2.8. It is worth mentioning that the detailed structure can be observed and highlighted.

Overall Quality Measure

On the basis of the above analysis, it is rational to merge the MASM and MISM models to make up for the shortcomings of each component and improve the prediction accuracy. In order to significantly facilitate the distortion comparison process, we distinguish insignificant structures from meaningful ones by linear mapping. By combining the psychometric function with the sigmoid colon [11], this article uses Galtons ogive [41], which is the cumulative normal distribution function (CDF) formula

$$C(s) = \frac{1}{\sqrt{2\pi}\phi} \int_{-\infty}^{s} \exp\left[-\frac{(t - \kappa)^2}{2\phi^2}\right] dt,$$ (2.54)

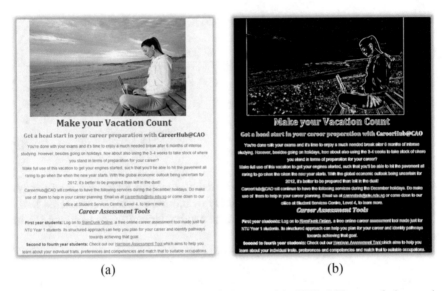

(a)   (b)

Fig. 2.8 Illustration of microscopic structures of SCIs. **a** A original SCIs. **b** The map of microscopic structures of (**a**) (©[2021] IEEE. Reprinted, with permission, from [39].)

where $C(S)$ denotes the prediction probability density used to distinguish the insignificant and significant structures. κ represents the modulation threshold; s is the stimulus amplitude; ϕ is the parameter that controls the slope of predicted change in probability. In this research, the authors allocate ϕ to a constant value fixed at 0.05 according to experience. By passing the maps of the MASM and MISM models through the CDF, we can obtain two important maps related to input SCI.

We adopt the above method of feature extraction on the original SCI $\dot{S}$ and its corresponding damaged version $\ddot{S}$. However, it is impractical to use the original image as pristine information for QA, which causes a huge transmission burden. To overcome this difficulty, this article uses a histogram to represent the distribution. Essentially, this approach targets at achieving an excellent compromise between the prediction and pristine information data score. We first study how to employ this approach to the MASM model. The distribution domain of $\phi([d_{min}, d_{max}])$ can be divided into N equal-length gaps. The histogram bin relies on the amount of factors by setting $\mathcal{W}_k$ as follows:

$$h_k = |\mathcal{W}_k|, \mathcal{W}_k = \{w|\Phi(w) \in J_k\}, \tag{2.55}$$

where

$$J_k = \{d_{min} + (k-1)\frac{\tilde{d}}{N}, d_{min} + k\frac{\tilde{d}}{N}\}, \tilde{d} = d_{max} - d_{min}. \tag{2.56}$$

The histogram bin of the lossless SCIs can be calculated as follows:

$$H_{\widetilde{S}}(k) = h_k / \sum_{l=1}^{N} h_l. \tag{2.57}$$

The same operation is applied to the damaged image $\ddot{S}$ to obtain $H_{\ddot{S}}(k)$. Each histogram bin's value is related to the interval probability. The score of the MASM model is obtained by comparing the following two histograms:

$$Q_{MASM}(\dot{S}, \ddot{S}) = \frac{1}{N} \sum_{k=1}^{N} \frac{min\{H_{\dot{S}}(k), H_{\ddot{S}(k)}\} + \mu}{max\{H_{\dot{S}}(k), H_{\ddot{S}(k)}\} + \mu}, \tag{2.58}$$

where $min\{\cdot, \cdot\}$ and $max\{\cdot, \cdot\}$ are utilized to observe the minimum and maximum values from two values, separately. μ is a tiny positive fixed value close to 0.

To prevent the denominator from being zero as $\{H_{\dot{S}}(k), H_{\ddot{S}}(k)\}$ approaches zero, set μ to a small normal number that approaches zero. At the same time, N is set to 2 to minimize the transmission burden. Obviously, the value of $Q_{MASM}(\dot{S}, \ddot{S})$ ranges from zero to one. The value of $Q_{MASM}(\dot{S}, \ddot{S})$ is larger, and the quality of the input SCI is much better. In addition, we adopt the uniform step to the map of MISM, and its score $Q_{MISM}(\dot{S}, \ddot{S})$ can be obtained. Next, we multiply the scores of the MASM and MISM models to derive the final overall image quality score:

$$Q(\dot{S}, \ddot{S}) = Q_{MASM}(\dot{S}, \ddot{S}) \cdot Q_{MISM}(\dot{S}, \ddot{S})^{\alpha}, \tag{2.59}$$

where α is an exponential parameter to adjust the validity of two models' score of the MASM $Q_{MASM}(\dot{S}, \ddot{S})$ and MISM $Q_{MISM}(\dot{S}, \ddot{S})$. If the two terms are assumed to be equally important, α can be set as 1.

2.2.3 No-Reference QA of Screen Content Images

As computer technology evolves with each passing day, different types of natural scenes, graphics, and SCIs are being created. Over the past decades, a quantity of image QA methods have been proposed to process the content of NSIs. However, there is limited research on the QA of SCIs. In SCIs, the original picture information is not available, so it is particularly important to propose NR QA algorithms.

Unified Blind QA of Compressed Natural, Graphic, and SCIs

To deal with the booming growth of SCIs, we will introduce a cross-content-type (CCT) database as well as an UCA NR image QA model that can be applied to multiple content categories.

Fig. 2.9 Pristine images in the CCT database. Top two rows: NSIs. Middle two rows: CGIs. Bottom two rows: SCIs (©[2021] IEEE. Reprinted, with permission, from [42].)

CCT Database

Due to the different characteristics shown by SCIs, existing objective image QA methods lack reliable mechanisms to obtain content category changes, which is a serious problem for generalizing from one category to another. To solve this issue, we established a CCT database consisting of 1,320 contaminated NSIs, computer graphic images (CGIs), and SCIs. We utilize the HEVC intracoding method and the screen content image compression (SCC) extension of HEVC.

In addition, we select three kinds of images from the above database. (1) 24 high-quality NSIs covering a variety of image content: nature and urban views, indoor and outdoor landscapes, and close-up and wide-angle shots. (2) 24 reference CGIs were captured from 15 computer games through screen shots. The types of games selected are diverse, including action, adventure, and strategy. (3) The last 23 reference SCIs are picked from the SCD database [21] and another one is collected via screen shot. The SCIs cover a wide range of usual computer operation scenes, such as web pages, Internet files, and software. All 72 pristine NSIs, CGIs, and SCIs are exhibited in Fig. 2.9. Similarly, the HEVC and HEVC-SC are utilized to compress the original SCIs. Generally, the CCT database totally composes of 72 original and 1,320 contaminated NSIs, CGIs, and SCIs.

The Proposed UCA Model

The designed UCA model contains two major parts: a feature extraction step implemented on multiple scales and an adaptive multi-scale weighting step integrating the results into a single quality score. A diagram of this model is exhibited in Fig. 2.10.

Feature Extraction From the perspective of the spatial domain, corners and edges may be the most significant image features. They are sensitive to multifarious image distortion types. New corners and edges are generated close to block boundaries, whereas real corners and edges will be smoothed inside blocks. We find it is easy to detect the differences in corners and edges between block boundaries and regions inside, which can effectively obtain the prediction of compressed images' perceptual quality.

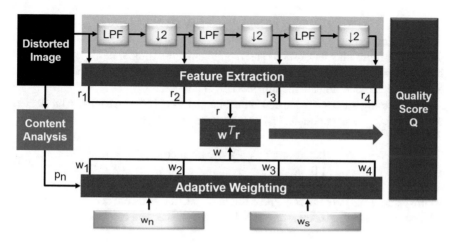

Fig. 2.10 Diagram of the designed UCA method. LPF: low-pass filtering. ↓ 2: downsampling by a parameter of 2. p_n: the likelihood of a contaminated image being NSI. w_n: multi-scale weights for NSI. w_s: multi-scale weights for SCI. w: final multi-scale weights. r: feature vector

Corner Feature We realize the recognition of corners in UCA model by using Shi and Tomasi's minimum eigenvalue method [28]. The corners in an image $P(x, y)$ can be identified by maximizing the weighted sum of squared differences:

$$S(a, b) = \sum_{x,y} \mathbf{A}(x, y)[\mathbf{P}(x + a, y + b) - \mathbf{P}(x, y)]^2, \quad (2.60)$$

where (a, b) denotes the spatial transform, and $\mathbf{A}(x, y)$ is a weighted parameter. We apply a Taylor series expansion to $I(x + u, y + v)$, and $S(a, b)$ can be estimated as follows:

$$S(a, b) \approx \begin{bmatrix} a\ b \end{bmatrix} \mathbf{H} \begin{bmatrix} a \\ b \end{bmatrix}, \quad (2.61)$$

where H is a Harris matrix:

$$\mathbf{H} = \sum_{x,y} \mathbf{w}(x, y) \begin{bmatrix} \mathbf{P}_x\mathbf{P}_x & \mathbf{P}_x\mathbf{P}_y \\ \mathbf{P}_x\mathbf{P}_y & \mathbf{P}_y\mathbf{P}_y \end{bmatrix}. \quad (2.62)$$

Corner has a more clear variance in $S(a, b)$ along all directions defined by (a, b). It means that the Harris matrix $\mathbf{H}$ should have two large eigenvalues. Hence, a corner metric can be expressed as follows:

$$\mathbf{H}_\lambda = \min(\lambda_1, \lambda_2), \quad (2.63)$$

where λ_1 and λ_2 are eigenvalues of $\mathbf{H}$. A corner map can be obtained by

$$\mathbf{C_{map}} = \left(c_{ij}\right)_{h \times w} = \mathrm{BW}\left(\mathbf{H_\lambda}\right), \tag{2.64}$$

where BW represents a threshold based on binarization function. $\mathbf{C_{map}}$ denotes the binary corner map, where $c_{ij} = 1$ means that a corner is recognized at location (i, j). h and w separately indicate the image's height and width.

For selecting the corners located at the boundaries of block, we make a mask map $\mathbf{M} = \left(m_{ij}\right)_{h \times w}$. The parameters can be expressed as follows:

$$m_{ij} = \begin{cases} 1 & \text{if } \mod (i, N) < 2 \text{ or } \mod (j, N) < 2 \\ 0 & \text{otherwise} \end{cases}, \tag{2.65}$$

where i and j indicate the row and column parameter, respectively. mod computes the rest; N means the block size. With the mask, the corners can be derived by

$$\mathbf{C_{map}}' = \left(c_{ij}'\right)_{h \times w} = \mathbf{C_{map}} \circ \mathbf{M} = \left(c_{ij} \cdot m_{ij}\right)_{h \times w}, \tag{2.66}$$

where $\circ$ means the Hadamard product. The corner feature is obtained by

$$r_c = \frac{\sum_{i,j} c_{ij}'}{\sum_{i,j} c_{ij}}. \tag{2.67}$$

Edge Feature Same as the corner feature, we have to enhance the edge of SCI and extract the edge feature. To this aim, we obtain the gradient magnitude of an image P from

$$\mathbf{G} = \sqrt{\mathbf{G}_x^2 + \mathbf{G}_y^2}, \tag{2.68}$$

where G_x and G_y represent the partial derivatives along horizontal and vertical directions, separately. An edge map is calculated as follows:

$$\mathbf{E_{map}} = \left(e_{ij}\right)_{h \times w} = \mathrm{BW}(\mathbf{G}), \tag{2.69}$$

where $\mathbf{E_{map}}$ is a binary map of edge, in which $e_{ij} = 1$ is an edge pixel located at (i, j). We recognize edges at the block boundaries with the uniform mask map $\mathbf{M}$ defined:

$$\mathbf{E_{map}}' = \left(e_{ij}'\right)_{h \times w} = \mathbf{E_{map}} \circ \mathbf{M} = \left(e_{ij} \cdot m_{ij}\right)_{h \times w}. \tag{2.70}$$

Similarly, we obtain the edge feature by calculating the ratio of the edges as follows:

$$r_e = \frac{\sum_{i,j} e_{ij}'}{\sum_{i,j} e_{ij}}. \tag{2.71}$$

Overall Quality Feature In Fig. 2.11, block boundaries take up $R = \frac{4(N-1)}{N^2}$ of an image. Normally, a high-quality image without block-based compression should have r_c and r_e, which values approximate R. The stronger the compression level

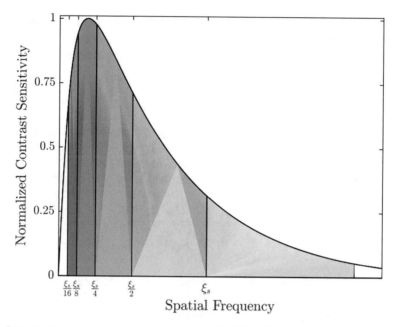

Fig. 2.11 Multi-scale weights for screen content (©[2021] IEEE. Reprinted, with permission, from [42].)

is, the easier the corners and edges are detected near the boundary, and the larger the values of r_c and r_e are. We calculate the overall quality or distortion feature as the product of r_c and r_e normalized with R^2 in order to make the eigenvalue of the high-quality image approach one:

$$r = \frac{r_c r_e}{R^2} = \frac{N^4 r_c r_e}{16(N-1)^2}.$$
(2.72)

The process of eigenvalue extract is implemented at four scales. The eigenvalue vector $\mathbf{r} = [r_1, r_2, r_3, r_4]^T$, where r_i means the overall quality eigenvalue at the ith scale.

Adaptive Multi-Scale Weighting

To thoroughly investigate the effect of human psychological behaviors and visual perception characteristics, we designed an adaptive multi-scale framework. This framework has been proved to improve quality prediction performance in many works.

Multi-Scale Weights for Screen Content Normally, humans behave very differently when watching SCIs. When people watch SCIs, the human brain is more inclined to focus attention, making the framework's performance of extracting the categories of information better. Our aim is to simulate the human brain's behavior in daily life and realize equal watching performance in natural scenes and screen content. For that, we fix the equivalent viewing distance of the screen content at half its actual viewing distance. The parameter of viewing distance is expressed by

$$\xi_s = \frac{\pi \cdot d \cdot n}{180 \cdot h_s \cdot 2},$$

(2.73)

where ξ_s is viewing distance factor, its unit is cycles per degree of visual angle (cpd); d means the viewing distance (inch); h_s indicates the screen's height (inch); n is the sum of pixels in the screen's vertical direction. We utilize ξ_s to split the domain for each scale, which covers one part of the contrast sensitivity function obtained by [43]

$$S(u) = \frac{5200exp\left(-0.0016u^2(1 + \frac{100}{L})^{0.08}\right)}{\sqrt{\left(1 + \frac{144}{X_0^2} + 0.64u^2\right)\left(\frac{63}{L^{0.83}} + \frac{1}{1-exp(-0.02u^2)}\right)}},$$

(2.74)

where u, L, and X_0^2 represent spatial frequency (cpd), luminance (cd/m^2), and angular object area, respectively. The weight of each block is computed as the area covered by the corresponding frequency under the CSF

$$w_i = \frac{1}{Z} \int_{\frac{\xi_s}{2^i}}^{\frac{\xi_s}{2^{i-1}}} S(u)du, \quad i \in \{1, 2, 3, 4\},$$

(2.75)

where w_i indicates the block's weight, and $\sum_i w_i = 1$. The value of i between 1 to 4 means the optimal to coarsest scale, separately. Z is a normalization parameter.

Reference-Free QA of SCIs

In this part, we introduce a new reference-free model to estimate the perceptual quality of SCIs by utilizing big data learning. The novel model extracts four categories of features including image complexity, screen content statistics, global brightness quality, and details' sharpness.

Feature Selection

Image Complexity Description Due to the fact that image complexity is a key parameter correlated to the influences of gaze direction and spatial masking, we consider it when devising SCI QA models. In this work, we define image complexity by calculating the discrepancy between an input image s and its measured output produced by an AR model:

$$y_q = \mathcal{Q}^n\left(x_q\right)\mathbf{a} + \tilde{t}_q,$$

(2.76)

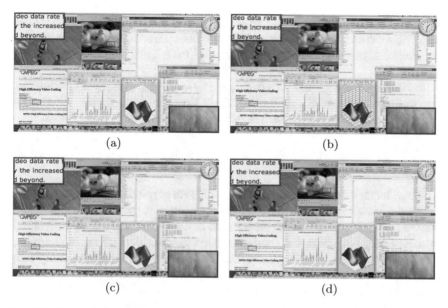

Fig. 2.12 Comparison of different filters: **a** a lossless SCI; **b–d** processed images generated by utilizing AR model, BL filter, and hybrid filter, separately (©[2021] IEEE. Reprinted, with permission, from [13].)

where q denotes pixel's index; y_q is a pixel's value located at x_q; $\mathcal{Q}^n(y_q)$ consists of the n surrounding pixels of x_q; $\mathbf{a} = (a_1, a_2, \ldots, a_n)^T$ represents a vector of AR parameter; $\tilde{t}_q$ means the residual error. We then derive the predicted image by

$$\hat{y}_q = \mathcal{Q}^n\left(x_q\right)\hat{\mathbf{a}}. \tag{2.77}$$

Figure 2.12a, b exhibits an example of the SCI and its corresponding output images generated by the AR model. To enhance the performance of near-image edges detection by using the AR model, we use a BL filter. BL filter has edge protecting capability and computational simplicity, which can modify the AR model toward preserving edges and restraining the effect of ringing artifacts. The BL filter can be expressed as follows:

$$y_q = \mathcal{Q}^n\left(x_q\right)\mathbf{b} + \hat{t}_q, \tag{2.78}$$

where $\mathbf{b} = [b_1, b_2, \ldots, b_n]^T$ are a series of parameters generated by BL filter; $\hat{t}_q$ means the error; $\mathbf{b}$ denotes the response of BL filter. The BL filter has better performance of closing luminance edges than does the predictor based on AR model. But it doesn't preserve texture details. In order to access the optimal performance of the two models, a hybrid filter is designed by combining the AR and BL filters systematically:

$$\hat{y}_q = \frac{\mathcal{Q}^n\left(x_q\right)\hat{\mathbf{a}} + \kappa \mathcal{Q}^n\left(x_q\right)\mathbf{b}}{1 + \kappa}, \tag{2.79}$$

where κ regulates the correlative force of the AR and BL filters' responses. We assign this value at 9, since its related to hybrid filter can attain the output image. The predicted output has a positive tradeoff between the AR and BL filters, as exhibited in Fig. 2.12d.

We then calculate the residual error map $\Delta y_q = y_q - \hat{y}_q$ by using Δy_q to improve the predicted accuracy of large absolute values. Next, the obtained feature descriptive of the image complexity is defined as the entropy of the residual error map E_r:

$$E_r = -\int_i p_i \log p_i di, \tag{2.80}$$

where p_i indicates the probability density of the ith grayscale in the Δy_q.

Previous research finds that the mechanisms selective to limited domains of spatial frequencies and orientations are the intrinsic attributes of the HVS. These research results develop into multi-scale cortical models that permeate advanced perception models and visual processing algorithms. So we calculate the image complexity at a reduced resolution by employing a subsample with a set of 16 pixels in each fundamental direction after using a 16×16 square to move the low-pass filter. We set the decreased resolution complexity as E_d. The overall image complexity is denoted as $F_c = \{E_r, E_d\}$.

Screen Content Statistics The degradation of image structure can be calculated in the following way. $\mathbf{s}$ is the input image, $\mu_\mathbf{s}$, $\sigma_\mathbf{s}$, and $\tilde{\sigma}_\mathbf{s}$ indicate local mean and variance maps:

$$\mu_\mathbf{s} = \sum_{r=1}^{R} w_r s_r, \tag{2.81}$$

$$\sigma_\mathbf{s} = \left[\sum_{r=1}^{R} w_r \left(s_r - \mu_s \right)^2 \right]^{\frac{1}{2}}, \tag{2.82}$$

$$\tilde{\sigma}_\mathbf{s} = \left[\sum_{r=1}^{R} \left(s_r - \mu_s \right)^2 \right]^{\frac{1}{2}}, \tag{2.83}$$

where $\mathbf{w} = \{w_r \mid r = 1, 2, 3, \ldots, R\}$ denotes a normalized Gaussian window. The structural degradation can be calculated by

$$S_\mu(\mathbf{s}) = \frac{1}{D} \sum \left(\frac{\sigma_{(\mu_\mathbf{s}\mathbf{s})} + \gamma}{\sigma_{(\mu_\mathbf{s})}\sigma_\mathbf{s} + \gamma} \right), \tag{2.84}$$

$$S_\sigma(\mathbf{s}) = \frac{1}{D} \sum \left(\frac{\sigma_{(\sigma_\mathbf{s}\tilde{\sigma}_\mathbf{s})} + \gamma}{\sigma_{(\sigma_\mathbf{s})}\sigma_{(\tilde{\sigma}_\mathbf{s})} + \gamma} \right), \tag{2.85}$$

where D means the pixels' amount in $\mathbf{s}$; γ indicates an extra positive stationary constant; $\sigma(\alpha_1, \alpha_2)$ denotes the local empirical covariance map between α_1 and α_2:

$$\sigma_{(\alpha_1,\alpha_2)} = \sum_{r=1}^{R} w_r \left(\alpha_r - \mu_{\alpha_1}\right)\left(\beta_r - \mu_{\alpha_2}\right). \tag{2.86}$$

Normally, SCIs are composed of pictorial and textual parts in the mean time. We use two Gaussian window functions to capture their microstructure and macrostructure, respectively. We also adopt different ways to process the interiors and edges of blocks when capturing structural degradation information. On this basis, we extract eight structural degradation features, named $S_{(a,b,c)}$, where $a = \{\mu, \sigma\}$ denotes information category, $b = \{3, 11\}$ represents kernel size, and $c = \{i, e\}$ means block interiors and edges, separately.

There are eight structural degradation features $S_{(a,b,c)}(s_0)$, in which s_0 indicates an uncontaminated SCI. We compare the image complexity features $E_r(s_0)$ by utilizing the obtained SCIs. The scatter plot is exhibited in Fig. 2.13. Blue dots are related to uncontaminated SCIs. It is obviously observed that there exists an approximate linear relationship between the image complexity feature E_r and the structural degradation $S_{(\mu,3,i)}$. It inspires us to predict distortions by estimating the departure of a distorted SCI with this linear relationship found in positive quality SCIs. We make efforts to fit the linear regression model:

$$E_r(\mathbf{s}_0) = \begin{bmatrix} A_{(a,b,c)} \\ B_{(a,b,c)} \end{bmatrix}^T \begin{bmatrix} S_{(a,b,c)}(\mathbf{s}_0) \\ 1 \end{bmatrix}, \tag{2.87}$$

where $\left[A_{(a,b,c)}, B_{(a,b,c)}\right]$ denotes one of eight factor pairs associated with (a, b, c).

Structural degradation characteristics obtain the changes in image structure, while the estimation of image complexity is sensitive to image details. Hence, the performance of these two features responds dissimilarly to the different levels and categories of distortion. As shown in Fig. 2.13, the near-linear relationship between pristine SCI features will be tampered when introducing diverse distortions.

Global Measurement of Brightness and Surface Quality These abovementioned features perform well for measuring many visual degradations, but cannot capture undesirable brightness changes or contrast changes. Among them, the contrast change is a challenge to detect, because it will also influence the complexity of the image: raised contrast will lead to the promotion of the image's complexity and vice versa. From that, we find that features are sensitive to contrast adjustments and not susceptible to noise, blur, and other artifacts. Here, we employ the sample mean of the image $\mathbf{s}$, defined as O_1:

$$O_1 = E(\mathbf{s}) = \frac{1}{D} \sum_{d=1}^{D} s_d. \tag{2.88}$$

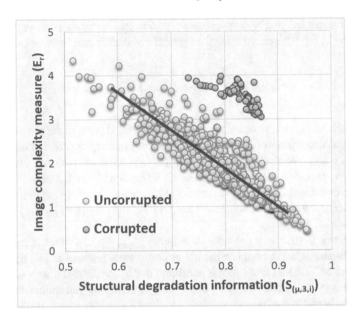

Fig. 2.13 Representative scatter plot of image complexity feature E_r versus structural degradation information $S_{(\mu,3,i)}$ on uncontaminated (blue points) and distorted (red points) SCIs (©[2021] IEEE. Reprinted, with permission, from [13].)

We also calculate the sample skewness of the image **s**:

$$O_3 = \frac{E\left[(\mathbf{s} - O_1)^3\right]}{\sqrt{E^3\left[(\mathbf{s} - O_1)^2\right]}}.$$ (2.89)

This feature is positively related to image contrast. After processing, the SCI with larger skew displays brighter and darker than its correlated pristine image. In summary, we estimate features associated with global brightness and surface quality, which are denoted as $F_{bs} = \{O_1, O_3\}$.

Detail Assessment of Sharpness and Corners With the development of picture compression technologies, more and more compression images are stored on our computers. Compression usually leads to complex interactions of multiple distortions. We utilize two types of features to percept two main categories of compression distortion: local sharpness loss and blocking. We measure the log-energy of wavelet subbands of an image at three scales, that is, $\{LL_3, LH_n, HL_n, HH_n\}$, and $n = 1, 2, 3$. At each level of decomposition, the log-energy can be computed as follows:

$$L_{m,n} = log_{10}\left[1 + \frac{1}{M_n}\sum_h m_n^2(h)\right],$$ (2.90)

where h indicates the pixel index; m represents LH, HL, and HH; and M_n denotes the sum of wavelet coefficients at the nth level. Each decomposition level's log-energy can be derived as follows:

$$L_n = \frac{L_{LH,n} + L_{HL,n} + \gamma L_{HH,n}}{2 + \gamma}, \tag{2.91}$$

where γ is set to 8 to apply a greater effect on the HH subbands. Only the second and third levels are adopted to obtain information associated with sharpness. We have observed that utilizing all levels cannot produce performance gains. The second compression feature detects corners to derive the measurement of blockiness. Min et al. [44] prove that SCI corners change with the variation of compression. Especially, there exist many sharp edges and regular patterns in the screen content image generated by the computer, which makes the increase of genuine corners. While the blockiness caused by compression will increase pseudo corners. We find that the real corners may occur anywhere, and the pseudo corners only appear at block boundaries. We define the image matrix $\mathbf{S} = (s_{ij})_{\tau \times v}$, where τ represents the image height and v indicates image width. We first adopt the Shi-Tomasi detector [28] to detect corners. The corner map $\mathcal{C} = (c_{ij})_{\tau \times v}$ can be obtained by

$$c_{ij} = \begin{cases} 1 & if \ s_{ij} \in \mathbb{C} \\ 0 & otherwise \end{cases}, \tag{2.92}$$

and the pseudo corner map $\mathcal{P} = (p_{ij})_{\tau \times v}$ denoted as follows:

$$p_{ij} = \begin{cases} 1 & if \ s_{ij} \in \mathbb{C}, mod(i, k) \leqslant 1 mod(j, k) \leqslant 1 \\ 0 & otherwise \end{cases}, \tag{2.93}$$

where $s_{ij} \in \mathbb{C}$ denotes a corner located at (i, j), mod keeps the rest part of the region, and k indicates the compression blocks' size, which normally is set to 8×8 in JPEG. As the degree of compression distortion increases, the number of pseudo corners will increase due to blockiness, while the number of genuine corners will decrease due to intrablock blurring. By combining these, we calculate the ratio of pseudo corners to all corners:

$$R = \sqrt{\xi_p / \xi_c}, \tag{2.94}$$

where $\xi_p = \sum_{i,j} p_{ij}$ and $\xi_c = \sum_{i,j} c_{ij}$, respectively, present the sum of pseudo corners and all corners. Thus, we utilize $F_{sc} = \{L_2, L_3, R\}$ to calculate the last features associated with image sharpness and corners.

In total, we extract 15 features, which contains image complexity (f_{01}-f_{02}), the statistics of SCIs (f_{03}-f_{10}), global brightness and surface quality (f_{11}-f_{12}), compression-induced image sharpness loss (f_{11}-f_{12}), and blocky corners (f_{15}).

Module Regression

In order to transform 15 features into a single index of the screen image quality, we adopt a regression model, that is, efficient SVR [14, 15, 45]. Concretely, we utilize the LibSVM package to execute the SVR with the radial basis function (RBF) kernel [46]. To observe the performance of the proposed model, we divide the 1,000 trials into two parts, 80% data for training and 20% data for testing. The contemporary database includes SCIs of less than 1500. The limited number of different scenes and distortion levels leads to the fact that the regression module cannot be successfully implemented in a larger domain of image scenes and distortion levels. To solve this issue, more opinion-unaware (OU) blind image QA models have been designed [47, 48]. Different from the opinion-aware (OA) methods, the OU method does not rely on human-labeled training images, which has greater generalization potential for large volumes of authentic world images.

We develop the OU-NR image QA model by a generic framework mentioned at the start of this section. The framework is flexible for developing the distortion-specific blind image QA approach that uses a larger number of training images with more distortion types. This general framework is adopted to train a highly efficient SVR to study a regression module with a large number of training images.

Training Samples Eleven kinds of distortions (namely, GN, JC, J2C, HEVC, SC, GB, MB, and four CC-correlated distortions including Gamma transfer, brightness intensity-shifting, and so on) are applied to distort 800 SCIs, producing a training sample including 100,000 distorted images. In [49], 1,000 "webpage" and "screen capture" images are gathered from the "Google Images" website. But these images were not tested to identify if they are contaminated with visible distortions. Apart from that, the image content is limited, and the resolution of some of the images is low. To overcome these limitations, we manually gather 800 undistorted SCIs including considerably richer content.

Training Labels Image QA training labels are usually obtained from subjective experiments. Subjective experiments are time-wasting and laborious, which is not suitable for labeling a high volume of training images. To avoid the problems associated with large-scale study participation, we implement an objective QA model to generate scores as training labels to take the place of subjective opinion scores. Ideally, human scorings can be approximated by using a well-performed FR image QA model. We apply the FR saliency-guided quality measure of screen content (SQMS) metric on SCI QA, which realizes an excellent performance. After clearing images outlier, we label about 100,000 training images by using predicted quality scores obtained from SQMS. By training the SVR with a large body of training data, we derive a constant regression module named screen image quality evaluator, which can transform the fifteen features into a single quality prediction score.

Data Cleaning Every FR metric on the basis of the learning framework may mislead the training process due to mislabeled training data. This indicates that it is meaningful to propose a mechanism to examine and reduce noisy training data [50]. We test the potentially noisy quality predictions by comparing the quality predictions generated from SQMS and structure-induced quality metric (SIQM) algorithms. Both

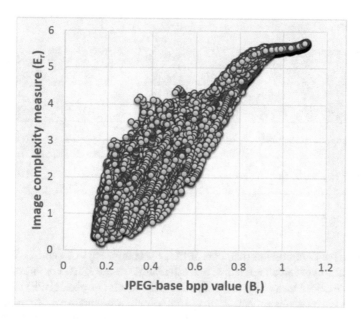

Fig. 2.14 Scatter plot of image complexity estimate (E_r) and JPEG-based bpp value (B_r) on 100,000 training images (©[2021] IEEE. Reprinted, with permission, from [13].)

algorithms have been proved that they can predict SCIs accurately. Specifically, we measure the PLCC between the SQMS and SIQM ratio on each of the 800 images. Figure 2.14 exhibits the plots of 800 images. It can be observed that the overwhelming most PLCC values are very high and only several values are under 0.9, as shown in red in Fig. 2.14. We hypothesize the low PLCC values as "noisy", then remove these images' content and their corresponding training images.

Complexity Reduction

The hybrid filter implements in local regions, which causes the SIQE inefficient. For an image of size 2560 × 1440, the time cost of calculating four kinds of features is exhibited in Table 2.1. For high-definition images, the SIQE's operating time is approximately 804 s. The time to estimate image complexity is over 600 times that of the other three feature categories.

There are two useful methods to reduce the computational complexity of the hybrid filter. One way is a simplified version of the simplified screen image quality evaluator (SSIQE), which removes the AR model while reserving the BL filter. The SSIQE only needs 42.2 and 0.19 s to operate on the image with the size of 2560 × 1440. Then the other way is to simulate the output of the hybrid filter by using highly efficient algorithms. Calculating the entropy of the difference Δy_q between an image and its corresponding estimation, which is sufficiently associated with predictive coding [8, 19]. Based on this idea, we deploy an image's compressibility to measure complexity.

Table 2.1 Computation time of fifteen types features

Feature type	Symbol	Feature ID	Time (second)
Image complexity	E_r	f_{01}	802.0
	E_d	f_{02}	
Screen content scene statistics	$T_{(a,b,c)}$	$f_{03} - f_{10}$	0.702
Brightness and surface quality	O_1	f_{11}	0.153
	O_3	f_{12}	
Sharpness and corners	L_2, L_3	$f_{13} - f_{14}$	0.462
	R	f_{15}	

We tested five compression methods: JPEG, J2, H.264, HEVC, and SC. To make a good balance between effectiveness and efficiency, we use JPEG compression in the "lossless" mode. Meanwhile, we utilize the derived bit per pixel (BPP) value as an alternative correlated approach of image complexity measurement. By utilizing the 100,000 training images, we draw the scatter plot between the JPEG-based bpp values B_r and the image complexity estimate E_r calculated through the hybrid filter. This scatter plot shows a broad linear relationship, which surpasses 95%. Like Eq. (2.87), we establish this linear model and explore the two parameters observed by least squares. Using the compression-backed B_r and B_d to replace the image complexity estimates E_r and E_d, we derive an alternate and quicker model named the accelerated screen image quality evaluator (ASIQE). For the same size image, the calculation only needs 0.125 and 0.022 s when calculating B_r and B_d separately, or approximately 6400 and 150 times the computational efficiency correlative to calculating E_r and E_d.

2.3 Comparison and Analysis of Algorithm Performance

In this section, we introduce an image database that is specific to SCIs and analysis of some modern reference-free and reference-based image QA methods. We concentrate on comparing and measuring the performance of the introduced QA models in this chapter with these methods. The analysis results show that the performance of these models in this chapter is quite well.

2.3.1 Testing Database

To verify the performance of the introduced SCIs QA models, we utilize the SIQAD [6] to compare and analyze. This database was established by Nanyang Technology University in 2015 and composes of 20 pristine screen images and 980 contaminated images. These 980 images are obtained by corrupting the original images with seven kinds of distortions at seven intensity grades according to those 20 reference images. The seven distortions include CC, GB, MB, GN, LC, JP, and J2. Over 20 subjects are invited to participate in the subjective scoring and rate these 980 corrupted images in 11 grades from zero to ten. The image with a higher score means a better quality, and the highest ten means the best quality. This scoring procedure is implemented in a quiet environment and the viewing distance is set to 2.25 times the screen height. The DMOS value of each image in the database is normalized to [24.2, 90.1].

2.3.2 Performance Comparison and Analysis

In order to reflect the validity and superiority of the models introduced in this chapter, we compare the introduced models with the state-of-the-art image QA models. They can be divided into three categories in Table 2.2. The first category is composed of 18 FR image QA models. The second category is composed of 10 RR image QA models. The third category is composed of 7 NR image QA models.

When we compare the above modern image QA methods, four commonly used metrics, namely PLCC, SRCC, KRCC, and RMSE, are used. The evaluation accuracy can be measured by PLCC and RMSE, while the monotonicity of the prediction can be found by SRCC and KRCC. A higher value of PLCC, SRCC, and KRCC and a lower value of RMSE represent better quality evaluation methods. The objective assessment scores are nonlinearity obtained by PLCC, SRCC, KRCC, and RMSE, so we use a logistic function to increase the linearity. We compute the image QA scores using these four criteria by the mapping including five parameters as follows:

$$f(x) = \tau_1 \left(\frac{1}{2} - \frac{1}{1 + \exp^{\tau_2 (x - \tau_3)}} + \tau_4 x + \tau_5 \right), \tag{2.95}$$

where $\tau_{i, i=1,2,3,4,5}$ represents the fitted parameter; $f(x)$ and x are subjective scores and its corresponding objective scores which are assessed by image QA algorithms.

The performance results of 28 competing image QA techniques are illustrated in Table 3.2 for comparison. We find the best-performing model in each category. The comparison results of the proposed introduced metrics in this chapter with existing image QA algorithms including three categories are presented. By analyzing the superiority of these models, we are able to derive some important conclusions as follows:

(1) Among these tested FR image QA models, the SQMS algorithm outperforms other models according to the value of SRCC, KRCC, PLCC, and RMSE, respec-

Table 2.2 Information of the metrics involved in the comparative experiment

Category	Abbreviation	Full Name	Refs.
FR	GSI	Gradient Similarity	[55]
FR	IGM	Internal Generative Mechanism	[66]
FR	VSI	Visual Saliency-induced Index	[5]
FR	PSIM	Perceptual SIMilarity	[40]
FR	ADD-GSIM	Analysis of Distortion Distribution GSIM	[67]
FR	SIQM	Structure-Induced Quality Metric	[68]
FR	SQMS	Saliency-guided Quality Measure of Screen content	[8]
FR	NQM	Noise Quality Measure	[53]
FR	SSIM	Structural SIMilarity	[2]
FR	VIFP	Visual Information Fidelity in Pixel domain	[31]
FR	VSNR	Visual Signal-to-Noise Ratio	[54]
FR	FSIMC	Feature SIMilarity in Color domain	[3]
FR	GSM	Gradient Similarity Measurement	[55]
FR	GMSD	Gradient Magnitude Similarity Deviation	[4]
FR	SPQA	Screen Perceptual Quality Assessment	[6]
FR	SVQI	Structural Variation-based Quality Index	[1]
FR	SQI	SCI Quality Index	[29]
FR	Xia et al.	–	[39]
RR	DNT-RR	Divisive NormalizaTion domain Reduced-Reference quality model	[57]
RR	VIF-RR	Visual-Information-Fidelity-based Reduced-Reference model	[58]
RR	WNISM	Wavelet-domain Natural Image Statistic Model	[59]
RR	FTQM	Fourier Transform-based scalable image Quality Metric	[60]
RR	SDM	Structural Degradation Model	[61]
RR	BMPRI	Blind Multiple Pseudo-Reference Image	[62]
RR	BPRI	Blind Pseudo-Reference Image	[63]
RR	RWQMS	Reduced-reference Wavelet-domain Quality Measure of Screen content pictures	[21]
RR	RQMSC	Reduced-reference Quality Measure of Screen Content pictures	[22]
RR	PBM	Prediction Backed Model	[65]
NR	NIQE	Natural Image Quality Evaluator	[47]
NR	IL-NIQE	Integrated Local-NIQE	[48]
NR	BQMS	Blind Quality Measure for Screen content images	[44]
NR	UCA	Unified Content-type Adaptive	[42]
NR	SIQE	Screen Image Quality Evaluator	[13]
NR	SSIQE	Simplified Screen Image Quality Evaluator	[13]
NR	ASIQE	Accelerated Screen Image Quality Evaluator	[13]

tively. SRCC and KRCC are widely used evaluation metrics that reflect the monotonicity of the measurements. From the viewpoint of this index, the proposed FR SVQI metric drives a remarkably high performance. The SRCC, KRCC, and PLCC value of the SVQI is significantly higher than all the three types of models on the SIQAD database.

(2) Since the RR image QA models use less reference information, the four metric value of this type of model is worse than FR image QA models. Among the ten RR image QA models, the RWQMS attains the best performance in the value of SRCC, KRCC, PLCC, and RMSE. From statistics, we can observe that the performance of the RR image QA models used for comparison is not only lower than that of the FR image QA models proposed, but also worse than that of the NR image QA models proposed. It is worth mentioning that SIQE is statistically superior to all the tested RR image QA models, even some FR image QA models.

(3) Considering the blind image QA model, the BQMS achieves the optimal results in the tested methods according to the value of SRCC, KRCC, PLCC, and RMSE. The SIQE is the best model in the proposed NR image QA model, whose SRCC, KRCC, and PLCC values are higher than the ones of BQMS.

2.4 Conclusion

SCIs are mainly generated by computers and mobile phone screens. Different from NSIs, their color change is not obvious and their shape is relatively simple. Thus, the QA metrics designed for NSIs may be difficult to show good performance on SCIs. This chapter introduces three types of methods to assess the quality of SCIs, namely FR, RR, and NR QA methods. Two FR image QA methods based on structural information are introduced. One of them not only associates perceived quality with structural variation, but also takes into account the HVS characteristics and the limitations of color change. The other one constructs a local QA based on structural similarity, which considers visual field adaptation and information content. Second, in order to accurately estimate image quality from a limited number of reference information, we introduce a RR image QA method with feature differences. It extracts the macrostructure of SCIs and calculates the feature difference between them and the corresponding distorted versions. Using similar processing for the microstructure, the overall image quality can be evaluated from these information. Finally, we introduce two NR QA methods of SCIs. One approach is to incorporate changes in human perception attributes into different image contents on a multi-scale weighted framework. The other method obtains the image quality score by four types of features: image complexity, screen content statistics, overall brightness quality, and detail clarity. Experimental results show that the FR, RR, and NR SCI QA models are better than the traditional SCI QA models. Despite the good performance of the measures described, there is still work to be done. In future work, we will consider how to develop universal image QA models that can accurately assess the visual quality of natural scenes and SCIs simultaneously.

References

1. Gu K, Qiao J, Min X et al (2017) Evaluating quality of screen content images via structural variation analysis. IEEE Trans Vis Comput Graph 24(10):2689–2701
2. Wang Z, Bovik AC, Sheikh HR et al (2004) Image quality assessment: from error visibility to structural similarity. IEEE Trans Image Process 13(4):600–612
3. Zhang L, Zhang L, Mou X et al (2011) FSIM: a feature similarity index for image quality assessment. IEEE Trans Image Process 20(8):2378–2386
4. Xue W, Zhang L, Mou X et al (2013) Gradient magnitude similarity deviation: a highly efficient perceptual image quality index. IEEE Trans Image Process 23(2):684–695
5. Zhang L, Shen Y, Li H (2014) VSI: a visual saliency-induced index for perceptual image quality assessment. IEEE Trans Image Process 23(10):4270–4281
6. Yang H, Fang Y, Lin W (2015) Perceptual quality assessment of screen content images. IEEE Trans Image Process 24(11):4408–4421
7. Ni Z, Ma L, Zeng H et al (2017) ESIM: edge similarity for screen content image quality assessment. IEEE Trans Image Process 26(10):4818–4831
8. Gu K, Wang S, Yang H et al (2016) Saliency-guided quality assessment of screen content images. IEEE Trans Multimedia 18(6):1098–1110
9. Fang Y, Yan J, Liu J et al (2017) Objective quality assessment of screen content images by uncertainty weighting. IEEE Trans Image Process 26(4):2016–2027
10. Ni Z, Zeng H, Ma L et al (2018) A Gabor feature-based quality assessment model for the screen content images. IEEE Trans Image Process 27(9):4516–4528
11. Fu Y, Zeng H, Ma L et al (2018) Screen content image quality assessment using multi-scale difference of Gaussian. IEEE Trans Circuits Syst Video Technol 28(9):2428–2432
12. Gu K, Zhai G, Yang X et al (2014) Using free energy principle for blind image quality assessment. IEEE Trans Multimedia 17(1):50–63
13. Gu K, Zhou J, Qiao J et al (2017) No-reference quality assessment of screen content pictures. IEEE Trans Image Process 26(8):4005–4018
14. Saad MA, Bovik AC, Charrier C (2012) Blind image quality assessment: a natural scene statistics approach in the DCT domain. IEEE Trans Image Process 21(8):3339–3352
15. Mittal A, Moorthy AK, Bovik AC (2012) No-reference image quality assessment in the spatial domain. IEEE Trans Image Process 21(12):4695–4708
16. Fang Y, Yan J, Li L et al (2017) No reference quality assessment for screen content images with both local and global feature representation. IEEE Trans Image Process 27(4):1600–1610
17. Shao F, Gao Y, Li F et al (2017) Toward a blind quality predictor for screen content images. IEEE Trans Syst Man Cybern Syst 48(9):1521–1530
18. Friston K, Kilner J, Harrison L (2006) A free energy principle for the brain. J Physiol Paris 100(1–3):70–87
19. Friston K (2010) The free-energy principle: a unified brain theory? Nat Rev Neurosci 11(2):127–138
20. Feynman BP (1998) Statistical mechanics: a set of lectures. Boca Raton
21. Wang S, Gu K, Zhang X et al (2016) Subjective and objective quality assessment of compressed screen content images. IEEE J Emerg Sel Top Circuits Syst 6(4):532–543
22. Wang S, Gu K, Zhang X et al (2016) Reduced-reference quality assessment of screen content images. IEEE Trans Circuits Syst Video Technol 28(1):1–14
23. Pan Z, Shen H, Lu Y et al (2013) A low-complexity screen compression scheme for interactive screen sharing. IEEE Trans Circuits Syst Video Technol 23(6):949–960
24. Jain R, Kasturi R, Schunck BG (1995) Machine vision. McGraw-hill, New York
25. Miller J (1989) The control of attention by abrupt visual onsets and offsets. Percept Psychophys 45(6):567–571
26. Harnad S (2003) Categorical perception. Encyclopedia of cognitive science. https://eprints.soton.ac.uk/257719/
27. Li L, Lin W, Zhu H (2014) Learning structural regularity for evaluating blocking artifacts in JPEG images. IEEE Signal Process Lett 21(8):918–922

28. Shi J (1994) Good features to track. In: Paper presented at the IEEE conference on computer vision and pattern recognition, pp 593–600, June 1994
29. Wang S, Gu K, Zeng K et al (2016) Objective quality assessment and perceptual compression of screen content images. IEEE Comput Graph Appl 38(1):47–58
30. Wang Z, Shang X (2006) Spatial pooling strategies for perceptual image quality assessment. In: Paper presented at the international conference on image processing, pp 2945–2948, Oct 2006
31. Sheikh HR, Bovik AC (2006) Image information and visual quality. IEEE Trans Image Process 15(2):430–444
32. Field DJ, Brady N (1997) Visual sensitivity, blur and the sources of variability in the amplitude spectra of natural scenes. Vis Res 37(23):3367–3383
33. Bosse S, Maniry D, Mller KR (2018) Deep neural networks for no-reference and full-reference image quality assessment. IEEE Trans Image Process 27(1):206–219
34. Zuo L, Wang H, Fu J (2016) Screen content image quality assessment via convolutional neural network. In: Paper presented at the IEEE international conference on image processing, pp 2082–2086, Sep 2016
35. Yue G, Hou C, Yan W (2019) Blind quality assessment for screen content images via convolutional neural network. Digit Signal Process 91:21–30
36. Chen J, Shen L, Zheng L (2018) Naturalization module in neural networks for screen content image quality assessment. IEEE Signal Process Lett 25(11):1685–1689
37. Zhang Y, Chandler DM, Mou X (2018) Quality assessment of screen content images via convolutional-neural-network-based synthetic/natural segmentation. IEEE Trans Image Process 27(10):5113–5128
38. Gu K, Xu X, Qiao J (2020) Learning a unified blind image quality metric via on-line and off-line big training instances. IEEE Trans Big Data 6(4):780–791
39. Xia Z, Gu K, Wang S (2020) Towards accurate quality estimation of screen content pictures with very sparse reference information. IEEE Trans Ind Electron 67(3):2251–2261
40. Gu K, Li L, Lu H (2017) A fast reliable image quality predictor by fusing micro- and macro-structures. IEEE Trans Ind Electron 64(5):3903–3912
41. Barten PG (1999) Contrast sensitivity of the human eye and its effects on image quality. SPIE Press
42. Min X, Ma K, Gu K et al (2017) Unified blind quality assessment of compressed natural, graphic, and screen content images. IEEE Trans Image Process 26(11):5462–5474
43. Barten PGJ (2003) Formula for the contrast sensitivity of the human eye. In: Paper presented at the international society for optical engineering, vol 5294, pp 231–238, Dec 2003
44. Min X, Zhai G, Gu K et al (2016) Blind quality assessment of compressed images via pseudo structural similarity. In: Paper presented at the IEEE international conference on multimedia and expo, 11–15 July 2016
45. Zhang Y, Moorthy AK, Chandler DM et al (2014) C-DIIVINE: no-reference image quality assessment based on local magnitude and phase statistics of natural scenes. Signal Process Image Commun 29(7):725–747
46. Chang C, Lin C (2011) LIBSVM: a library for support vector machines. ACM Trans Intell Syst Technol 2(3):1–27
47. Mittal A, Soundararajan R, Bovik AC (2012) Making a completely blind? image quality analyzer. IEEE Signal Process Lett 20(3):209–212
48. Zhang L, Zhang L, Bovik AC (2015) A feature-enriched completely blind image quality evaluator. IEEE Trans Image Process 24(8):2579–2591
49. Gu K, Zhai G, Lin W et al (2016) Learning a blind quality evaluation engine of screen content images. Neurocomputing 196(5):140–149
50. Han J, Pei J, Kamber M (2011). Data mining: concepts and techniques. https://doi.org/10.1016/C2009-0-61819-5
51. ITU-R BT Recommendation (2012) The subjective evaluation method of television image quality. https://www.itu.int/rec/R-REC-BT.500-13-201201-S/en

52. Attias H (1999) A variational baysian framework for graphical models. In: Paper presented at the conference and workshop on neural information processing systems, Colorado, USA, pp 209–215
53. Damera-Venkata N, Kite TD, Geisler WS (2000) Image quality assessment based on a degradation model. IEEE Trans Image Process 9(4):636–650
54. Chandler DM, Hemami SS (2007) VSNR: a wavelet-based visual signal-to-noise ratio for natural images. IEEE Trans Image Process 16(9):2284–2298
55. Liu A, Lin W, Narwaria M (2012) Image quality assessment based on gradient similarity. IEEE Trans Image Process 21(4):1500–1512
56. Zhang L, Shen Y, Li H (2014) VSI: a visual saliency induced index for perceptual image quality assessment. IEEE Trans Image Process 23(10):4270–4281
57. Li Q, Wang Z (2009) Reduced-reference image quality assessment using divisive normalization-based image representation. IEEE J Sel Top Signal Process 3(2):202–211
58. Wu J, Lin W, Shi G (2013) Reduced-reference image quality assessment with visual information fidelity. IEEE Trans Multimedia 15(7):1700–1705
59. Wang Z, Simoncelli EP (2005) Reduced-reference image quality assessment using a wavelet-domain natural image statistic model. In: Paper presented at the international society for optical, pp 149–159, Mar 2005
60. Narwaria M, Lin W, McLoughlin IV (2012) Fourier transform-based scalable image quality measure. IEEE Trans Image Process 21(8):3364–3377
61. Gu K, Zhai G, Yang X (2013) A new reduced-reference image quality assessment using structural degradation model. In: Paper presented at the 2013 IEEE international symposium on circuits and systems, pp 1095–1098, May 2013
62. Min X, Zhai G, Gu K (2018) Blind image quality estimation via distortion aggravation. IEEE Trans Broadcast 64(2):508–517
63. Min X, Gu K, Zhai G (2018) Blind quality assessment based on pseudo-reference image. IEEE Trans Multimedia 20(8):2049–2062
64. Ni Z, Ma L, Zeng H (2017) ESIM: gradient direction for screen content image quality assessment. IEEE Signal Process Lett 23(10):1394–1398
65. Jakhetiya V, Gu K, Lin W (2018) A prediction backed model for quality assessment of screen content and 3-D synthesized images. IEEE Trans Ind Inf 14(2):652–660
66. Wu J, Lin W, Shi G (2013) Perceptual quality metric with internal generative mechanism. IEEE Trans Image Process 22(1):43–54
67. Gu K, Wang S, Zhai G (2016) Analysis of distortion distribution for pooling in image quality prediction. IEEE Trans Broadcast 62(2):446–456
68. Gu K, Wang S, Zhai G (2015) Screen image quality assessment incorporating structural degradation measurement. In: Paper presented at the 2015 IEEE international symposium on circuits and systems, pp 125–128, May 2015

Chapter 3
Quality Assessment of 3D-Synthesized Images

3.1 Introduction

The recent decade has witnessed the rapid development of three-dimension (3D) video applications, such as 3D-TV and free viewpoint video (FVV), and this makes 3D imaging and display technologies draw an immense amount of consideration in a broad scope of fields, including remote education, entertainment, remote monitoring, and so on. Among them, FVV uses the depth image-based rendering (DIBR) technology to synthesize new viewpoint images of the same scene from a limited number of multiple views with no-reference (NR) images, and this can solve the problems of high cost and complexity caused by camera settings [1]. However, the introduction of DIBR brings distortion to 3D-synthesized images, particularly the geometric distortion, making the image appear unforeseeable degradation. With this concern, it is necessary to conduct objective QA models which can more effectively and efficiently compute the quality of 3D-synthesized images generated with DIBR.

In the past decades, various image QA models have received extensive attention. For example, after designing the image QA of structural similarity (SSIM) [2], Wang et al. further proposed the model and weighting strategy of information weighted SSIM (IW-SSIM) [3] with the model of natural scene statistics (NSS). However, most of these traditional image QA models were designed for specific scenes or typical distortions (such as noise and blurriness). By contrast, when DIBR uses depth information to transfer occluded areas that mainly appear on the foreground object contour to the virtual view, the resultant image inevitably introduces geometric distortion due to technical deficiencies. This distortion, belonging to local distortion, is more likely to destroy the semantic structure of an image than typical distortions, and cannot be captured effectively using traditional image QA models.

To address the above-mentioned issues, researchers have done a lot of work on the design of 3D-synthesized image QA based on DIBR. For example, in [4], Battisti et al. developed a new full-reference (FR) image QA model called 3D synthesized view image quality metric (3DSWIM) by comparing the statistical characteristics of wavelet subband of the original image and the synthetic image via DIBR. In [5], Li et al. designed a new algorithm by estimating local geometric distortion and global sharpness changes to infer the quality of 3D-synthesized images. In [6], the influences of direction, contrast, and texture were used to correct the distorted view or similarity view from the composite view and the associated reference view, so as to design the view synthesis quality prediction (VSQA) measure of view comprehensive QA. In [7, 8], the morphological wavelet peak signal-to-noise ratio (MW-PSNR) model was designed by applying morphological wavelet decomposition on DIBR composite image, and then the morphological pyramid peak signal-to-noise ratio (MP-PSNR) model was developed by using morphological pyramid instead of morphological wavelet to obtain better performance. Apart from the FR QA model, the reduced-reference (RR) QA model is also followed. In [9], through improving MP-PSNR, a RR image QA algorithm, namely morphological pyramid peak signal-to-noise ratio (MP-PSNR-RR), with better performance was proposed to solve DBIR influence and effectively overcome geometric distortion in 3D-synthesized image quality. All the above-mentioned QA models require the participation of reference images, but FVV images synthesized based on DIBR are carried out in the absence of reference images, so it is necessary to design NR QA models for evaluating 3D-synthesized images.

Considering the aforementioned real scenarios, new progress has also been made in QA of 3D-synthesized images based on DIBR without reference. First, the model of NSS is used in modeling NR QA of 3D-synthesized images. In [10], Gu et al. proposed a NR image QA model with local image description based on autoregression (AR), where the geometric distortion can be obtained from the residual value between one 3D-synthesized image and its AR reconstructed image. In [11], Gu et al. devised a blind image QA model based on multi-scale natural scene statistical analysis (MNSS) using two new NSS models. In [12], a high efficiency view synthesis quality prediction (HEVSQP) model was designed to gauge the effects of depth and color distortion on the perceptual quality of 3D-synthesized image, towards achieving automatic prediction of 3D-synthesized images. Note that local geometric distortion is the major distortion introduced by DIBR and global information influences the quality of 3D-synthesized images as well, so some work has also been done on local and global structures. In [13], Yue et al. proposed a new image QA model, which combined local and global models to evaluate geometric distortion and sharpness changes, solving the problem that the traditional NR model is not effective for DIBR correlation distortion. In [14], Yan et al. measured the quality of NR 3D-synthesized views by extracting local changes in structure and color and global changes in brightness. In [15], in addition to geometric distortion and global sharpness, Wang et al. also considered image complexity to design NR synthetic image QA model. For evaluating the performance of those QA models, we also compared them with state-of-the-art competitors using four extensive employed standards, i.e., Spearman rank correlation coefficient (SRCC), Kendall rank correlation coefficient (KRCC), Pearson linear correlation coefficient (PLCC), and root mean square error (RMSE).

The organization of this chapter is arranged below. Section 3.2 introduces in detail the modeling process and experimental analysis of three types of NR 3D-synthesized image QA models, namely the model based on NSS, transform domain and structural variation. Section 3.3 illustrates the comparison with those state-of-the-art image QA models of 3D-synthesized images. Section 3.4 finally draws the conclusive remarks and provides future applications.

3.2 Methodology

In this section, we introduce six state-of-the-art NR QA models of 3D-synthesized images generated based on DIBR. We divide these QA models into three categories, namely the models relying on NSS, the models based on domain transformation, and the models based on structural transformation. More specifically, we first introduce two NR models based on NSS for evaluating the quality of images. The natural features of the image are affected by geometric distortion. Second, we introduce two NR models based on domain transformation. The models are by combining pixels' change with human perception. Third, we introduce two NR models based on structural transformation for evaluating the quality of synthetic image from the perspective. DIBR may not only cause local geometric distortion but also affect global clear information. We compare and analyze their performance with the typically methods by indices of PLCC, SRCC, KRCC, and RMSE.

3.2.1 NSS-Based NR 3D-Synthesized Image QA

The geometric distortion introduced due to the use of DIBR is very likely to seriously damage the natural characteristics of images. The NSS can be used to capture environmental statistical characteristics changes caused by distortion, and make further measurement distortion information [16, 17]. Specifically, based on NSS modeling and reliable visual perception, image QA model can strengthen the consistency with subjective evaluations [18]. NSS-based image QA model has become one of the most important models of image QA and has been widely used in NR image QA tasks [16, 19]. In the following content, we will introduce two kinds of NR 3D-synthesized image QA based on NSS models.

NR 3D-Synthesized Image QA Using Local Image Description

The geometric distortion of 3D-synthesized images is a key problem affecting the quality of 3D-synthesized images [20], which usually causes serious damage to the natural attributes of the image. It is natural to consider using the NSS model to solve the above problems. However, most of the current NSS models were designed to extract the structural corruption, unable to accurately extract the geometric corruption commonly occurred in the synthesized image. Therefore, we proposed a NR QA model of 3D-synthesized image called AR-plus threshold (APT), which is based on local AR model and an adaptive threshold can effectively catch the geometric distortion. The implementation details of our proposed model mentioned above will be elaborated as follows.

AR-Based Neighborhood Relationship

In natural images' local region, there is a certain correlation between surrounding image pixels, which is very akin to the correlation of other adjacent pixels. On this basis, the introduction of local image similarity can help to solve the image degradation problem such as disproportion and distortion of synthesized images. There are many models used to describe local similarity, such as AR operator, bilateral filter, and non-local mean filter. The AR model has good invariance to translation, rotation, scaling and other transformations, and can describe local similarity well of an input 3D-synthesized image. In addition, free energy theory [21] states that the human brain divides an input image into ordered and disordered components in a constructive way. The process of minimizing free energy can be seen as predictive coding [22], which can well simulate quality assessment and saliency detection based on AR models. The above content also facilitates the selection of AR operator for local image description [23, 24]. So, the AR operator is employed to capture the local similarity of the synthetic image.

Autocorrelation means there exists the serial correlation between one signal and itself. In a natural image I, we denote the index and value of a specific pixel's location to be k and x_k. The relationship between pixels and their neighborhood can be defined as

$$x_k = \Omega_\theta(x_k)s + d_k, \tag{3.1}$$

where $\Omega_\theta(x_k)$ is a neighborhood vector of the θ pixels region. The patch size is $\sqrt{\theta+1} \times \sqrt{\theta+1}$; the $s = (s_1, s_2, \ldots, s_\theta)^T$ forms a vector of AR parameters need to be confirmed; the d_k indicates the error discrepancy of the values between the current pixel and the associated AR predicted version. Increasing the size of local patch adjacent to more pixels greatly increases the computational cost, and moreover, it cannot achieve the higher performance. With this view, we consider a maximum of 8 pixels adjacent to the current pixel in this algorithm, and set $\theta = 8$.

Determination of AR Parameters

After obtaining the pixel neighborhood relationship, we focus on the value of AR parameters. Towards estimating the reliable AR parameters' vector, we use a matrix to define the linear system:

$$\hat{s} = arg \min_s ||x - X_s||_2, \tag{3.2}$$

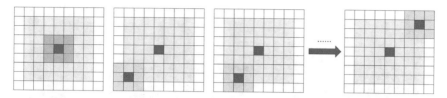

Fig. 3.1 Local AR model implementation process

where $x = (x_{i,1}, x_{i,2}, \ldots, x_{i,\varphi})^T$, $X(j, :) = \Omega_\theta(x_{i,j})$, and $j = \{1, 2, \ldots, \varphi\}$. After that the least square method is used to derive the linear system above and deduce the best estimation of the AR parameter as

$$\hat{s} = (X^T X)^{-1} X^T x, \tag{3.3}$$

where $\varphi = 48$ represents the pixels surrounding the present pixel. The 48 pixels can be used to confirm the relationship among pixels by using Eq. (3.1), and further utilize Eq. (3.3) to predict the vector of AR parameters $\hat{s}$. For better understanding, we exhibit Fig. 3.1 as an implementation schematic diagram of the local AR model. Each small block in the figure represents a pixel, and the local patch consists of 7×7 light blue blocks in the middle. The dark blue blocks are the pixel under the processing procedure currently. In the first subgraph, local 3×3 patch includes the center dark blue block and adjacent 8 green blocks from the local $\sqrt{\theta + 1} \times \sqrt{\theta + 1}$ patch, where $\theta = 8$. In the subsequent subgraph, the red block and 8 yellow blocks also constitute the same local 3×3 patch. Thus, a total of 49 conditions are provided within 7×7 patch.

In general, the AR prediction image can be considered as an ordered whole, but the absolute value $|d_i|$ in the error map between the input image and its predicted image with AR is regarded as the disordered part. The AR-based models applied for local image description can effectively illustrate the content of natural image, such as smoothness, texture, and edge. Consequently, the value of error map is significantly reduced to a very small range. In Fig. 3.2a, we labeled three typical natural image blocks and one geometric distortion block with a smooth block in red, a texture block in green, a edge block in orange, and a geometric distortion block in blue. There are four corresponding error histograms illustrated in Fig. 3.2b, e. One can observe from Fig. 3.2b, d that the majority values in the three error histograms are zero and the small numerical cannot exceed 20. In terms of the errors maps' histogram of geometric distortion shown in Fig. 3.2e, we can observe that graph includes big values of error difference, even outstrips 100.

Based on the observation, we reach the following two conclusions: (1) Natural images ordinarily contain disorder parts, and the size of disordered parts depends on the type of natural image contents, e.g., smoothness, texture, or edge; the values in the error histograms are rarely non-zero, and in most cases are small values beneath twenty; (2) The geometric distortion destroy the local image similarity. In geometric

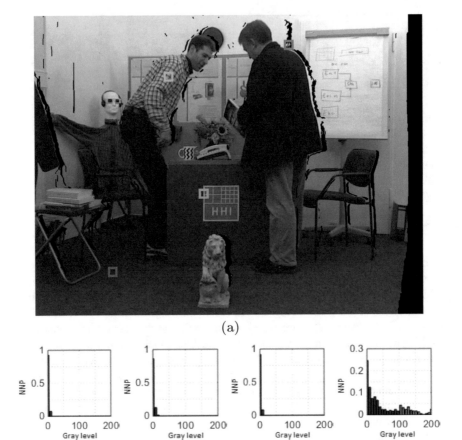

(a)

(b) Red patch   (c) Green patch (d) Orange patch (e) Blue patch

Fig. 3.2 Comparison of geometric distortion patches and its associated natural image patches: **a** is a typical 3D-synthesized distortion image with edge, texture, smooth, and geometric distortion patches' labels; **b–e** are the error histograms of red, green, orange, and blue patches, respectively, where NNP represents the normalized pixel number (©[2021] IEEE. Reprinted, with permission, from [10].)

distortion regions, the values of the error suddenly accelerate, some of which are even larger than one hundred. We can observe an interesting thing is the AR predictor has very strong ability to describe local image and highlight geometric distortions.

AR-Based Thresholding

The distribution of error difference values shown in the histogram of Fig. 3.2e reveals the AR model cannot predict regions with geometric distortion effectively. Some values in the histogram even outstrip 100, and indicate that the AR predictor is sufficient to emphasize geometric distortion. Based on these phenomena and analyses provided above, the AR model can be used to ascertain the quality of 3D-synthesized image effectively. Furthermore, a few modifications are necessary to modify the calculated error map. We utilize the AR model to estimate the input image synthesized with DIBR, derive the error map from that procedure. Firstly, we adopt Gaussian filter for deleting some single small "noise" in the error map. Secondly, the FES model [24] is used to detect the most salient regions for removing the corresponding parts in the error map, because these regions without geometric distortion probably have large error values that should be set aside. Finally, a threshold is adopted to obtain a "0–1" binary filtered error map:

$$
M_d = \begin{cases} 1 & , \text{if } M_e < \gamma_t \\ 0 & , \text{otherwise} \end{cases} \tag{3.4}
$$

where M_e is the error map after the Gaussian filter processing; γ_t is a fixed threshold. The burrs of M_d are then removed by a median filter.

Estimation of Quality Score

Towards estimating the final quality score, we pool the binary maps M_d generated by Eq. (3.4). The majority of the existing image QA models have been devised based on NSS models. Several FR image QA models are realized by computing the difference of structural change between the corrupted images and their original (natural) images. The RR image QA metrics estimate the image quality by computing the distance between the two feature vectors, which are extracted from the corrupted and original images. In the absence of reference images, NR image QA model can generally extract certain statistical rules from natural images and estimate the quality of distorted images according to the deviation between them and the above natural statistical rules. Thus, we observe a reliable method to evaluate the visual quality by comparing the distance between the distorted image and its related natural image statistics (i.e., natural image structure, RR vector, and statistic domains). In Eq. (3.4), the error map's small values are correlated to the natural image parts. Based on this, when geometric distortion occurs in the image, its value derived from Eq. (3.4) should be set to zero, and all the undistorted natural image should be set as one. We achieve the 3D-synthesized image quality prediction by comparing M_d with the binary map of natural images M_r.

In order to obtain the differences between the binary map of geometric distortion images M_d and the binary maps of natural images M_r. The natural image can generate the binary map of reference M_r with Eqs. (3.1)-(3.4). The quality model of distorted 3D-synthesized images is defined as follows:

$$
Q_s = \frac{1}{H} \sum_{h=1}^{H} \left(\frac{2M_d(h) \cdot M_r(h) + \varepsilon}{M_d(h)^2 + M_r(h)^2 + \varepsilon} \right)^\alpha , \tag{3.5}
$$

where H means the number of the image pixels; h is the index of image pixel; α is a non-negative indicator correlated with the Minkowski summation; ε is a small fixed number to avoid the issue of dividing by zero. Typical values of α range from one to four.

In the natural images without the corrupt of geometric distorted, the residual error values are below the threshold. We hypothesis that all values of M_r are a unity and set the value to 1. The ε is a small variable. It is obvious that the denominator cannot be zero, since the $M_d(h)^2 + 1$ not less than 1. So we subtract ε and the Eq. (3.5) can be simplified as

$$
\begin{aligned}
Q_s &= \frac{1}{H} \sum_{h=1}^{H} \left(\frac{2M_d(h)}{M_d(h)^2 + 1} \right)^{\alpha} \\
&= \frac{1}{H} \sum_{h \in H_0} \left(\frac{2M_d(h)}{M_d(h)^2 + 1} \right)^{\alpha} + \frac{1}{H} \sum_{h \in H_1} \left(\frac{2M_d(h)}{M_d(h)^2 + 1} \right)^{\alpha},
\end{aligned}
\tag{3.6}
$$

where H_0 and H_1 represent regions with and without geometric distortion, in which the corresponding values are 0 and 1, respectively, and $H = H_0 + H_1$; when α is positive, Eq. (3.6) can be simplified as

$$
Q_s = \frac{1}{H} \sum_{l \in H_0} \left(\frac{2 \cdot 0}{0 + 1} \right)^{\alpha} + \frac{1}{H} \sum_{l \in H_1} \left(\frac{2 \cdot 1}{1 + 1} \right)^{\alpha} = \frac{H_1}{H}.
\tag{3.7}
$$

We remove the α since the Minkowski pooling has no effect on the image quality predicting. The quality score can be easily derived to be the ratio of the single pixels to the size of the entire map. In a 3D-synthesized image, the similarity of the binary maps between the distorted image and its pure natural image can be obtained from the region without geometric distortion to the whole pixel region. The score Q_s refers to the 3D-synthesized image quality, the closer the value is to 1, the higher the image quality. Figure 3.3 presents the block diagram of the proposed blind APT model. The AR model is used to predict the input image, and remove some unnecessary noise with the Gaussian filter. The saliency detection model is used to avoid the geometric distorted free region with large value error being misjudged as distortion region. After these steps, a preliminary modified error map is obtained. Then, we adopt a threshold to implement binary error map, and further remove burrs with the median filtering. Finally, we pool the binary map generated by Eq. (3.7) to obtain the quality score.

Multi-scale NSS Analysis for NR 3D-Synthesized Image QA

Another NR QA for 3D-synthesized images was developed by combining two new NSS models, both of which were designed for 3D-synthesized image QA task. The first NSS model extracts local statistical features according to the self-similarity of

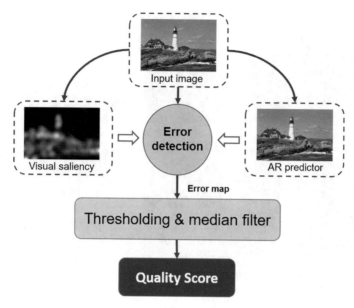

Fig. 3.3 Block diagram of our proposed APT model

natural images, and the second NSS model extracts global statistical features based on the consistency of the main structure of natural images. With the features extracted from the two NSS models, we propose a new blind image QA model based on multi-scale statistical natural scenes analysis. This method has obtained greater accuracy than each of its two components and modern image QA models. The implementation details of the proposed model mentioned above will be elaborated as follows.

Self Similarity-Based NSS Modeling

Local self-similarity is an important characteristic of natural images, which has been widely used in the image description, compression, and other fields [3]. Compared with the effects of Gaussian blur or white noise on the global self-similarity of images, geometric corruption only varies the characteristics of self-similarity in some commonly seen local areas but does not affect other regions.

As shown in Fig. 3.4, Y is a 3D-synthesized image generated from its reference one X. When they are analyzed at multiple scales, the distance between them rapidly shrinks as the scale decreases. Among them, SSIM value [25] can accurately reflect the above variation trend. This is more obvious in scenes with reference images, but practice reference images are usually hard to obtain when synthesizing images by DIBR. Therefore, finding an approximate reference to replace the reference image can be considered as a simple and effective model.

As shown in Fig. 3.4, X_5 and Y_5 have high SSIM values, namely high similarity. Considering Y_5 as a reference and taking X_3 and Y_3 division as an example, the

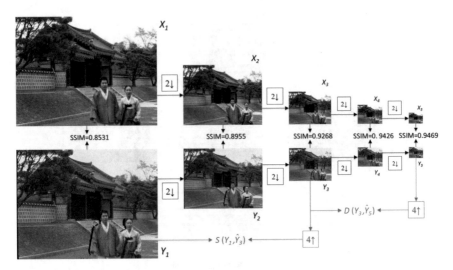

Fig. 3.4 Comparison of a 3D-synthesized image and its associated reference one at multi-scales. $2\downarrow$ is downsampling by 2. $4\uparrow$ is upsampling by 4 (©[2021] IEEE. Reprinted, with permission, from [11].)

following approximate relation $D(Y_3, X_3) = D(Y_3, \hat{X}_5) \approx D(Y_3, \hat{Y}_5)$ can be deduced, where '^' is an upsampling operator that can fully recover details lost due to down-sampling and makes the two inputs match in size. In other words, X_i can be replaced by $Y_5, i = \{1, 2, \ldots, 5\}$. This similarity measure can be used to approximate replace the relationship between the synthesized image and its associated original version when the original image is missing.

In the human visual system (HVS), the multi-scale analysis is an important char-acteristic. It has been broadly leveraged in many image processing tasks, e.g., quality assessment [26] and significance detection [27]. According to the multi-scale analysis model in [26], each similarity map is integrated to derive:

$$\overline{S}_j = \prod_{i=1}^{N} [S_j(Y_1, \widehat{Y}_i)]^{\gamma_i}, \tag{3.8}$$

where j indicates the pixel index and $N = 5$; $S(Y_1, \hat{Y}_i)$ is the similarity measure between Y_1 and upsampled Y_i. $\gamma_i \in \{\gamma_1, \gamma_2, \gamma_3, \gamma_4, \gamma_5\}$, and they are defined as $\{0.0448, 0.2856, 0.3001, 0.2363, 0.1333\}$ according to psychophysical experiments [27]. Then, the common similarity measure (not SSIM) having the three advantages of unique maximum, boundedness and symmetry, are used as the measure of distance:

$$S(Y_1, \widehat{Y}_i) = \frac{2Y_1 \cdot \widehat{Y}_i + \varepsilon}{Y_1^2 + \widehat{Y}_i^2 + \varepsilon} \tag{3.9}$$

where ε is a fixed number to avoid being divided by zero. The range of Eq. (3.9) belongs to [0, 1] and it equals 1 when two inputs are identical. Therefore, this equation can also be simplified as

$$\overline{S}_j = \prod_{i=2}^{N} [S_j(Y_1, \widehat{Y}_i)]^{\gamma_i}. \tag{3.10}$$

In the 3D-synthesized image, there are isolated noises that have effect on the perceived quality. So there should be a median filter to remove the noisy pixels in $\overline{S}_j$ and generate $\dot{S}$. For natural images, the fused $\overline{S}_j$ will contain distortion that is not present in the original. So, a threshold value is added to the filtered graph to extract the geometric distortion region:

$$\ddot{S}_j = \begin{cases} 0 & \text{, if } \dot{S}_j < T \\ 1 & \text{, otherwise} \end{cases} \tag{3.11}$$

where T is a threshold below which the geometric distortion region will be retrained and the blur distortions will be deleted. The value of T depends on a new NSS regularity. 300 high-quality natural images were randomly selected from Berkeley image segmentation database [28] and their $\dot{S}_j$ images were calculated. Assuming that there are no geometric distortion areas in most selected natural images, that is, most pixels (about 50 million) are higher than T. A histogram of all pixel $\dot{S}$ values are shown in Fig. 3.5, and we can obviously find that the pixels with $\dot{S}$ values above 0.1 account for 99.85% of the overall pixels, so set T to 0.1.

Finally, we extract local statistical features from the self-similarity of natural images to evaluate the quality fraction Q_1 of the input 3D-synthesized image:

$$Q_1 = \frac{1}{K} \sum_{k=1}^{K} \ddot{S}_k, \tag{3.12}$$

where L is the number of the overall pixels in $\ddot{S}$. When Q_1 and the subjective average opinion score is larger, the geometric distortion is smaller.

Main Structure Consistency-Based NSS Modeling

The structure in the image conveys important visual information, which is of great significance for analyzing and understanding scenes. The structure diagram with different measurement values (such as gradient and covariance) is applied in some classical image QA models, such as SSIM, feature similarity (FSIM) index, and gradient magnitude standard deviation (GMSD). Damaged structure, especially major structures, such as contour, will have a large impact on image quality and may lead to the reduction of semantic information [29]. The geometric distortion is the key corruption of the 3D-synthesized image. Occlusion is an inevitable issue in image rendering on account of the limited number of cameras available to capture the view.

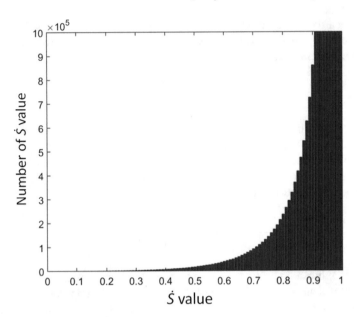

Fig. 3.5 Distribution of From $\dot{S}$ values of about fifty million pixels from three hundreds natural images (©[2021] IEEE. Reprinted, with permission, from [11].)

This usually produces some holes, such as geometric corruption, in binary synthesized images, particularly at the contour of foreground objects, even the application of advanced repair and interpolation techniques to fix these holes does not work very well.

If possible, it is a simple way to directly compare the main structure consistency between one 3D-synthesized image and its corresponding reference version. However, in most cases, due to the fact that only a limited number of cameras are available for view capture, images with reference-free viewpoints cannot be accessible. Therefore, a new NSS model should be devised carefully to obtain the consistency of the main structures. By comparing the differences between the main structure of 3D-synthesized images and the NSS model based on a huge number of natural images with high quality, we can estimate the degradation degree of the main structure caused by the DIBR model and infer the quality of the 3D-synthesized image.

The distortion intensity and even the quality of 3D-synthesized images can be estimated by using the difference of major structure degradation between 3D-synthesized images and reference images at multiple scales. It is a simple model to directly compare the differences of the main structure diagrams at various scales. Due to the mismatch issue caused by occlusion, we need distortion operation to solve the problem. In this case, there must be reference images to adjust the 3D-synthesized views so that they can match well. Towards achieving the design of image QA models without any reference information, alternative solutions were considered. More specifically, we gauge the degeneration similarity between the 3D-synthesized images and its reference versions on major structures with the distance measure:

$$Q_2(Y, X) = \frac{1}{U} \sum_{u=1}^{U} \left(\frac{2m_Y(u) \cdot m_X(u) + \varepsilon}{m_Y(u)^2 + m_X(u)^2 + \varepsilon} \right), \tag{3.13}$$

where ε is a small constant that avoids being divisible by zero; $U = 5$ represents five scales; u is a measure of similarity; m_Y is the degradation vector in the main structure of Y; m_X is similarly defined for X. The similarity between the two main structure maps on the Uth scale and the uth scale is compared. It is defined as follows:

$$m_Y(u) = \sum_{v=1}^{V} M_U(v) \oplus M_u(v) \tag{3.14}$$

where M_u is the uth main structure map; V is the number of all pixels; v stands for pixels' index in M_u and there are only two values for v, 1 or 0, indicating whether the main edge is included. It is not difficult to find that Eq. (3.13) contains m_X, that is, the calculation of Q_2 still depends on some information of the reference image. We need to find other factors to replace m_X, so that Q_2 can get good results even in the absence of a reference image.

The vector m_X is also obtained based on three hundred natural images from the Berkeley segmentation database. Then the major structural degradation curves of three hundred images on 5 scales were drawn in the same image. Finally, the median value of 300 values at five scales are calculated, and the NSS vector m_P is derived. The better the image quality, the closer the curve to the median value. On this basis, Q_2 is modified to

$$Q_2(Y, X) = \frac{1}{U} \sum_{u=1}^{U} \left(\frac{2m_Y(u) \cdot m_P(u) + \varepsilon}{m_Y(u)^2 + m_P(u)^2 + \varepsilon} \right)^{\gamma_u}, \tag{3.15}$$

where $\{\gamma_1, \gamma_2, \gamma_3, \gamma_4, \gamma_5\}$ are also defined as $\{0.0448, 0.2856, 0.3001, 0.2363, 0.1333\}$. Like Q_1, the Q_2 means that the more similar between reference image X and 3D-synthesized image Y, and the higher image quality.

Estimation of Quality Score

In the previous part, we introduced two new NSS models for 3D-synthesized image QA and obtained the corresponding quality scores Q_1 and Q_2. The first NSS model extracts local statistical features based on self-similarity of natural images. The second model is to extract global statistical features based on the consistency of the main structure of natural images. If these two models are combined together, a better blind image QA model can be constructed. We use a simple product to combine them, and their weighted multiplication is in the same range as Q_1 and Q_2, which is [0, 1]. The final model for MNSS is

$$Q_{MNSS} = Q_1^{\phi} \cdot Q_2, \qquad\qquad (3.16)$$

where ϕ is a positive constant parameter used for balancing the relative weight of each component. The larger the Q_{MNSS}, the higher the quality of the composite image.

3.2.2 Transform Domain-Based NR 3D-Synthesized Image QA

The HVS is the final receiver of visual information such as images and videos, so the most reliable evaluation method should be subjective assessment. Objective QA by using mathematical models for simulating the HVS is more efficient than the expensive and time-consuming subjective assessment. The human eye is more sensitive to low-frequency errors than high-frequency ones. As for the image, the pixel in the image with mutation or rapid change belongs to the high-frequency part, while the flat part belongs to the low-frequency part. Considering these, image quality evaluation models based on transform domain design have been widely studied [30]. A new information entropy calculation model based on the improved reconstructed discrete cosine transform (RDCT) domain has been developed for evaluating the quality of RR images [31]. The improved RDCT was used to decompose the reference image into 10 subbands, which was consistent with the channel decomposition characteristics of the HVS. Sendashonga and Labeau [32] used an image measurement model based on the discrete wave transform (DWT) domain, which requires the participation of the reference image. In the following content, we will introduce two kinds of NR image QA models based on transform domain.

NR 3D-Synthesized Video QA with Color-Depth Interactions

In a system of 3D-synthesized video, many data formats have been used to express 3D scenes. Among these formats, there is a format of multi-view video plus depth (MVD) that can merely encode typical 2 or 3 views of color and depth videos. From an arbitrary viewpoint, the DIBR technique can generate the virtual view. In order to provide users a good quality of experience (QoE), the perceptual quality is a significant index for evaluating the merit of 3D-synthesized videos based on MVD. Therefore, we introduce an automatical and blind QA model of 3D-synthesized video directly from the input color and depth videos, namely HEVSQP. Such model has great accuracy measured based on the whole synthesized video QA dataset, as compared to classical FR and NR video QA models. The implementation details of the proposed model mentioned above will be elaborated in the following paragraphs.

View Synthesis Quality Prediction Model

The distortions in color and depth independently lead to the uncertainty of human scoring. The distortions in color and depth together also lead to the difference between subjective rating. Therefore, measuring the quality of synthesized video seems more challenging than straightforwardly measuring the color or depth sequences. We need to find the relationship between the distortions in color and depth and even their interactions. The view synthesis quality prediction (VQSP) model was developed to resolve such problem. It explains the impacts of distortions in color and depth on the quality and their interactions [33, 34].

Let I_v represents a virtual view composed of the original depth maps and the primeval/undistorted color images, $\tilde{I}_v$ represents a virtual view composed of the distorted depth maps and the original color images, $\check{I}_v$ represents a virtual view composed of the original depth maps and the distorted color images, and $\hat{I}_v$ represents a virtual view composed of the distorted depth maps and the distorted color images. Since color distortion directly affects the synthesized view, it can be assumed that the virtual view synthesized from the distorted color image adds color distortion ΔD_c to the original synthesized image. So, $\tilde{I}_v \approx I_v + \Delta D_c$, $\hat{I}_v \approx \check{I}_v + \Delta D_c$. Then the view synthesis distortion (VSD) can be described approximately as

$$
D_v = E\left\{\left(I_v - \hat{I}_v\right)^2\right\} \approx \underbrace{E\left[\left(I_v - \tilde{I}_v\right)^2\right]}_{D_v^c} + \underbrace{E\left[\left(I_v - \check{I}_v\right)^2\right]}_{D_v^d}, \tag{3.17}
$$

where D_v^c is the VSD caused by color video coding error, D_v^d is the VSD caused by depth map coding error. The former part is the color-involved VSD (CI-VSD), the latter part is the depth-involved VSD (DI-VSD). Since $E[(I_v - \hat{I}_v)^2]$ is the error of the color images, D_v^c is independent of D_v^d [35].

In a NR manner, it is essential to build the specific relation between the VSD and the quality of 3D-synthesized view. Considering that D_v^c and D_v^d may affect the quality of synthesized view, such as subjective score ϑ, we want to describe the relationship between the perceived quality and CI-VSD (or DI-VSD). Based on the Bayesian model, the process of quality prediction can be modeled as a posterior probability

$$
P_{(\vartheta|D_v)} = \underbrace{\omega_v^c \cdot p_{\vartheta|D_v^c}}_{\text{Color quality}} + \underbrace{\omega_v^d \cdot p_{\vartheta|D_v^d}}_{\text{Depth quality}} -
$$
$$
\underbrace{\omega_v^{c,d} \cdot p_{\vartheta|D_v^c} \cdot p_{\vartheta|D_v^d}}_{\text{Quality related to color} - \text{dept interactions}}, \tag{3.18}
$$

where ω_v^c, ω_v^d, and $\omega_v^{c,d}$ are the weights of color, depth, and their interactions, respectively. This can be considered as a typical VSQP model. The first term is VSQP (CI-VSQP) involved in color, the second term is VSQP (DI-VSQP) involved in depth, and the third is their color-depth interaction term. The key idea of the VSQP model is that, although the distortions in color and depth are independent, the effects of them on the perceptual quality of 3D-synthesized view are not independent. Therefore, the proposed VSQP is flexible in dealing with color and depth distortion and their interaction by decomposing into three independent terms.

The VSQP model in Eq. (3.18) still requires synthesized images to predict perceived quality, but we do not know the view synthesis process in the practical applications. It is significant to evaluate the synthesized view by arbitrary compressed color and depth sequences. It is efficient to evaluate the quality without view synthesis. Such approaches would considerably reduce the amount of computation required to make more accurate predictions. Therefore, the above-mentioned VSQP model needs to be improved.

Due to the fact that the intermediate reference view is applied to compose both the left and right virtual views, and that the distance between the intermediate reference view and the virtual view is the equivalent, let's redefine the total D_v^c and D_v^d in another form:

$$D_v^c = D_{v,L}^c + D_{v,R}^c \triangleq \sum_\phi \omega_\phi^2 \cdot D_{c,\phi}, \tag{3.19}$$

$$D_v^d = D_{v,L}^d + D_{v,R}^d \triangleq \sum_\phi (\omega_\phi \cdot k_\phi \cdot \nabla I_{c,\phi})^2 \cdot D_{d,\phi}, \tag{3.20}$$

where $\phi \in \{1, 2, 3\}$; $D_{c,\phi}$ and $D_{d,\phi}$ are the coding distortion of color map and depth map, respectively; ω_ϕ is the weight associated with the synthetic view position; $\nabla I_{c,\phi}$ is a parameter related to the color content, which can be calculated according to the gradient of the reconstructed color image. The CI-VSD and DI-VSD models mentioned above still require the participation of original virtual view to calculate the distortion. To solve the problem, we suppose the HEVSQP model, in which the feature vectors can represent the distortions.

High-efficiency View Synthesis Quality Prediction Model

Figure 3.6 illustrates the framework of the the HEVSQP model that automatically predicts the quality of 3D-synthesized video based on the input of color and depth video. First, a color and depth dictionary was constructed during the training phase, which contained a set of feature vectors and associated human evaluation scores. The dictionary revealed their relationship. For the color and depth videos tested, we calculate their sparse code on the constructed dictionary and predict CI-VSQP and DI-VSQP indexes, respectively. Then, the HEVSQP exponent is obtained by combining the CI-VSQP exponent and DI-VSQP exponent based on the derived VSQP model. There are three steps to explain details.

In feature representation step, we extract perceptual quality features which can well stand for the view synthesis quality prediction. Considering that spatial and temporal distortions in color and depth sequences can affect the quality of composite view, we extract spatial and temporal features from the sequences, respectively,

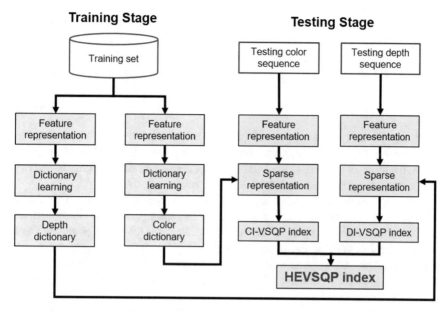

Fig. 3.6 The framework of the HEVSQP model

and combine them to obtain overall features. In the previous section, we used the likelihood function to reveal the relationship between VSD and perceived quality. Therefore, we calculate the feature vectors from the color and depth sequences with the same weights in Eqs. (3.19) and (3.20) for predicting the feature vectors of the synthesized views induced by color or depth distortions. For purpose of exploring spatial and temporal redundancy simultaneously, video sequences need to be divided into non-overlapped group of frames (GoFs), within which spatial and temporal distortions are analyzed. In order to extract the spatial features of the view, the magnitude of gradient is calculated by the gradient vector of each frame:

$$\nabla I_{x,y,t}^{spatial} = \sqrt{(\overrightarrow{\nabla} I_{x,y,t}^{hor})^2 + (\overrightarrow{\nabla} I_{x,y,t}^{ver})^2}, \tag{3.21}$$

where $\overrightarrow{\nabla} I_{x,y,t}^{hor}$ and $\overrightarrow{\nabla} I_{x,y,t}^{ver}$ respectively represent the horizontal and vertical gradient vectors of the pixel point (x, y) at frame t. Then, the following three parts are calculated:

(1) With reference to [18], 16 asymmetric generalized Gaussian Distribution (AGGD) fitting parameters are calculated according to the gradient magnitude map;

(2) By convolving each frame with a Laplacian of Gaussian (LOG) operator, 16 similar AGGD fitting parameters are calculated;

(3) Calculate 16-dimensional local binary mode features for each frame.

Consequently, each frame will generate a 48-dimensional spatial and temporal feature vector. The average spatial feature vector of all frames in a GoF is represented by $f^{spatial}$. Likewise, we extract the temporal features using the frame error $\overrightarrow{\nabla} I_{x,y,t}^{temporal} = I(s, y, t) - I(x, y, , t-1)$ as temporal gradient vector. The average temporal feature vector of all frames in a GoF is represented by $f^{temporal}$. They constitute the 96-dimensional GoF feature vector, f^{GoF} is defined as follows:

$$f^{GoF} = [f^{spatial}, f^{temporal}], \tag{3.22}$$

In this research, we use temporal gradient information to derive the similar statistical features, which is different from the existing video QA methods [34, 36] to design the temporal feature representation by spatio-temporal complexity or activity. By the way, an open framework for NR VSQP model is provided.

In the dictionary construction step, the training data were obtained from 42 combinations of compressed color and original depth sequence pairs and 42 combinations of original color and compressed depth sequence pairs. Due to the relatively small number of training data in sparse representation, they do not follow the general dictionary learning process to generate dictionaries. Instead, the color dictionary and depth dictionary are directly defined as the feature vectors of N training color samples and N training depth samples.

More than 90 dimensions of features are extracted from each sequence, and inevitably, some features may be associated with other features. In order to reduce the feature dimension, principal component analysis (PCA) is performed on the feature vector. Then, the dictionary learning process is simplified to directly combine the feature vectors of the training samples and the opinion scores of the related people. For example, the color dictionary $[\tilde{D}_c, q_c]$ can be defined:

$$\begin{bmatrix} \tilde{D}_c \\ q_c \end{bmatrix} \doteq \begin{bmatrix} \tilde{f}_{c,1} & \tilde{f}_{c,2} & \cdots & \tilde{f}_{c,N} \\ \vartheta_{c,1} & \vartheta f_{c,2} & \cdots & \vartheta f_{c,N} \end{bmatrix}, \tag{3.23}$$

where $\tilde{D}_c$ denotes the dimension-reduced color dictionary; $\vartheta_{c,i}$ represents the human opinion score corresponding to reduced feature vector $f_{c,i}$. By the same way, we can obtain the depth dictionary learning model $\tilde{D}_d$. These similar deep lexicographical learning models establish the relationship between the feature distribution and the perceived quality score. They can be regarded as regression models for $p(\vartheta | D_v^c)$ and $p(\vartheta | D_v^d)$.

In the quality pooling step, it is assumed that the three-view MVD data have no prior information about the distortion strengths. Then, we compute the feature vectors of the color and depth sequences from the reference views with the same weights in Eqs. (3.19) and (3.20). Based on the assumption that videos with the same quality value will have similar feature distributions, the quality prediction process only needs to weigh the human opinion scores of the training samples based on the sparse coefficient. After acquiring the CI-VSQP index Q_c^{GoF} and DI-VSQP index Q_d^{GoF}, we need to integrate them together to predict the overall quality score. According to Eq. (3.18), the three weights, ω_c, ω_d and $\omega_{c,d}$, are combined into a quality score to calculate the final HEVSQP index of a GoF:

$$Q^{GoF} = \omega_v^c \cdot Q_c^{GoF} + \omega_v^d \cdot Q_d^{GoF} - \omega_v^{c,d} \cdot Q_c^{GoF} \cdot Q_d^{GoF} \tag{3.24}$$

Finally, the average of all GoF is taken to calculate the perceived quality of full sequences:

$$Q^{Seq} = \frac{1}{M} \sum_m^M Q_m^{GoF}, \tag{3.25}$$

where M is the number of GoF in the full sequences. The HEVSQP model has the following features:

(1) Trained CI-VSQP or DI-VSQP models attempt to establish the relationship between feature distribution and quality score, rather than relying on synthesized views to evaluate the perceived quality;

(2) By evaluating the quality scores based on CI-VSQP or DI-VSQP models and using different weights of color or depth quality scores to integrate them together, which reveals the interaction of color-depth. We achieve an efficient QA method of the 3D-synthesized view without view synthesis;

(3) Since the HEVSQP model refers to the distortion of the view to predict VSD, the estimated parameters will lead to certain deviation from the actual VSD. The same parameters are also used to combine the feature distributions, which can lead to inaccurate predictions. The effect of the above approximation can be reduced by using the same rules to predict VSD during training and testing, but we should try to train separate models of CI-VSQP and DI-VSQP.

NR 3D-Synthesized Image QA in the DWT Domain

FVV has aroused a huge amount of attention for its wide applications. Because they are synthesized through a DIBR procedure without reference images, a real-time and reliable QA metric is desperately required. Existing QA methods failed to reach the requirements since they are not able to detect the geometric distortion caused by DIBR. To address aforementioned problem, [37] proposed a novel blind method of 3D-synthesized images. To begin with, in order to quantize the geometric distortions, the image is decomposed into wavelet subbands via DWT. To be followed, the global sharpness is obtained by calculating the log-energies of the wavelet subbands. Finally, image complexity is calculated through a hybrid filter. The overall assessment depends on the normalized result of geometric distortion and global sharpness by image complexity. This method has made remarkable improvements on existing NR image QA models, and proved to be especially adaptive for 3D-synthesized images. The implementation details of the proposed model mentioned above will be elaborated in the following paragraphs.

Detection and Quantization of Geometric Distortion

In order to accurately detect geometric detection, we utilize the Cohen-Daubechies-Feauveau 9/7 filter [38] on 3D-synthesized images to decompose the image into low-frequency (LL) and high-frequency (LH,HL,HH) subbands as shown in Fig. 3.7. To further extract the edges of the geometric distortion from LL subband, it needs to be binarized as shown in Fig. 3.7f. Then we utilized the Canny operator [39] to detect the edges of the binarized LL (BLL) subband as well as high-frequency wavelet subbands through Eq. (3.26)

$$C_{sub} = Canny(sub), \tag{3.26}$$

in which *sub* denotes the BLL, HL, LH, and HH subbands.

It can be seen from Fig. 3.7g–j that the edges of BLL subband only consists of geometric distortion edges, while the high-frequency subbands' (HL, LH, and HH) edges are a mixture of both 3D-synthesized view itself and geometric distortions. Therefore, digging into the edge similarity between BLL and high-frequency subbands can be of crucial importance to calculate how much geometric distortion account for the overall effect of DIBR-synthesis images. To simulate HVS, we quantized the geometric distortion from horizontal, vertical and diagonal directions, and the similarity between C_{BLL} and C_{HL}, C_{LH}, C_{HH} is obtained by the functions listed below

$$S_H = \frac{1}{L} \sum_{l=1}^{L} (\frac{2C_{BLL}(l) \cdot C_{HL}(l) + \varepsilon}{C_{BLL}(l) + C_{HL}(l) + \varepsilon}), \tag{3.27}$$

$$S_V = \frac{1}{L} \sum_{l=1}^{L} (\frac{2C_{BLL}(l) \cdot C_{LH}(l) + \varepsilon}{C_{BLL}(l) + C_{LH}(l) + \varepsilon}), \tag{3.28}$$

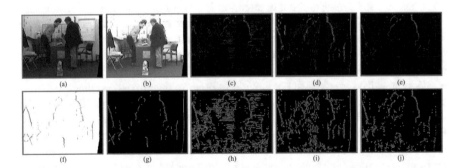

Fig. 3.7 An example of 3D-synthesized image and its wavelet subbands. **a** 3D-synthesized image, **b–e** are LL, HL, LH, and HH subbands of (**a**) respectively, **f** is LL subband after binarization, **g–j** are edge detection results of the subbands (**f**) and (**c**)–(**e**) (©[2021] IEEE. Reprinted, with permission, from [15].)

$$S_D = \frac{1}{L} \sum_{l=1}^{L} (\frac{2C_{BLL}(l) \cdot C_{HH}(l) + \varepsilon}{C_{BLL}(l) + C_{HH}(l) + \varepsilon}), \tag{3.29}$$

where L stands for the number of pixels in an image and l is the index of pixels, ε is a constant in case the denominator is zero. The final quantization that combined the calculation results above is as follows:

$$Q_1 = \sum (\alpha_i \cdot S_i), \tag{3.30}$$

where $i = H, V$ and D; α_i denotes the weight coefficient used to adjust the proportions of similarities in each direction.

Evaluation of Global Sharpness

The process of 3D-synthesis also brings inevitable image quality problems like blurring which mainly happens around the transitions of background and foreground. Thus, we also evaluated the factor of sharpness. Unlike some mainstream methods [25, 42] that only analyze high-frequency information of the blurred images (for blurring mainly occurs in the high-frequency part), we took low-frequency information into consideration by imposing different weights to the log-energies of low-frequency and high-frequency subbands.

There are two steps to evaluate global sharpness, to begin with, we calculate the log-energy at each wavelet subband, and the major operation follows the equation below:

$$E_{XY} = log_{10}(1 + \frac{1}{L} \sum_{l=1}^{L} XY^2(l)), \tag{3.31}$$

where XY refers to LL, LH, HL, or HH subband; l is the pixel index; L denotes the number of wavelet coefficients in each subband. Furthermore, we measured the total logarithmic energies of all decomposed wavelet subbands via Eq. (3.32). Q_2 is used to evaluate the global sharpness of 3D-synthesized images, and HH subband plays a more important role in blurring, the parameters are arranged as $a = 0.5$, $b = 0.3$, and $c = 0.2$.

$$Q_2 = a \cdot E_{HH} + b \cdot \frac{E_{HL} + E_{LH}}{2} + c \cdot E_{LL}. \tag{3.32}$$

Image Complexity Estimation

Image complexity is of key importance when assessing 3D-synthesized image quality, for it relates to the effects of gaze direction and spatial masking. Generally speaking, higher-complexity images contain more high-frequency information compared to low-complexity images, such as edges and textures. A hybrid filter is used to estimate image complexity by combining AR filter and BL filter, since the AR filter performs well on texture regions and on the contrary, BL filter is more satisfied in edge-preserving function. The hybrid filter plays as a tradeoff towards better results on the two aspects. The hybrid filter is defined as follows:

$$\hat{y}_i = \frac{\phi^n(x_i)\hat{a} + k\phi^n(x_i)b}{1+k},$$

(3.33)

where x_i denotes the ith pixel value, while $\phi^n(x_i)$ contains the n pixels of the neighborhood of the center x_i. $\hat{a}$ is a set of AR parameter vector, calculated by model [24], in the form of $(a_1, a_2, \ldots, a_n)^T$. This gives a description of predicted image result by AR filtering. In addition, b is a set of coefficients produced by BL filtering, which followed the assignment in [40]. This term provides the prediction image by BL filter, which gives more explicit results around luminance edges than AR ones. k adjusts the proportion of the responses of AR and BL filters, here we define $k = 9$. The specific process and parameter settings of parameter k can be seen in [41].

The final image complexity is estimated as follows:

$$Q_3 = -\int H'_{(\rho)} \log H'_{(\rho)} d\rho,$$

(3.34)

where $H'_{(\rho)}$ represents the probability density of grayscale ρ in the error map between the synthesized image and its filtered result, i.e., $\delta y_i = y_i - \hat{y}_i$; y_i is the value of pixel x_i.

Estimation of image QA

From the metrics above, we can integrate geometric distortion (Q_1), global sharpness (Q_2) and image complexity (Q_3) to form a overall quality score. Higher Q_1 implies more severe geometric distortion of the image, and higher Q_2 value denotes higher degree of global sharpness. To eliminate the interference of the variety of image content, image complexity Q_3 is induced to normalize the quantized geometric distortion and global sharpness, based on aforementioned consideration, we defined overall quality score function:

$$Q = \frac{Q_1 + p \cdot Q_2}{1 + p} \cdot \frac{1}{Q_3},$$

(3.35)

where p is a normalized parameter which adjusts the contributions of Q_1 and Q_2. Lower Q indicates better quality for having less geometric distortions and global sharpness. The overall architecture of proposed 3D-synthesized image QA metric is shown in Fig. 3.8.

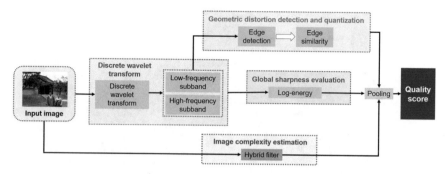

Fig. 3.8 The overview of the proposed QA model of 3D-synthesized images

3.2.3 Structure Variation-Based NR 3D-Synthesized Image QA

There are two stages to DIBR synthesis: First, the aim of warping is to map the reference view to a 3D Euclidean space by the supervision of depth information. Then, the target view is generated from the 3D Euclidean space through inverse mapping. These operations may produce geometric displacement in the form of the disoccluded regions. DIBR usually introduces blur, discontinuity, blocking, stretching, and other effects that reduce the quality of the synthetic images. Many work has been done to solve these problems [6–8]. These methods only consider the changes from the global scope and ignore the effect of local distortion on image quality. Here, we will introduce two NR image QA models that consider both local and global structural changes.

Fusing Local and Global Measures for NR 3D-Synthesized Image QA

The measurement of geometric distortion and global sharpness are considered as the key problems to evaluate the quality of synthetic images. In the proposed method, the geometric distortion is measured by three methods: disoccluded region evaluation, stretching strength evaluation, and global sharpness evaluation. Figure 3.9 systematically describes the framework of the proposed approach. This method is better than all competing methods except APT in terms of effectiveness, but greatly exceeds APT in terms of implementation time. The implementation details of the proposed model mentioned above will be elaborated in the following paragraphs.

Disoccluded Region Evaluation

Digital images have complex structures and textures, and there is a strong correlation between pixels, which means that one pixel is very similar to its neighbors within a local region. We try to detect the disoccluded regions by analyzing the similarity of

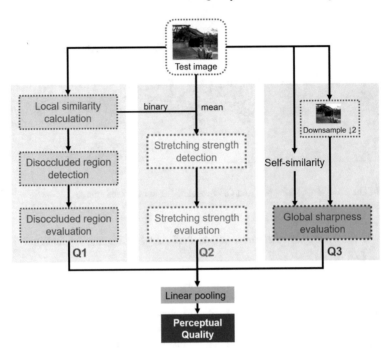

Fig. 3.9 The framework of the proposed scheme

local images. Figure 3.10 provides a brief illustration about the analysis procedure. In the image, the light blue circle refers to the central pixel, while the rest of the circles are its adjacent pixels. In this part, local binary pattern (LBP) is used to measure local correlation. Although some work has used LBP to solve image QA problems [42–45], there are inherent differences compared to this work. Comparing with others, this method only uses LBP to the disoccluded region. First of all, we encode the surrounding pixels. According to different positions, the gray value of the central pixel $I(n_c)$ is taken as the threshold value, and the gray value of the adjacent 8 pixels $I(n_i)$ is compared with it. If the surrounding pixel value is greater than or equal to the central pixel value, the position of the pixel is marked as 1, otherwise, it is marked as 0. These comparison results can be encoded using binomial factor 2^i according to their location:

$$\Lambda_P = \sum_{i=0}^{P-1} s(I(n_i), I(n_c)) \cdot 2^i. \tag{3.36}$$

LBP only has gray level invariance, but lacks good object transformation property, i.e., the rotation invariance. To compensate for this, we use a rotation invariant uniform LBP, which are defined as follows:

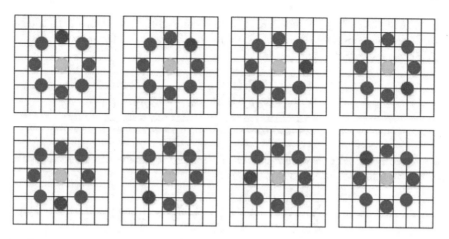

Fig. 3.10 The process of measuring the relationship between a pixel and its neighboring pixels (©[2021] IEEE. Reprinted, with permission, from [13].)

$$
\Lambda_P^{riu2} = \begin{cases} \sum_{i=0}^{P-1} s(I(n_i), I(n_c)) & \text{, if } \mu(\Lambda_P) \leq 2 \\ P+1 & \text{, otherwise} \end{cases}
\tag{3.37}
$$

where μ is the number of bitwise transitions.

Generally speaking, LBP clarifies different natural images or patches by analyzing texture information, and can be used as an effective tool to distinguish natural and disoccluded image patches. In addition, LBP can effectively detect disoccluded regions. After the LBP map is obtained, the disoccluded region map D_r can be obtained by a binary operation:

$$
D_r = \begin{cases} 0 & \text{, if } \Lambda p^{riu2} = 8 \\ 1 & \text{, otherwise} \end{cases},
\tag{3.38}
$$

where value 0 represents the dissociation region. After getting the disoccluded region map D_r, our next concern is how to use it to estimate image quality. In this part, we simulate the benchmark work (that is SSIM) and define a quality evaluator for the disoccluded region. The quality (Q_1) of the synthesized image in terms of measuring the disoccluded region can be calculated as follows:

$$
Q_1 = \frac{1}{K} \sum_{k=1}^{K} \left(\frac{2D_r(k) \cdot D_R(k) + \varepsilon}{D_r(k)^2 \cdot D_R(k)^2 + \varepsilon} \right)
\tag{3.39}
$$

where k indicates the pixel index, K is the total number of pixels in an image, and is a small positive constant to ensure the stability. All the values of Dr are one. Equation (3.39) can be rewritten as follows:

$$Q_1 = \underbrace{\frac{1}{K} \sum_{k \in K_0} \frac{2D_r(k)}{D_r(k)^2 + 1}}_{Non-disoccluded\,region} + \underbrace{\frac{1}{K} \sum_{k \in K_1} \frac{2D_r(k)}{D_r(k)^2 + 1}}_{Disoccluded\,region} \qquad (3.40)$$

K_0 is the pixel set of the non-disoccluded region, K_1 is the disoccluded region, $K = K0 + K1$. We further simplify the equation:

$$Q_1 = \frac{1}{K} \sum_{k \in K_0} \frac{2 \cdot 1}{1^2 + 1} + \frac{1}{K} \sum_{k \in K_1} \frac{2 \cdot 0}{0^2 + 1} = \frac{K_0}{K} = 1 - \frac{K_1}{K} \qquad (3.41)$$

From this equation, we can see that the value of Q_1 does not require reference information. In addition, the synthesized quality Q_1 depends on the area K_1 of the disoccluded region. K_1 gets bigger as Q_1 gets smaller.

Stretching Strength Evaluation

The stretching caused by the failure of in-painting operation mainly occurs on the left or right side of the image. A case in point is given in Fig. 3.11a. In this part, we propose a simple and effective measurement to evaluate the stretching strength.

First, given an image, we calculate its LBP map. Then, the LBP mapping is binarized to obtain the coarse stretch region map:

$$D_s = \begin{cases} 1 & \text{, if } \Lambda p^{riu2} = 8 \\ 0 & \text{, otherwise} \end{cases} . \qquad (3.42)$$

It can be seen that in Fig. 3.11b, the outline of the stretch region is mainly drawn by the white regions. In natural regions, almost all elements are zero. From this observation, the average values of the elements in each column are calculated to detect fine stretch regions. As shown in Fig. 3.11c, the average value of elements in the stretched region is very high compared with the natural region. After capturing the stretching region, our next concern is how to evaluate its strength, which indicates its impact on perceptual quality. Since the HVS is more sensitive to structures, we calculate similarity in the gradient domain. Given a stretching region S_I, its gradient can be calculated as

$$G_s = \sqrt{(S_I \otimes p_x)^2 + (S_I \otimes p_y)^2}, \qquad (3.43)$$

where p_y and p_x are filter the kernel in vertical and horizontal directions, respectively. Through the above Eq. (3.43), we can also obtain the gradient map G_n of the adjacent

(a)   (b)   (c)

Fig. 3.11 Illustration of the stretching region. **a** One typical image contains a stretching region. Two sub-regions are highlighted by colorful rectangles: **b** Coarse stretching region map. **c** Average element values of each column in (**b**) (©[2021] IEEE. Reprinted, with permission, from [13].)

natural region with the same size as the stretching region. Then, the similarity between them is estimated:

$$S_g = \frac{2G_s \cdot G_n + T_2}{G_s^2 + G_n^2 + T_2}, \tag{3.44}$$

where $T_2 = 0.01$. Finally, the standard deviation Q_2 of S_g is used to evaluate tensile strength.

$$Q_2 = \sqrt{\frac{1}{J} \sum_{j=1}^{J} (S_j - \overline{S_g})^2}, \tag{3.45}$$

where S_j is the jth element in S_g, which including J elements.

Global Sharpness Evaluation

In the quality evaluation of 3D-synthesized images based on DIBR, besides disoccluded region and stretched region, sharpness is another factor that cannot be ignored. Here, we provide a simple and efficient method to measure the global sharpness of synthesized images. The key strategy of this method is the estimation of self-similarity between scales. Given an image I_0, let's just get a condensed version I_1 of it by a down sampling operation with factor 2. Then there's global sharpness (Q_3) of I_0 is evaluated by estimating its self-similarity, i.e., measuring the standard deviation distance between I_0 and I_1:

$$Q_3 = \frac{1}{N} \sum_{n=1}^{N} \sqrt{|\delta_{0,n}^2 - \delta_{1,n}^2|}, \tag{3.46}$$

where N represents the total number of non-overlapping blocks. $\delta_{0,n}^2$ and $\delta_{1,n}^2$ represent the standard deviation of the ith given image and the downsampling image, respectively.

Estimation of Quality Score

In the previous part we obtained the quality scores of the disoccluded region Q_1, stretching strength Q_2, and global sharpness Q_3. It can be seen from the above formulas that these scores remain monotonic with the perceived quality. So we can effectively integrate these three quality scores linearly:

$$Q = \alpha_1 \cdot Q_1 + \alpha_2 \cdot Q_2 + \alpha_3 \cdot Q_3, \tag{3.47}$$

where α_1, α_2, and α_3 are used to allocate the relative contribution of the quality scores of each part.

NR 3D-Synthesized Image QA by Local Structure Variation and Global Naturalness Change

Yan et al. proposed an effective NR QA algorithm for 3D-synthesized images based on local structure variation and global naturalness change [14]. In terms of local variation, Gaussian derivative is used to extract structural features and chromatic features. Then, LBP operator is used to encode the two feature maps. Finally, quality-aware features are calculated through these feature maps to measure the local structure distortion and chromatic distortion. In the global change aspect, the luminance map is calculated by local normalization, and then the naturalness of the 3D-synthesized image is represented by the fitted Gaussian distribution parameters. After obtaining these features, random forest regression is used to train quality prediction models from visual features to human ratings. It demonstrates the superior performance of the proposed metric against state-of-the-art image QA metrics and the effectiveness of the proposed metric by combining local and global features. The implementation details of the proposed model mentioned above will be elaborated in the following paragraphs.

Structure Features

It is shown that the local structure of an image can be represented by local Taylor series expansion from local Gaussian derivative [46]. The Gaussian derivative of an image I is defined as follows:

$$I^{\sigma}_{x^m y^n} = \frac{\partial^{m+n} G^{\sigma}(x, y, \sigma)}{\partial^m x \partial^n y} * I(x, y), \tag{3.48}$$

where m and n with non-negative values are the orders of derivatives along the x (horizontal) and y (vertical) directions, respectively. '$*$' is the convolution operation. The Gaussian function $G^{\sigma}(x, y, \sigma)$ with standard deviation σ can be defined as follows:

$$G^\sigma(x, y, \sigma) = \frac{1}{2\pi\sigma^2} exp\left(-\frac{x^2 + y^2}{2\sigma^2}\right). \tag{3.49}$$

Inspired by researches [47] and [48], the second-order Gaussian derivative is used to extract the structural features. First, we calculate the resulting matrix $J^\sigma_{m,n}$ obtained by the Gaussian derivative when $1 \le m + n \le 2$:

$$J^\sigma_{m,n} = [J^\sigma_{m,n}(x, y) | (x, y) \in I, 1 \le m + n \le 2]. \tag{3.50}$$

Then, we can calculate the uniform local binary pattern (ULBP) value of each pixel of $J^\sigma_{m,n}$, and use local rotation invariant ULBP operator [47] to achieve its rotational invariability. Applying the absolute value of $J^\sigma_{m,n}$, we calculate the feature maps $SW^s_{m,n}$:

$$SW^s_{m,n} = LBP^{riu2}_{D,E}(|J^\sigma_{m,n}|), \tag{3.51}$$

where $s \in \{s_1, s_2, s_3, s_4, s_5\}$, LBP is the LBP operator, $riu2$ represents uniform patterns with rotation invariant. D and E are the number of adjacent elements and their radius, respectively. After setting $D = 8$, $E = 1$ and $1 \le m + n \le 2$, we can obtain five feature maps, they are $SW^{s_1}_{1,0}$, $SW^{s_2}_{0,1}$, $SW^{s_3}_{2,0}$, $SW^{s_4}_{1,1}$ and $SW^{s_5}_{0,2}$. Eq. (3.51) describes the relationship between the central pixel and adjacent pixels of a local region. Complex degradation caused by different distortion types can be captured effectively by using local detail information.

LBP can detect differences between the center pixel and its neighbors. It cannot accurately obtain magnitude information. Using LBP to encode differences among adjacent pixels weakens LBP's ability to distinguish local changes. However, that are highly correlated with the visual quality of the image. Therefore, we add the pixels in $SW^s_{m,n}$ with the same LBP pattern to obtain a weighted histogram, which can be defined as

$$H^s(k) = \sum_{i=1}^{N} w^s_i(x, y) \Gamma(SW^s_{m,n}(x, y), k), \tag{3.52}$$

$$\Gamma(x, y) = \begin{cases} 1 & , x = y \\ 0 & , \text{otherwise} \end{cases}, \tag{3.53}$$

where N represents the number of image pixels; k represents the possible LBP index, $k \in [0, D + 2]$; w^s_i denotes the weight assigned to the LBP value. According to the intensity value of LBP map, we aggregate the pixel values in Gaussian derivative [46], fuse LBP map with Gaussian derivative, and obtain the feature vector by normalization. Through these operations, image regions with high contrast changes can be enhanced.

Chromatic Features

Two color photometric-invariant descriptors are used on the first-order Gaussian derivative of the chromatic channels [49, 50] to extract the chromatic features. Here, the first part of chromatic features representing hue information is defined as

$$\chi_1 = \frac{1}{(O_1)^2 + (O_2)^2}, \tag{3.54}$$

where $O_1 = \frac{R-G}{\sqrt{2}}, O_2 = \frac{R+G-2B}{\sqrt{6}}$. R, G, and B represent red, green, and blue channels in RGB color space, respectively.

The operator LBP^{riu2} is used to extract feature map $CW^{c_1}_{m,n}$ on χ_1, where $CW^{c_1}_{m,n} = LBP^{riu2}_{D,E}(\chi_1)$. The feature maps are converted into feature vectors by the following formula:

$$H^{c_1}_{m,n}(k) = \sum_{i=1}^{N} w^{c_1}_i(x, y)\Gamma(CW^{c_1}_{m,n}(x, y), k), \tag{3.55}$$

where $w^{c_1}_i$ is the weight assigned to the LBP value corresponding to feature map $CW^{c_1}_{m,n}$.

The second feature is the color angle χ_2 [49], defined as follows:

$$\chi_2 = \arctan\frac{\phi}{\psi}, \tag{3.56}$$

where

$$\phi = \frac{R \times (B' - G') + G \times (R' - B') + B \times (G' - R')}{\sqrt{2(R^2 + G^2 + B^2 - R \times G - R \times B - G \times B)}}, \tag{3.57}$$

and

$$\psi = \frac{R \times \rho + G \times \delta + B \times \tau}{\sqrt{6(R^2 + G^2 + B^2 - R \times G - R \times B - G \times B)}}, \tag{3.58}$$

R', G', and B' are the first-order values of the Gaussian derivatives along horizontal direction with R, G, and B channels. And $\rho = 2R' - G' - B'$, $\delta = 2G' - R' - B'$, $\tau = 2B' - R' - G'$.

Then the operator LBP^{riu2} is used to extract feature map $CW^{c_2}_{m,n}$ on χ_2 where $CW^{c_2}_{m,n} = LBP^{riu2}_{D,E}(\chi_2)$. And its corresponding weighted histogram $H^{c_2}_{m,n}$ is calculated as follows:

$$H^{c_2}_{m,n}(k) = \sum_{i=1}^{N} w^{c_2}_i(x, y)\Gamma(CW^{c_2}_{m,n}(x, y), k), \tag{3.59}$$

where $\omega_i^{c_2}$ is the weight assigned to the LBP value corresponding to feature map $CW_{m,n}^{c_2}$. Finally, combining the above two features, a single feature vector representing the image chroma information can be calculated:

$$H^c(k) = [H_{m,n}^c | m + n = 1, c \in \{c_1, c_2\}]. \tag{3.60}$$

Note that color features are invariant to accidental effects of scenes (such as shadows) related to luminosity and illumination. Therefore, they are almost unaffected by illumination and can convey robust structural information. In addition, image distortion caused by independent factors (such as ambiguity) may destroy the image structure, but they are not necessarily related to the influence of illumination.

Image Naturalness

In a 3D-synthesized view, the loss of brightness may affect naturalness. It is assumed that a high-quality 3D-synthesized view looks more natural than a low-quality view. We use quality-aware features based on luminance to evaluate the naturalness of 3D-synthesized view. Considering that the luminance coefficient of natural image obeys Gaussian distribution [19], we use the luminance coefficient to compute the naturalness of synthetic view. The definition for luminance coefficient L' is as follows:

$$L(i, j)' = \frac{L(i, j) - \mu(i, j)}{\sigma(i, j) + 1}, \tag{3.61}$$

where

$$\mu(i, j) = \sum_{a=-3}^{3} \sum_{b=-3}^{3} w_{a,b} L_{a,b}(i, j), \tag{3.62}$$

and

$$\sigma(i, j) = \sqrt{\sum_{a=-3}^{3} \sum_{b=-3}^{3} w_{a,b} [L_{a,b}(i, j) - \mu_{a,b}(i, j)]^2}, \tag{3.63}$$

where (i, j) represents the spatial indices, $i \in \{1, 2, \ldots, H\}$ and $j \in \{1, 2, \ldots, W\}$, H and W is the image height and width. w is a 2D circularly symmetric Gaussian weighting function, which is sampled out to three standard deviations and re-scale to unit volume, $w = \{w_{a,b} | a \in [-3, 3], b \in [-3, 3]\}$.

Zero-mean general Gaussian distribution (GGD) [47] can also model the luminance coefficient:

$$f(x; \alpha, \sigma^2) = \frac{\alpha}{2\beta\Gamma(\frac{1}{\alpha})} exp[-(\frac{|x|}{\beta})^\alpha], \tag{3.64}$$

where $\beta = \alpha\sqrt{\frac{\Gamma(1/\alpha)}{3/\alpha}}$ and $\Gamma(x) = \int_0^\infty t^{x-1} e^{-1} dx (x > 0)$. α affects the shape of the distribution, and σ adjusts the variance. We can obtain the two parameters by

Table 3.1 Summary of features for NR image QA of 3D synthesized views

Feature type	Structure	Color	Naturalness
Symbol	H^s	H^c	$\alpha,\ \sigma^2,\ k,\ s$
Feature ID	$f_1 \sim f_{250}$	$f_{251} \sim f_{270}$	$f_{271} \sim f_{310}$

fitting the GGD model. The kurtosis and skewness of the luminance coefficients are calculated by empirical distribution on five scales, resulting in a total of 20 features.

In addition, using the difference between the synthesized image and the low-pass filter image can calculate the Laplace pyramid image (LPI). The distribution of pixel values in LPI can be fitted by a GGD model. The estimated parameters (α, σ^2) and the kurtosis and skewness of LPI are used as features. A total of 20 quality-sensitive features are extracted from 5 scales, respectively.

Regression Model and Quality Prediction

The study [26] has shown that when we perceive visual information, there are multi-scale features in HVS. So, the authors use multi-scale to extract the visual features of the image for better representing it. Through feature extraction, they can get a 310-dimensional feature vector, as shown in Table 3.1, in which 270-dimensional features (structure and color) are used for local change, and 40-dimensional features (naturalness) are used for global naturalness. Then, the visual quality prediction model is trained by RFR [51], and the quality-aware features are mapped to subjective evaluation. In the experiment, the 3D-synthetic view quality database was randomly divided into training set and test set for 1000 times, of which 80% of the image samples and corresponding subjective scores were used for training, and the remaining 20% of the samples were used for testing.

The framework of the proposed model is shown in Fig. 3.12, which is divided into training stage and test stage. In the training phase, quality perception features representing structure, color, and naturalness information were extracted, and the visual quality prediction model of 3D-synthesized view was trained using RFR. In the test phase, we input the features of the test images into the trained RFR model to calculate the estimated quality score.

3.3 Comparison and Analysis of Algorithm Performance

In this section, we introduce an image database aiming at 3D-synthesized image QA and some modern reference-free and reference-based image QA methods. We concentrate on comparing and analyzing the performance of the proposed quality

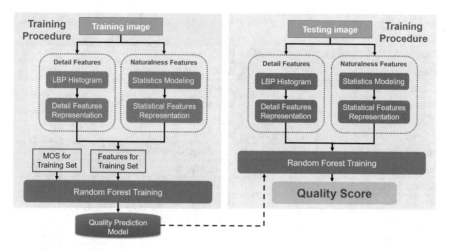

Fig. 3.12 The framework of the proposed model

assessment models in this chapter with these methods. The analysis results show that the performance of these models in this chapter performs quite well.

3.3.1 DIBR-Synthesized Image Database

There are 12 original images and its corresponding 84 DIBR-synthesized images on the IRCCyN/IVC DIBR-synthesized database [20]. The 84 DIBR-synthesized images were generated by 7 different DIBR algorithms which are represented by A1-A6 [52–57] and A7 (warping without rendering). The subjective evaluation of the IRCCyN/IVC DIBR database [20] was denoted by mean opinion score (MOS) form according to the absolute category rating-hidden reference (ACR-HR) algorithm [58]. Every observer used a discrete category rating scale to score the test image.

3.3.2 Performance Comparison and Analysis

In order to reflect the models introduced in this chapter validity and superiority, we compare the proposed introduced models with the state-of-the-art image QA models, which can be divided into five categories in Table 3.2. The first category is composed of nine FR image QA models of natural scene images. The second category is composed of four RR image QA models of natural scene images. The third category is composed of seven NR image QA models of natural scene images. The fourth category is composed of eight image QA models of 3D-synthesized images. The fifth category is composed of six NR image QA models of 3D-synthesized images.

Table 3.2 The introduced algorithms with modern developed QA models for both natural and DIBR-Synthesized images

Desiged for	Category	Abbreviation	Full Name	Refs.
Natural image	FR	PSNR	Peak signal-to-noise ratio	[60]
Natural image	FR	SSIM	Structural similarity	[2]
Natural image	FR	IW-SSIM	Information weighted SSIM	[3]
Natural image	FR	ADD-SSIM	Analysis of distortion distribution-based SSIM	[17]
Natural image	FR	VSNR	Visual signal-to-noise ratio	[61]
Natural image	FR	FSIM	Feature similarity	[62]
Natural image	FR	GMSD	Gradient magnitude standard deviation	[83]
Natural image	FR	PSIM	Perceptual similarity	[29]
Natural image	FR	MAD	Most apparent distortion	[63]
Natural image	RR	RRED	Reduced-reference algorithms	[64]
Natural image	RR	FEDM	Free energy-based distortion metric	[65]
Natural image	RR	OSVP	Orientation selectivity-based visual pattern	[66]
Natural image	RR	FTQM	Fourier transform-based quality measure	[67]
Natural image	NR	NIQE	Natural image quality evaluator	[68]
Natural image	NR	IL-NIQE	Integrated local NIQE	[69]
Natural image	NR	QAC	Quality-aware clustering	[70]
Natural image	NR	NIQMC	No-reference image quality metric for contrast distortion	[71]
Natural image	NR	ARISM	AR-based image sharpness metric	[72]
Natural image	NR	SISBLIM	Six-step blind metric	[73]
Natural image	NR	BIQME	Blind image quality measure of enhanced images	[74]
DIBR-Synthesized	FR	VSQA	View synthesis quality assessment	[6]
DIBR-Synthesized	FR	3DSWIM	3D synthesized view image quality metric	[4]
DIBR-Synthesized	FR	Bosc11	–	[20]
DIBR-Synthesized	FR	MW-PSNR	Morphological wavelet peak signal-to-noise ratio	[75]
DIBR-Synthesized	FR	MP-PSNR	Morphological pyramid peak signal-to-noise ratio	[5]
DIBR-Synthesized	FR	LOGS	Local geometric distortions and global sharpness	[5]
DIBR-Synthesized	RR	MW-PSNR-RR	Reduced version of MW-PSNR	[76]
DIBR-Synthesized	RR	MP-PSNR-RR	Reduced version of MP-PSNR	[76]

(continued)

Table 3.2 (continued)

Desiged for	Category	Abbreviation	Full Name	Refs.
DIBR-Synthesized	NR	NIQSV	No-reference image quality assessment of synthesized views	[77]
DIBR-Synthesized	NR	NIQSV+	No-reference image quality assessment method for 3-D synthesized views	[78]
DIBR-Synthesized	NR	NRSL	No-reference quality assessment using statistical structural and luminance features	[79]
DIBR-Synthesized	NR	GM-LOG	Gradient magnitude map and the Laplacian of gaussian response	[80]
DIBR-Synthesized	NR	CLGM	Combining local and global measures	[13]
DIBR-Synthesized	NR	OUT	Outliers in 3-D synthesized images	[81]
DIBR-Synthesized	NR	APT	Autoregression plus threshold	[10]
DIBR-Synthesized	NR	MNSS	Multi-scale natural scene statistical analysis	[11]
DIBR-Synthesized	NR	Wang et al.	–	[15]
DIBR-Synthesized	NR	Yue et al.	–	[13]
DIBR-Synthesized	NR	Yan et al.	–	[14]

When we compare the above modern image QA methods, four commonly used metrics, namely PLCC, SRCC, KRCC, and RMSE, are used. The evaluation accuracy can be measured by PLCC and RMSE, while the monotonicity of the prediction can be found by SRCC and KRCC. A higher value of PLCC, SRCC, and KRCC and a lower value of RMSE represent a better quality evaluation methods. The objective assessment scores are nonlinearity obtained by PLCC, SRCC, KRCC, and RMSE, so we use a logistic function to increase the linearity. We compute the image QA scores using these four criteria by the mapping including five parameters as follows:

$$f(x) = \tau_1 \left(\frac{1}{2} - \frac{1}{1 + \exp^{\tau_2(x - \tau_3)}} + \tau_4 x + \tau_5 \right), \tag{3.65}$$

where $\tau_{i,i=1,2,3,4,5}$ represents the fitted parameter; $f(x)$ and x are subjective scores and its corresponding objective scores which are assessed by image QA algorithms.

The performance results of 34 competing image QA techniques are illustrated in Table 3.2 for comparison. We find the best-performing model in each category. The comparison results of the proposed introduced metrics in this chapter with existing image QA algorithms including five categories are presented. By analyzing the superiority of these models, we are able to derive some important conclusions as follows:

(1) Those existing image QA algorithms designed for NSIs (in the first category), which perform effectively in natural image processing, cannot be adopted in DIBR-Synthesized image satisfactorily. We employ four widely employed evaluation criterion to evaluate the performance of these methods, among which SRCC is one of the most significant index. From the viewpoint of this index, we analyze the performance of FR image QA methods. The most apparent distortion (MAD) algorithm [63] performs the best, and the analysis of distortion distribution based structural similarity (ADD-SSIM) in second place on SRCC index among nine FR image QA models of NSIs. The proposed NR MNSS metric achieves performance improvement compared with FR MAD algorithm and gets higher performance gains beyond the ADD-SSIM.

(2) Across four RR image QA metrics, those methods have a visible performance degradation. The Fourier-transform-based scalable image quality metric (FTQM) methods lead to the optimal results in its personal type from the viewpoint of PLCC. However, it is unable to perform better than the introduced methods in this chapter.

(3) For NR image QA, the blind image quality measure of enhanced images (BIQME) method in the third category of image QA metrics leads to the optimal results from SRCC, PLCC, and RMSE perspective, respectively, while the value of SRCC still does not exceed one of introduced models in this chapter.

The above methods, including FR, RR, and NR metrics, are designed for natural 2D images. That maybe explain why they don't work very well on DIBR-Synthesized images. More specifically, those existing algorithms in the first three categories cannot catch the geometric distortions. And badly, geometric distortions are the predominant artifacts contained in the DIBR-synthesized images.

(4) The image QA methods in the fourth category are designed for the DIBR-synthesized images, and they gain better average performance than those designed for natural images. For example, the 3DSWIM (not the best algorithm in this category) algorithm performs better than all of the algorithms designed for natural images except BIQME, and the other methods show the same trend. In spite of this, compare with the methods introduced in this chapter, the performance indices of those algorithms are not sufficient yet. For instance, as a reduced-reference method, the morphological pyramid peak signal-to-noise ratio (MP-PSNR-RR) gets the best performance among the image QA models designed for DIBR-synthesized views. But values of its PLCC, SRCC, and KRCC are still smaller than the values acquired by APT algorithm. For FR image QA, the local geometric distortions and global sharpness (LOGS) method obtain the best overall performance as compared with other competing image QA algorithms in the first four categories. Furthermore, for LOGS, it belongs to FR image QA algorithms, which means it requires complete information about the reference synthesized views, but that information is generally not accessible in most real application scenarios, which makes it less significant than the reference-free image QA models for DIBR-synthesized views.

(5) Finally, we have validated the NR image QA methods for DIBR-Synthesized images. Except for the last five methods introduced in this chapter, the OUT method achieves the best performance among the remaining NR methods. Overall, the methods proposed in this chapter obtain higher performance than almost all other methods. More specifically, the above-proposed methods achieve inspiringly high value of PLCC and SRCC and low value of RMSE, which makes it greater than all image QA algorithms considered in the first four categories except for LOGS. As compared with Wang et al. proposed method, although the performance of APT and MNSS algorithm leave a slight gap to the Wang et al. proposed method, they are still greater than all methods in the first four categories except for LOGS. The index values acquired by the method proposed by Yue et al. are not as high as APT or MNSS, but it is still greater than most methods in the first four categories. While ensuring low implementation time, it still achieves high-performance values. Yan et al. proposed method obtains the greatest superiority in the overall 34 image QA methods. The method learns from local and global features adaptively to acquired quality scores, which lets the method overcome the shortcomings of simple weighting scheme for aggregating local quality scores in current related research. Besides, the structure, chromatic, and naturalness features extracted from an image can represent the local distortion of 3D synthesized views than other existing related works. Combining these advantages, Yan et al. proposed method obtains the best values of PLCC, SRCC, KRCC, and RMSE, respectively.

3.4 Conclusion

3D-synthesized images are the basis of 3D-related technologies such as FVV, 3D TV, and so on. In this chapter, we introduce three NR QA models of 3D-synthesized images based on NSS, domain transformation, and structure transformation, respectively. Considering that geometric distortion caused by DIBR can seriously damage the natural characteristics of images, we first introduce a NSS model based on AR and a MNSS model based on two new NSS models for DIBR-synthesized images. Secondly, in order to better combine the pixel changes in images with human perception, we introduce two models based on transform domain to evaluate the quality of 3D-synthesized images. One model is to extract temporal and spatial features from color and depth sequences to represent quality perception features. Another model is to evaluate the quality of 3D-synthesized images by calculating the edge similarity and logarithmic energy level of wavelet subbands obtained after processing the synthetic image with discrete wavelet transform. Finally, considering that DIBR not only introduces local geometric distortion, but also affects global sharpness, we introduce two evaluation models from local and global structures. One is to infer the overall perceived quality from the similarity between local similarity and model scale. The other one evaluates 3D-synthesized images quality based on DIBR by extracting structure, color, and brightness features. Experimental results show that the NR 3D-synthesized image QA model based on geometric distortion design introduced by DIBR is better than the traditional DIBR model. Despite the good performance of the measures described, there is still work to be done. In future work, we will consider how to effectively evaluate high-quality 3D-synthesized images or videos while reducing the complexity of models.

References

1. Battisti F, Callet PL (2016) Quality assessment in the context of FTV: challenges, first answers and open issues. IEEE ComSoc MMTC Commun Front 11(2):22–27
2. Wang Z, Bovik AC, Sheikh HR et al (2004) Image quality assessment: from error visibility to structural similarity. IEEE Trans Image Process 13(4):600–612
3. Wang Z, Li Q (2011) Information content weighting for perceptual image quality assessment. IEEE Trans Image Process 20(5):1185–1198
4. Battisti F, Bosc E, Carli M et al (2015) Objective image quality assessment of 3D synthesized views. Signal Process Image Commun 30:78–88
5. Li L, Zhou Y, Gu K et al (2018) Quality assessment of DIBR-synthesized images by measuring local geometric distortions and dlobal sharpness. IEEE Trans Multimedia 20(4):914–926
6. Conze PH, Robert P, Morin L (2012) Objective view synthesis quality assessment. In: Paper presented at the international society for optics and photonics, pp 8256–8288, Feb 2012
7. Sandic-Stankovic D, Kukolj D, Callet PL (2015) DIBR synthesized image quality assessment based on morphological wavelets. In: Paper presented at the seventh international workshop on quality of multimedia experience, 1–6 May 2015
8. Sandic-Stankovic D, Kukolj D, Callet PL (2015) DIBR synthesized image quality assessment based on morphological pyramids. The True Vision - Capture, Transmission and Display of 3D Video 1:1–4
9. Jakhetiya V, Gu K, Lin W et al (2018) A prediction backed model for quality assessment of screen content and 3-D synthesized images. IEEE Trans Ind Inf 14(2):652–660
10. Gu K, Jakhetiya V, Qiao J et al (2018) Model-based referenceless quality metric of 3D synthesized images using local image description. IEEE Trans Image Process 27(1):394–405
11. Gu K, Qiao J, Lee S et al (2020) Multiscale natural scene statistical analysis for no-reference quality evaluation of DIBR-synthesized views. IEEE Trans Broadcast 66(1):127–139
12. Shao F, Yuan Q, Lin W et al (2018) No-reference view synthesis quality prediction for 3-D videos based on color-depth interactions. IEEE Trans Multimedia 20(3):659–674
13. Yue G, Hou C, Gu K et al (2019) Combining local and global measures for DIBR-synthesized image quality evaluation. IEEE Trans Image Process 28(4):2075–2088
14. Yan J, Fang Y, Du R et al (2020) No reference quality assessment for 3D synthesized views by local structure variation and global naturalness change. IEEE Trans Image Process 29:7443–7453
15. Wang G, Wang Z, Gu K et al (2020) Blind quality metric of DIBR-synthesized images in the discrete wavelet transform domain. IEEE Trans Image Process 29:1802–1814
16. Moorthy AK, Bovik AC (2011) Blind image quality assessment: from scene statistics to perceptual quality. IEEE Trans Image Process 20(12):3350–3364
17. Gu K, Wang S, Zhai G et al (2016) Analysis of distortion distribution for pooling in image quality prediction. IEEE Trans Image Broadcast 62(2):446–456
18. Saad MA, Bovik AC, Charrier C (2012) Blind image quality assessment: a natural scene statistics approach in the DCT domain. IEEE Trans Image Process 21(8):3339–3352
19. Mittal A, Moorthy AK, Bovik AC (2012) No-reference image quality assessment in the spatial domain. IEEE Trans Image Process 21(12):4695–4708
20. Bosc E, Pepion R, Le Callet P et al (2011) Towards a new quality metric for 3-D synthesized view assessment. IEEE J Sel Top Signal Process 5(7):1332–1343

21. Friston K (2010) The free-energy principle: a unified brain theory? Nat Rev Neurosci 11(2):127–138
22. Attias H (2000) A variational Bayesian framework for graphical models. Adv Neural Inf Process Syst 12:209–215
23. Gu K, Zhai G, Yang X et al (2015) Using free energy principle for blind image quality assessment. IEEE Trans Multimedia 17(1):50–63
24. Gu K, Zhai G, Lin W et al (2015) Visual saliency detection with free energy theory. IEEE Signal Process Lett 22(10):1552–1555
25. Li L, Lin W, Wang X et al (2016) No-reference image blur assessment based on discrete orthogonal moments. IEEE Trans Cybern 46(1):39–50
26. Wang Z, Simoncelli EP, Bovik AC (2003) Multiscale structural similarity for image quality assessment. In: Paper presented at the the thrity-seventh asilomar conference on signals, systems and computers, vol 2, pp 1398–1402, Nov 2003
27. Kim C, Milanfar P (2013) Visual saliency in noisy images. J Vis 13(4):5–5
28. Martin D, Fowlkes C, Tal D et al (2001) A database of human segmented natural images and its application to evaluating segmentation algorithms and measuring ecological statistics. In: Proceedings eighth IEEE international conference on computer vision, vol 2, pp 416–423
29. Gu K, Li L, Lu H et al (2017) A fast reliable image quality predictor by fusing micro- and macro-structures. IEEE Trans Ind Electron 64(5):3903–3912
30. Guo T, Seyed MH, Monga V (2019) Adaptive transform domain image super-resolution via orthogonally regularized deep networks. IEEE Trans Image Process 28(9):4685–4700
31. Wang Z, Xu K, Yan S (2015) Reduced-reference image quality assessment in modified reorganized DCT domain. In: Paper presented at IEEE international conference on computer and communications, pp 161–165, Jan 2016
32. Sendashonga M, Labeau F (2006) Low complexity image quality assessment using frequency domain transforms. In: Paper presented at international conference on image processing, pp 385–388, Feb 2007
33. Jang WD, Chung TY, Sim JY et al (2015) FDQM: fast quality metric for depth maps without view synthesis. IEEE Trans Circuits Syst Video Technol 25(7):1099–1112
34. Liu X, Zhang Y, Hu S et al (2015) Subjective and objective video quality assessment of 3D synthesized views with texture/depth compression distortion. IEEE Trans Image Process 24(12):4847–4861
35. Yuan H, Kwong S, Liu J et al (2013) A novel distortion model and Lagrangian multiplier for depth maps coding. IEEE Trans Circuits Syst Video Technol 24(3):443–451
36. De Silva V, Arachchi HK, Ekmekcioglu E et al (2013) Toward an impairment metric for stereoscopic video: a full-reference video quality metric to assess compressed stereoscopic video. IEEE Trans Image Process 22(9):3392–3404
37. Wang G, Wang Z, Gu K et al (2020) Blind quality metric of 3D-synthesized images in the discrete wavelet transform domain. IEEE Trans Image Process 29:1802–1814
38. Cohen A, Daubechies I, Feauveau JC (1992) Biorthogonal bases of compactly supported wavelets. Commun Pure Appl Math 45(5):485–560
39. Canny J (1986) A computational approach to edge detection. IEEE Trans Pattern Anal Mach Intell 6:679–698
40. Tomasi C, Manduchi R (1998) Bilateral filtering for gray and color images. In: Paper presented at international conference on computer vision, Aug 2002
41. Gu K, Zhou J, Qiao JF et al (2017) No-reference quality assessment of screen content pictures. IEEE Trans Image Process 26(8):4005–4018
42. Hassen R, Wang Z, Salama MMA (2013) Image sharpness assessment based on local phase coherence. IEEE Trans Image Process 22(7):2798–2810
43. Li Q, Lin W, Fang Y (2016) BSD: blind image quality assessment based on structural degradation. Neurocomputing 236:93–103
44. Yue G, Hou C, Gu K et al (2018) Analysis of structural characteristics for quality assessment of multiply distorted images. IEEE Trans Multimedia 20(10):2722–2732

45. Fang Y, Yan J, Li L et al (2018) No reference quality assessment for screen content images with both local and global feature representation. IEEE Trans Image Process 27(4):1600–1610
46. Koenderink JJ, van Doorn AJ (1987) Representation of local geometry in the visual system. Biol Cybern 55(6):367–375
47. Ojala T, Pietikainen M, Maenpaa T (2002) Multiresolution gray-scale and rotation invariant texture classification with local binary patterns. IEEE Trans Pattern Anal Mach Intell 24(7):971–987
48. Griffin LD (2005) Feature classes for 1D, 2nd order image structure arise from natural image maximum likelihood statistics. Netw Comput Neural Syst 16(2-3):301–320
49. Weijer J, Schmid C (2006) Coloring local feature extraction. In: Paper presented at the European conference on computer vision. Springer, Berlin, Heidelberg, pp 334–348, May 2006
50. Montesinos P, Gouet V, Deriche R (1998) Differential invariants for color images. In: Proceedings of the fourteenth international conference on pattern recognition, vol 1, pp 838–840
51. Criminisi A, Shotton J, Konukoglu E (2011) Decision forests for classification, regression, density estimation, manifold learning and semi-supervised learning. Microsoft Research Cambridge, Tech. Rep. MSRTR-2011-114 5(6):12
52. Fehn C (2004) Depth-image-based rendering (DIBR), compression, and transmission for a new approach on 3D-TV. In: Paper presented at SPIE, vol 5291(2), pp 93–104
53. Telea A (2012) An image inpainting technique based on the fast marching method. J Graph Tools 9(1):23–34
54. Mori Y, Fukushima N, Yendo T et al (2009) View generation with 3D warping using depth information for FTV. Signal Process Image Commun 24(1–2):65–72
55. Müller K, Smolic A, Dix K et al (2008) View synthesis for advanced 3D video systems. EURASIP J Image Video Process 2008:1–11
56. Ndjiki-Nya M, Koppel M, Doshkov D et al (2010) Depth image based rendering with advanced texture synthesis. In: Paper presented at IEEE international conference on multimedia and expo, pp 424–429, July 2010
57. Koppel M, Ndjiki-Nya P, Doshkov D et al (2010) Temporally consistent handling of disocclusions with texture synthesis for depth-image-based rendering. In: Paper presented at IEEE international conference on image processing, pp 1809–1812, Sept 2010
58. ITU-T RECOMMENDATION P (1999) Subjective video quality assessment methods for multimedia applications. International Telecommunication Union, 1999
59. Cermak G, Thorpe L, Pinson M (2009) Test plan for evaluation of video quality models for use with high definition TV content. Video Quality Experts Group, 2009
60. Budrikis ZL (1972) Visual fidelity criterion and modeling. In: Proceedings of the IEEE, vol 60(7), pp 771–779
61. Chandler DM, Hemami SS (2007) VSNR: a wavelet-based visual signal-to-noise ratio for natural images. IEEE Trans Image Process 16(9):2284–2298
62. Zhang L, Zhang L, Mou X et al (2011) FSIM: a feature similarity index for image quality assessment. IEEE Trans Image Process 20(8):2378–2386
63. Larson EC, Chandler DM (2010) Most apparent distortion: full reference image quality assessment and the role of strategy. J Electron Imaging 19(1):011006
64. Soundararajan R, Bovik AC (2021) RRED indices: reduced reference entropic differencing for image quality assessment. IEEE Trans Image Process 21(2):517–526
65. Zhai G, Wu X, Yang X et al (2012) A psychovisual quality metric in free-energy principle. IEEE Trans Image Process 21(1):41–52
66. Narwaria M, Lin W, McLoughlin IV et al (2012) Fourier transform-based scalable image quality measure. IEEE Trans Image Process 21(8):3364–3377
67. Wu J, Lin W, Shi G et al (2016) Orientation selectivity based visual pattern for reduced-reference image quality assessment. Inf Sci 351:18–29
68. Mittal A, Soundararajan R, Bovik AC (2013) Making a "completely blind" image quality analyzer. IEEE Signal Process Lett 20(3):209–212
69. Zhang L, Zhang L, Bovik AC (2015) A feature-enriched completely blind image quality evaluator. IEEE Trans Image Process 24(8):2579–2591

70. Xue W, Zhang L, Mou X (2013) Learning without human scores for blind image quality assessment. In: Proceeding of the IEEE conference on computer vision and pattern recognition, pp 995–1002
71. Gu K, Lin W, Zhai G et al (2017) No-reference quality metric of contrast-distorted images based on information maximization. IEEE Trans Cybern 47(12):4559–4565
72. Gu K, Zhai G, Lin W et al (2015) No-reference image sharpness assessment in autoregressive parameter space. IEEE Trans Image Process 24(10):3218–3231
73. Gu K, Zhai G, Yang X et al (2014) Hybrid no-reference quality metric for singly and multiply distorted images. IEEE Trans Broadcast 60(3):555–567
74. Gu K, Tao D, Qiao J et al (2018) Learning a no-reference quality assessment model of enhanced images with big data. IEEE Trans Neural Netw Learn Syst 29(4):1301–1313
75. Sandic-Stankovic D, Kukolj D, Le Callet P (2015) DIBR synthesized image quality assessment based on morphological wavelets. In: Paper presented at seventh international workshop on quality of multimedia experience, pp 1–6
76. Sandic-Stankovic D, Kukolj D, Callet Le et al (2016) Multi-scale synthesized view assessment based on morphological pyramids. J Electr Eng 67(1):3
77. Tian S, Zhang L, Morin L et al (2017) NIQSV: A no reference image quality assessment metric for 3D synthesized views. In: Paper presented at IEEE international conference on acoustics, speech signal processing, pp 1248–1252, March 2017
78. Tian S, Zhang L, Morin L et al (2018) NIQSV+: a no reference synthesized view quality assessment metric. IEEE Trans Image Process 27(4):1652–1664
79. Li Q, Lin W, Xu J et al (2016) Blind image quality assessment using statistical structural and luminance features. IEEE Trans Multimedia 18(12):2457–2469
80. Xue W, Mou X, Zhang L et al (2014) Blind image quality assessment using joint statistics of gradient magnitude and Laplacian features. IEEE Trans Image Process 23(11):4850–4862
81. Jakhetiya V, Gu K, Singhal T et al (2019) A highly efficient blind image quality assessment metric of 3-D synthesized images using outlier detection. IEEE Trans Ind Inf 15(7):4120–4128
82. Sheikh HR, Sabir MF, Bovik AC (2006) A statistical evaluation of recent full reference image quality assessment algorithms. IEEE Trans Image Process 15(11):3440–3451
83. Xue W, Zhang L, Mou X et al (2013) Gradient magnitude similarity deviation: a highly efficient perceptual image quality index. IEEE Trans Image Process 23(2):684–695

Chapter 4
Quality Assessment of Sonar Images

4.1 Introduction

In recent years, sonar has been more and more widely applied in underwater navigation, ocean exploration and underwater acoustic communication, and so on. Sonar
images contain much important information such as submarine geomorphology,
marine life, and wreck debris, which can well reflect underwater scenes acquired
in relatively dim light. In the aforementioned applications [1, 2], sonar images will
be transmitted by the underwater acoustic channel (UAC) to users for further analysis. The UAC is one of the most complicated channels. The reason is that (1) the
sonar signal takes multiple paths to transfer because of reflections on the surface
and the bottom of the sea; (2) the UAC itself has instability and random change
resulting in the loss of information; (3) the bandwidth provided by the current underwater acoustic communication technology is limited and the link is unstable [3, 4].
All these factors can cause distortions such as noise blur and structure degradation
of the sonar images in the transmission process, reducing the quality of the collected images and affecting the further analysis. Therefore, the sonar image quality
assessment (SIQA) plays an important role in maintaining the satisfactory quality of
received sonar images.

Many image quality assessment (QA) models have been proposed specifically for
camera-captured natural scene images (CC-NSIs). According to the accessibility of
reference information, image QA methods can be divided into three categories. The
first one is full-reference (FR) image QA methods, which can compare the complete
reference information with the test image to improve the quality score of images [5–
7]. The second one is reduced-reference (RR) image QA methods, which are further
categorized into semi-reference image QA methods and partial-reference (PR) image
QA methods. The quality score of the image can be obtained by comparing the subset
of the reference images with the test images [8–10]. The third one is no-reference
(NR) image QA methods, which can assess quality without reference images [11–
15]. Despite the previously mentioned efforts, the state-of-the-art natural scene image

© The Author(s), under exclusive license to Springer Nature Singapore Pte Ltd. 2022 95
K. Gu et al., *Quality Assessment of Visual Content*, Advances in Computer Vision
and Pattern Recognition, https://doi.org/10.1007/978-981-19-3347-9_4

(NSI) QA models are not suitable for assessing sonar images [16]. The reasons can be discussed from the following points: (1) CC-NSIs are generated by light reflection, while sonar images are formed by converting echo into a digital image; (2) the pixels of CC-NSIs have a very high dynamic variation range, however, sonar images reflect tiny pixel changes; (3) CC-NSIs are commonly used in human recreation, and the aesthetic elements contained in them have attracted more attention, while observers pay more attention to the information contained therein as sonar images are usually applied to underwater missions; (4) compared with the formation and transmission of CC-NSIs, the sonar images collected and transmitted underwater have a higher distortion rate due to the harsh environment; (5) CC-NSIs show the scene that photographers see, while sonar images show the turbid underwater scene that photographers cannot see directly.

From the perspective of sonar equipment, some SIQA methods are based on specific equipment. Considering the application of synthetic aperture sonar (SAS) images, [17] calculated the quality of SAS images by measuring the motion of the sonar platform, the level of navigation error, and environmental characteristics. In [18], an image QA metric was constructed based on the degree of navigation errors. From the characteristics of images, a lot of information contained in the sonar images is reflected by the structure, which has a great influence on QA of grayscale sonar images. In [19], a no-reference sonar image quality metric (NSIQM) was proposed to evaluate image quality by measuring the degree of contour degradation between the test image and the filtered image. In [4], Han et al. proposed a sparse wave-plate transformation matrix, which is able to represent the image in the sparsest representation while retaining the edge information of the image well. In [20], Zhang et al. presented a new SIQA algorithm, which carries out pixel fusion on the extracted multi-scale structure.

In fact, little effort has been devoted to quality metrics of sonar images in accordance with the characteristics of human visual system (HVS). Chen et al. proposed four categories of SIQA methods, namely FR SIQA methods, semi-reference SIQA methods, PR SIQA methods, and NR SIQA methods. In [24], Chen et al. put forward an FR image QA method which measures the similarity information between the distorted image and the reference image from both global and detailed aspects. In [25], a RR SIQA method was proposed. It simultaneously considered the features of sonar images and the HVS, and used base learners to get the image quality metric. In [26], Chen et al. proposed a semi-reference task- and perception-oriented SIQA (TPSIQA) method to achieve a better estimation of high-resolution sonar images' utility quality. In [27], a no-reference contour degradation measurement (NRCDM) for SIQA was designed. For evaluating the performance of those QA models, we also compared them with state-of-the-art competitors using four typically used metrics, namely Pearson linear correlation coefficient (PLCC), Spearman rank correlation coefficient (SRCC), Kendall rank correlation coefficient (KRCC), and root mean square error (RMSE).

The organization of this chapter is arranged as below. Section 4.2 introduces a sonar image quality database (SIQD) in detail and the modeling process of four types of SIQA models, namely the FR SIQA, the semi-reference SIQA, the PR SIQA, and the NR SIQA. Section 4.3 illustrates the comparison of the state-of-the-art QA methods of sonar images. Section 4.4 finally draws the conclusion and provides the future work.

4.2 Methodology

In this section, we first present a sonar image database named SIQD, and then introduce some SIQA methods. We divide these SIQA methods into four categories according to the accessibility of reference information, namely FR SIQA methods, semi-reference SIQA methods, PR SIQA methods, and NR SIQA methods. Specifically, we first introduce an FR image QA method, which measures the similarity information between the distorted image and the reference image from both global and detailed aspects. Second, we illustrate two RR SIQA methods that simultaneously consider the features of sonar images and the HVS. One of them uses base learners to get the final quality metric. The other method utilizes a watermarking strategy that replaces the auxiliary channel and generates quality scores combining information, comfort, and structural similarity (SSIM). Finally, an NR SIQA method is introduced to judge the quality of sonar images from the degree of contour degradation. We compare and analyze their performance with the typical methods by indices of PLCC, SRCC, KRCC, and RMSE.

4.2.1 Full-Reference QA of Sonar Images

With the development of underwater detection technology, more and more sonar images are used to analyze underwater scene information. The distortion often occurs during the formation and transmission of sonar images. In order to ensure that the images contain sufficient information, we need to evaluate the quality of the captured image. The FR image QA method is introduced in this part, which can compare the complete reference information obtained with the test image. FR image QA, as a method with the longest research time, has the advantages of high accuracy, strong robustness, and low operation difficulty. To the best of our knowledge, the establishing turbid underwater image quality dataset is still at an initial stage. This part mainly introduces a sonar image database created by Chen et al. [16] and the sonar image quality predictor (SIQP) method.

The Sonar Image Quality Database

The SIQD database contains 840 images, each of which is an 8-bit grayscale image, and has the same fixed resolution. Among them, 800 images are test images, and their distortions from the actual compression coding and image transmission process.

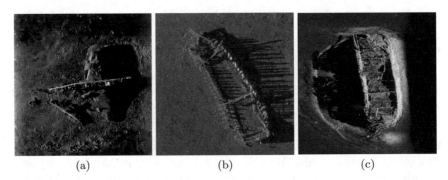

(a)   (b)   (c)

Fig. 4.1 Examples of sonar image quality database (©[2021] IEEE. Reprinted, with permission, from [24, 25, 27].)

The remaining 40 images captured by various sonar are reference images. Underwater life, shipwrecks, seabed, and other scenarios are covered in the database. In addition, it also includes the existence of target (EOT) information in each image to indicate whether the target is present in the subjective opinion of the sonar image. Figure 4.1 shows several sample diagrams of the database. The SIQA methods mentioned in this chapter are all experimented on this database.

In actual scenes, every transfer chain is the main source of errors and perceptual distortion. So the source compression before transmission and packet loss during transmission need to be considered when building the database. The SIQD database uses set partitioning in hierarchical trees (SPIHT) [21] and ComGBR [22] to generate compressed images. It also simulates packet loss by making imitated bit errors on coding streams of two aforementioned compression coding methods. The bit error information is collected according to the recent exploits about UAC. We divide each distortion into four or five levels to produce 20 distorted images from a single pristine image.

Subjective SIQA for Underwater Acoustic Transmission

The single stimulus with multiple repetitions method described in [23] is adopted in the SIQD database. All the images in the database are divided into 20 groups, and each group has 42 images, including reference images and distorted images. The same image does not appear twice in a row. In order to obtain a stable result, each audience evaluates the quality of the same image at two different stages. The sequence of images displayed at each stage is different. The score of the image is calculated by averaging the data from the two stages. In addition, each session consists of two presentations. The first one shows five different images from the group of 42. The second presentation is composed of the above 42 images awaiting subjective ratings and 5 images with repeated rejections. As viewing sonar images requires certain prior knowledge, the 25 selected viewers are all engaged in the UAC field. They are asked to take subjective tests based on their viewing habits. When the target in the image can be clearly seen, the observer can use the "with target" tag to mark the image. When the target cannot be recognized or does not exist, the observer can use the "without target" tag to mark the image.

The marking effort metrics above reflect the EOT metrics. In order to test the label with the largest probability of image selection, the EOT can be defined as follows:

$$EOT = \arg \max_{L} P_L(i), \tag{4.1}$$

where i denotes the test image. $P_L(\cdot)$ is the proportion of viewers using the label L to mark image i. It approximates the label L of image I. In addition to the EOT, the mean opinion score (MOS) of the image can also be utilized as an indicator to evaluate the image quality. It shows the visual perception of each viewer about the test image.

Objective SIQA for Underwater Acoustic Transmission

Chen et al. presented a new objective sonar image quality predictor. It can predict the image quality of sonar transmitted in harsh UAC based on the sonar image features from statistical information and structural information [24]. In this part, we will introduce the SIQP method from both global and detailed aspects. In the global aspect, we extract the similarity of the local entropy map between the distorted image and corresponding reference image as statistical information. In the detailed aspect, we extract the similarity of edge map between distorted image and corresponding reference image in the salient region as structural information. Finally, the sonar image quality can be predicted by integrating statistical information and structural information. Compared with the traditional QA model, the proposed SIQP has a better performance. The framework of this method is shown in Fig. 4.2.

Statistical Information Extraction

The formation and transmission principles of sonar images are shown in Fig. 4.3. Due to the uncertainty of the sonar object, we can model the object as a random source and its reflected echo as the output of the random source according to the information theory [28]. The amount of information sent by a random source will increase as its uncertainty increases. Entropy can measure the disorder degree of random source information. If the distortion does not occur during transmission, the entropy of the received graph is equal to the information contained in the object. Otherwise, the entropy of the received image is not consistent with that of the original object. In other words, the distortion will add some useless information or reduce useful information. Most of the existing algorithms based on image entropy regard image entropy as a statistical feature [29–33]. These methods ignore the characteristics of sonar images

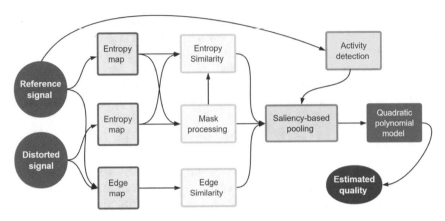

Fig. 4.2 Block diagram of the proposed SIQP metric

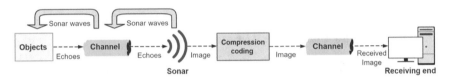

Fig. 4.3 The formation and transmission principles of sonar images

in the design. In order to evaluate the quality of sonar images effectively, we first extract the local entropy map containing statistical information about sonar images.

Some studies have shown that the HVS can recognize targets through feature detection and combination [34]. When objects are packed too closely together, several of their features tend to get jumbled up. The phenomenon of "crowding" occurs. Usually, most of the human vision field is crowded, except for a central "uncrowded window". At a specific viewing distance, only the local area of the "uncrowded window" can be clearly distinguished, while the area far away from it cannot be distinguished. We have to move our eyes and place our window on an object outside the window so that we can capture information outside the window [35]. Based on these, we apply local entropy in the SIQP method to measure the amount of information in the local area.

In the image block of size $(2m + 1) \times (2m + 1)$, the local entropy of its central position (x, y) is defined as follows:

$$Ent_l(x, y) = -\sum_{i=0}^{255} d_i log d_i, \tag{4.2}$$

where d_i is the gray-level distribution of the image block. m can be any number of window sizes, and its value is related to the content and resolution of the sonar image. When $m = 4$, the results show the best performance. This equation distributes the output entropy to the center position. So we can move the region of size $(2m + 1) \times (2m + 1)$ pixel by pixel to the entire image to get the local entropy map. Then we use a feature mask to mark key positions, which is implemented by the edge detector followed by the dilation operation. The feature mask is defined as

$$M_r(x, y) = h_s \circ Edge_r, \tag{4.3}$$

$$M_d(x, y) = h_s \circ Edge_d, \tag{4.4}$$

where $Edge_r$ is the result of edge detection on the reference image, and $Edge_d$ is the result of edge detection on the distorted image. h_s denotes a structural element, and "$\circ$" is the AND operation between the structural element and the binary edge map. Based on the local entropy and feature mask, we can obtain the mask entropy maps $\widehat{Ent}_{I_r}$ and $\widehat{Ent}_{I_d}$ for the reference image I_r and the distorted image I_d. The specific expressions are as follows:

$$\widehat{Ent}_{I_r}(x, y) = Ent_{I_r}(x, y) \cdot M_r(x, y), \tag{4.5}$$

$$\widehat{Ent}_{I_d}(x, y) = Ent_{I_d}(x, y) \cdot M_d(x, y). \tag{4.6}$$

As shown in Fig. 4.4, (a) is the reference image, (b)–(e) are four distorted images. (f)–(j) and (k)–(o) are the corresponding local entropy mapping and feature mask, respectively. It can be seen from the above images that the local entropy map of the reference image is in an ordered state with clear edges. However, when the image distortion occurs, the image changes from the ordered state to the disordered state [36]. This means that the change of entropy caused by distortion can affect the extraction of useful information. When the quality of the sonar image is lower, the information represented by the local entropy map is more chaotic.

Finally, we can use $\widehat{Ent}_{I_r}$ and $\widehat{Ent}_{I_d}$ to derive the similarity between the entropy map of the reference image and the distorted image. The similarity of the global information of the image can be given by

$$\hat{S}(x, y) = \frac{2\widehat{Ent}_{I_r}(x, y) \cdot \widehat{Ent}_{I_d}(x, y) + a_1}{\widehat{Ent}_{I_r}^2(x, y) + \widehat{Ent}_{I_d}^2(x, y) + a_1}, \tag{4.7}$$

where a_1 is specified as a small constant in order to avert instability when $\widehat{Ent}_{I_r}^2(x, y) + \widehat{Ent}_{I_d}^2(x, y)$ is very close to zero. It is easy to overlook the small changes of information in the information clustered area since they cannot affect the extraction of most information in the high entropy image block. For an image block with low entropy, the small information changes will be easily detected. Because they account for a large percentage of the total information, that is, they have more influ-

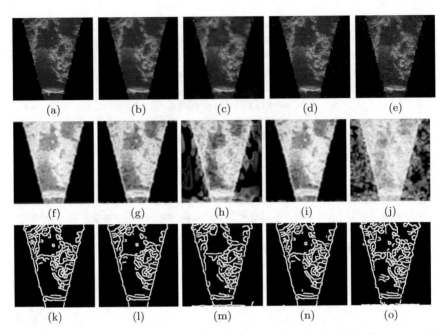

Fig. 4.4 **a** is a reference image, **b–e** are four distorted images, **f–j** represent the local entropy graphs corresponding to sonar images **a–e**, **k–o** represent the feature masks corresponding to sonar images **a–e**; **b** is a distorted image with MOS value of 61.31, **c** is a distorted image with MOS value of 30.4, and **d** is a distorted image whose MOS value is 57.15 (©[2021] IEEE. Reprinted, with permission, from [24].)

ence on the extraction of information in this block. The a_1 is revised in consideration of visual masking:

$$a_1 = K * min(Ent_{I_r}, Ent_{I_d}),\tag{4.8}$$

where the value of K should be set within a reasonable range, otherwise the degree of image distortion may be overestimated because of visual masking. Some studies have shown that the reasonable value range of K is between 40 and 90, and the performance difference caused by the change of K value is very small. Specific theoretical analysis can be referred to in [6].

Structural Information Extraction

We have used the entropy of images to measure statistical information from the global perspective in the above-mentioned method. Structural information plays a vital role in quantifying image quality when considering the HVS features. For high-quality sonar images, HVS tries to extract global information. For low-quality sonar images, HVS pays more attention to structural information. The contour of the main object in the image can also be regarded as a kind of structural information, which can

Fig. 4.5 Examples of the most active regions in different sonar images (©[2021] IEEE. Reprinted, with permission, from [24].)

be extracted by edge mapping. In order to be closer to the HVS features of sonar images with low quality, we combine the method based on edge with the local entropy method mentioned above.

The first step of this approach is to extract salient regions. In most cases, active areas containing important information are more salient than inactive areas. Here, image activity measurement (IAM) is used to detect the active area of a sonar image [37]. The activity of an image block I (represented by IAM_0) with the size of $m \times n$ is defined as

$$
IAM_0 = \frac{1}{m \times n} \left[\sum_{i=1}^{m-1} \sum_{j=1}^{n} |I(i, j) - I(i + 1, j)| + \sum_{i=1}^{m} \sum_{j=1}^{n-1} |I(i, j) - I(i, j + 1)| \right].
$$

(4.9)

The sonar image is divided into $k_1 \times k_1$ blocks, represented by $IAM(b_1)$, $IAM(b_2)$, ..., $IAM(b_n)$, respectively. $IAM(b_n)$ can be computed by Eq. (4.9). b_i represents the image block ($i = 1, 2, \ldots, n$) and n is the number of image blocks in the sonar image. $IAM(\cdot)$ denotes the active operator that evaluates IAM_0. Considering the content and resolution of the selected sonar image, we set k_1 to 64 for the best results.

The most active areas in different sonar images are highlighted in Fig. 4.5, including swimmers, aircraft wreckage, and ship wreckage. The Canny edge detector is utilized for edge mapping extraction of the most active image block b_{lm}. m refers to the block with the largest IAM_0 value. The edges of the original sonar image and the contaminated version are represented as $E_r = Edge_r^m$ and $E_d = Edge_d^m$, respectively. The SIMM can be defined as follows:

$$
\widehat{Edge}(x, y) = \frac{E_r(x, y) \& E_d(x, y) + a_2}{E_r(x, y) \| E_d(x, y) + a_2},
$$

(4.10)

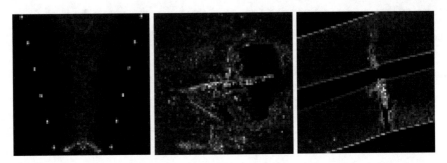

Fig. 4.6 Examples of activity maps for different sonar images (©[2021] IEEE. Reprinted, with permission, from [24].)

where a_2 is the small constant to avoid instability as the denominator goes to zero. $E_r(x, y)$ and $E_d(x, y)$ are logical mapping. "&" represents logical AND, and "||" is logical OR.

Feature Integration

In this part, we first introduce the pooling method based on saliency to obtain two feature parameters. And then a quadratic polynomial model is established to integrate the extracted features.

Salient areas should be given more attention, since the HVS is more likely to be attracted to salient features. In this method, the image activity theory is used to reflect the saliency of images. It is deduced that the saliency level of pixels in the same type of window is very similar. The activity operator is applied to each image block with the size of $k_2 \times k_2$. The IAM_0 value of the block is assigned to each pixel in the block as its activity. Then the IAM_{map} of the activity map of the image can be obtained. k_2 is equal to 4 here. The normalized activity map $\overline{IAM}_{map}$ can be used as the weight function of the feature pool:

$$\overline{IAM}_{map}(x, y) = \frac{IAM_{map}(x, y)}{\sum_x \sum_y IAM_{map}(x, y)}. \tag{4.11}$$

The activity diagram of Fig. 4.5 is shown in Fig. 4.6, where brighter pixels represent higher activities. The normalized activity graph is used to calculate statistical information feature s and structural information feature e, respectively:

$$s = \sum_x \sum_y \hat{S}(x, y)\overline{IAM}_{map}(x, y), \tag{4.12}$$

$$e = \sum_x \sum_y \widehat{Edge}(x, y)\overline{IAM}'_{map}(x, y), \tag{4.13}$$

where $\overline{IAM}'_{map}(x, y)$ is the normalized activity map of the most active block of the sonar image.

In the end, the quadratic polynomial model with the best performance is selected from different parameter models. And the extracted features are integrated to generate SIQP metrics:

$$SIQP = \sum_{n=1}^{2} \left(\alpha_{1n} s^n + \alpha_{2n} e^n \right) + \alpha_3 se, \qquad (4.14)$$

where α_{1n}, α_{2n} and α_3 are the parameters of quadratic polynomial model, $n = 1, 2$.

4.2.2 Semi-Reference QA of Sonar Images

As mentioned before, image QA methods can be classified into three categories. The first type is FR image QA, in which the test image can compare with complete reference information. In underwater transmission scenarios, it is difficult to obtain a reference map without damage. The use of FR image QA is limited. The second type is RR image QA, in which the test image can compare with a subset of reference information. To be specific, the RR image QA is divided into two groups, namely semi-reference image QA and PR image QA. They are generally inferior to FR image QA because of no prior knowledge of the content. The third type is NR image QA, in which there is no reference information for the comparison of test images. In poor conditions of UAC, it is difficult to obtain complete reference image information. Without any reference information, the performance of the metrics designed may not be as good as expected. After balancing the accuracy of the assessment with the amount of reference data required, we introduce an SR approach.

Toward Accurate Quality Evaluation of Sonar Images Based on Task and Visual Perception

Some task-oriented image QA methods are proposed to solve the problem of image low accuracy and resolution in SAS and forward-looking sonar. For example, the image quality of SAS can be represented by the information of sonar platform motion, environment characteristics, and navigation error [17, 18]. In underwater missions, sonar image-related tasks require analysis and decision-making by professionals. Sonar images need to be analyzed and decisions made by professionals. So, the perception information is also very important for the evaluation of sonar image quality. Perception-oriented SIQA methods have been emerging worldwide in [24, 25, 27]. In order to better evaluate the quality of sonar image, the SIQA method needs to add perceptual information and also consider the task situation. We will introduce a TPSIQA method, whose pipeline is shown in Fig. 4.7.

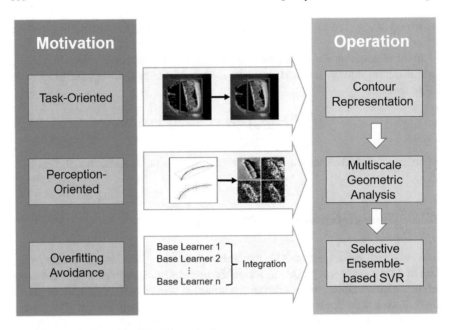

Fig. 4.7 The pipeline of the TPSIQA method

Task- and Perception-Aware Feature Extraction

The structures of the image can be divided into two parts, the global structure and the local structure. The former is very important for the representation of the target in the image, while the latter affects the visual effect of an image [27]. Considering the requirements of target recognition, features extracted in this method should be related to the global structural [38–41]. In addition, according to the content of sonar images, we extract contour information as one of the main representations of the global structure.

As one of the main features of global structure, contour is often used as an index to evaluate the quality of images. 2D wavelet can be used to capture directional information, but its power is limited. To get better results, the methods that use contourlet construction to describe the shape and directions of images are proposed in [42, 43]. Contourlets provide sets of directionality and geometry. Contours can be represented by contourlet transform. The schematic diagram of feature extraction is shown in Fig. 4.8. As we can see from the first column, each image has 10 subbands, all of which contain reference information on the contours.

In order to compress the amount of reference information, the statistical characteristics Ent_i, the energy fluctuation E_i, and the amplitude magnitude of the contourlet transform coefficients η_i are calculated, respectively:

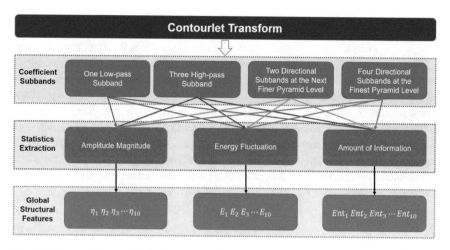

Fig. 4.8 A general framework for feature extraction

$$Ent_i = \sum_{x=1}^{M} \sum_{y=1}^{N} d(c_i(x, y)) logd(c_i(x, y)), \tag{4.15}$$

$$E_i = \frac{1}{MN} \left(\sum_{x=1}^{M} \sum_{y=1}^{N} log|c_i(x, y) - \frac{1}{MN} \sum_{x=1}^{M} \sum_{y=1}^{N} c_i(x, y)| \right), \tag{4.16}$$

$$\eta_i = \frac{1}{MN} \sum_{x=1}^{M} \sum_{y=1}^{N} log|c_i(x, y)|. \tag{4.17}$$

In the ith ($i \in [1, 10]$) subband, $c_i(x, y)$ is the coefficient at position (x, y), and $d(c_i(x, y))$ refers to the probability distribution of the coefficients in the subband of size $M \times N$. We stack the reference information including Ent_i, E_i, and η_i, which are extracted from the reference image:

$$G_r = \{Ent_1, Ent_2, \ldots, Ent_{10}; E_1, E_2, \ldots, E_{10}; \eta_1, \eta_2, \ldots, \eta_{10}\}, \tag{4.18}$$

$$\Delta G = |G_r - G_d|, \tag{4.19}$$

where the above information G_r is obtained from the reference image, and the information G_d is extracted from the test image in the same way. It is known from this equation that ΔG is related to the quality of distorted sonar image.

Selective Ensemble Learning

During the process of model training, not all features are equally important to image contour. Using all feature sets will not only make the quality prediction overfitting but also reduce the efficiency of the algorithm. Based on the above reasons, we use partial subsets of features to generate the base learner ensemble. The feature selection and base learner training process are repeated m times. In this part, we exclude lower performing base learners using a selection technique. The generalization error is employed as the performance indicator to get the corresponding performance threshold. $B_i(x)$ is the output of the ith base learner, where $i \in [1, m]$. x follows a distribution $\Psi(x)$, and $\tilde{x}$ and $B_i(x)$ are expected and actual outputs, respectively. The ensemble output on x is calculated as follows:

$$\hat{B}(x) = \sum_{i=1}^{m} \omega_i B_i(x), \tag{4.20}$$

where $0 \le \omega_i \le 1$ and $\sum_{i=1}^{m} \omega_i = 1$. The generalization error of the ith base learner $(er_i(x))$ and the ensemble on x $(\widehat{er}_i(x))$ are defined as follows:

$$er_i(x) = (B_i(x) - \tilde{x})^2, \tag{4.21}$$

$$\widehat{er}_i(x) = (\hat{B}_i(x) - \tilde{x})^2. \tag{4.22}$$

The correlation between the ith and the jth base learners can be defined as

$$cor_{ij} = \int \Psi(x)(B_i(x) - \tilde{x})(B_j(x) - \tilde{x})dx. \tag{4.23}$$

It is easy to prove that $cor_{ij} = cor_{ji}$ and $cor_{ii} = er_i$. Combining Eqs. (4.20)–(4.22), $\widehat{er}_i(x)$ can be given by

$$\widehat{er}(x) = \left(\sum_{i=1}^{m} \omega_i B_i(x) - \tilde{x}\right)\left(\sum_{j=1}^{m} \omega_j B_j(x) - \tilde{x}\right). \tag{4.24}$$

We make all the base learners with the same initial weights, namely $\omega_i = \frac{1}{m}(i = 1, 2, \ldots, m)$; we obtain

$$\widehat{er} = \frac{1}{m^2} \sum_{i=1}^{m} \sum_{j=1}^{m} cor_{ij}. \tag{4.25}$$

Then, we examine each base learner to determine whether it should be excluded. When testing kth learners, the generalization error after excluding some base learners can be defined as

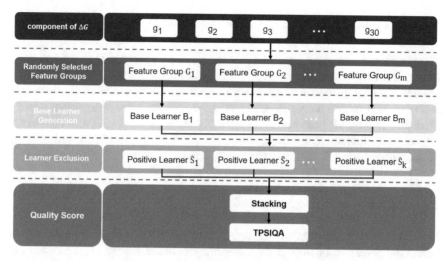

Fig. 4.9 The general framework of the selective ensemble learning technique

$$\widehat{er}^+ = \frac{1}{(m-1)^2} \sum_{\substack{i=1 \\ i \neq k}}^{m} \sum_{\substack{j=1 \\ j \neq k}}^{m} cor_{ij}. \tag{4.26}$$

After excluding the kth base learner to make the final ensemble better, $\widehat{er}$ should be greater than $\widehat{er}^+$ or equal to $\widehat{er}^+$. We can derive

$$er_k \geq \frac{2m-1}{m^2} \sum_{i=1}^{m} \sum_{j=1}^{m} cor_{ij} - 2 \sum_{\substack{i=1 \\ i \neq k}}^{m} cor_{ik}. \tag{4.27}$$

The threshold T_e is defined as

$$T_e = \frac{2m-1}{m^2} \sum_{i=1}^{m} \sum_{j=1}^{m} cor_{ij} - 2 \sum_{\substack{i=1 \\ i \neq k}}^{m} cor_{ik}. \tag{4.28}$$

If the generalization error of the base learner is greater than this threshold, the base learner will be discarded. After excluding some negative base learners, the output of the remaining positive base learners is averaged to achieve the ensemble. Figure 4.9 depicts a general framework of selective ensemble learning technology. g_i is a component of ΔG of the features extracted from all training images, $i \in [1, 30]$. After selecting the feature set of G_i, the base learners trained by the ith selected feature group are screened to obtain the positive base learners, which can be used to integrate and realize the TPSIQA methods.

4.2.3   Partial-Reference QA of Sonar Images

The poor environment of UAC prevents the receiver from obtaining the reference image. However, part of the original image information can be sent to the receiver through the auxiliary channel as reference information or as a robust watermark hidden in the transmitted image. Based on this, a partial-reference sonar image quality predictor (PSIQP) [25] can be used to remit the adverse effects of UAC on the transmission. This method also takes into account the clarity, information, and comfort of sonar images. In this part, we will mainly introduce a novel PR SIQA method.

PR SIQA for Underwater Transmission

In the first stage of this method, the information and comfort index are extracted to reflect the perceived quality of the sonar images. In the second stage, we use the structure similarity between the original and distorted sonar images to reflect the validity of the sonar images. In the third stage, we utilize the image information, the comfort index, and the structure similarity index to predict the image quality. For reference signals, most previous efforts have been made to protect them by assuming a low data rate error-free auxiliary channel.

RR Image QA-Based Underwater Transmission System

In practice, captured sonar images need to be sent to a remote location for further analysis by professionals. However, the communication environment of UAC is more restricted than that of terrestrial channels, which makes the transmitted image quality not always efficient. As Fig. 4.10 shows, a three-bit error in a compressed stream can seriously impair image quality. Since not all reference signals can be used for underwater transmission, RR image QA is used here to monitor the quality of sonar images transmitted through UAC. The application of RR image QA to monitor real-time video quality on wireless communication channels was first proposed by [44]. Subsequently, this principle is then extended to different applications [9, 45]. For underwater transmission systems, RR image QA can be used as a guide for post-processing. At the sender side, the reference signal of the sonar image is first extracted. Then the image is compressed and transmitted via UAC to a remote location for further analysis. At the receiver side, we perform feature extraction on the received distorted image. The features extracted from both the original and distorted sonar images are used for sonar image QA methods. Finally, we perform a post-processing operation according to the results of the RR sonar image QA method [46, 47].

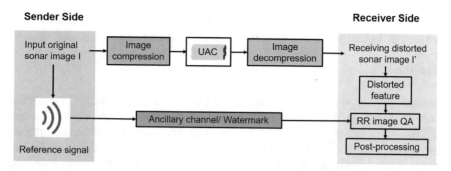

Fig. 4.10 Framework of a sonar image transmission system based on RR image QA

Information and Comfort Indices

In the first stage, we consider two factors: the amount of information extracted from the image and the comfort of the image. The information content can be measured by image entropy, and the comfort degree is related to some higher order statistics. We first calculate the entropy of the sonar image I:

$$Q_1 = -\sum_{i=0}^{255} d_i \log d_i, \tag{4.29}$$

where i is the pixel value, and d_i represents the gray-level distribution of the sonar image I.

Recent studies in neuroscience have found that higher order statistics are associated with human "comfort". Skewness measures the direction and degree of skewness of the data distribution. There is a relationship between skewness statistics and glossiness [48]. When the sonar image has negative skewed statistics, it is often brighter and smoother than similar images with higher skewness. We use the following definition of skewness in the PSIQP metric as the first comfort index:

$$Q_2 = E\left[\left(\frac{I - E(I)}{\sigma(I)}\right)^3\right], \tag{4.30}$$

where $\sigma(I)$ is the variance value of the sonar image I. In mathematics, kurtosis is used to measure the "tailedness" of the probability distribution of a real-valued random variable. In this part, we use kurtosis as the second comfort index, which is defined as

$$Q_3 = E\left[\left(\frac{I - E(I)}{\sigma(I)}\right)^4\right] - 3. \tag{4.31}$$

We extract the information and the comfort index at the receiver side. They are separately integrated into the proposed quality predictor with structural similarity.

Structural Similarity

According to the source image category, there are many QA methods. For example, there are QA methods based on natural scene images (NSIs), screen content images (SCIs), stereo images, and medical images. Generally speaking, different types of images acquired in different scenes have different characteristics. For example, 3D images have higher dimensional information. Sonar images are mostly grayscale images and the structure of sonar images is more prominent, etc. The image QA metrics designed according to these characteristics have their own advantages and corresponding limitations, so the traditional image QA method may not be suitable for sonar images. Therefore, it is very important to design the QA metric for underwater sonar image according to the application scenes and image characteristics.

In sonar images, the structure is the key to target recognition. We take the structure as the evaluation index of image quality, and utilize edge mapping to represent the structure information of the sonar image. Among the existing edge detection algorithms, Canny is adopted in PSIQP for its good performance. In addition, considering the interaction between adjacent pixels, the median filter F is used to reduce the influence of "blocking" artifacts. The edge graph E of sonar images extracted by the Canny operator can be expressed as

$$E_F = E * F_n, \tag{4.32}$$

where n represents the size of the filter and "$*$" is the convolution operator. The distribution of E_F is represented by a normalized histogram. Here, we select the probability of "edges" to represent the normalized histogram of each block. The normalized histograms of reference sonar image and distorted image edge maps are represented by $H_f(i)$ and $H_d(i)$. Finally, we calculate the similarity between $H_f(i)$ and $H_d(i)$ to measure the structural similarity $S(i)$ of each block I:

$$S(i) = \frac{2H_f(i) \cdot H_d(i) + \delta}{H_f^2(i) \cdot H_d^2(i) + \delta}, \tag{4.33}$$

where δ is a constant with small value that prevents division by zero.

Active areas will attract more visual attention on account of their greater salience. We can assign weights according to the activities of the corresponding image blocks. IAM is used to calculate the activity diagram $\overline{IAM}_{map}$ for each block in the received image. The standardized activity graph $\overline{IAM}_{map}$ is implemented as a weighting function of S.

$$\overline{IAM}_{map}(i) = \frac{IAM_{map}(i)}{\sum\limits_{i=1}^{n} IAM_{map}(i)}. \tag{4.34}$$

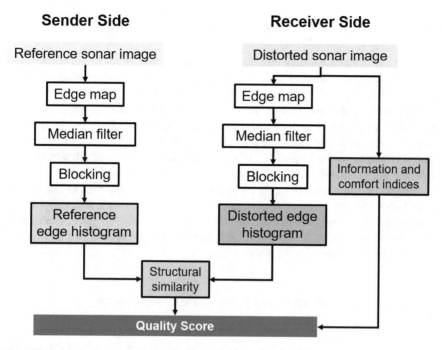

Fig. 4.11 Framework of the proposed PSIQP metric

The weighted structural similarity of the received sonar image is obtained by using the normalized activity map, shown as follows:

$$Q_4 = \hat{S} = \sum_{i=1}^{n} S(i)\overline{\text{IAM}}_{\text{map}}(i). \qquad (4.35)$$

Integration

Finally, the above information indicators, namely comfort index and structural similarity index, are integrated to obtain PSIQP:

$$PSIQP = \sum_{i=1}^{4} \beta_i \cdot Q_i, \qquad (4.36)$$

where β_i is the weight of the four indicators. The proposed PSIQP measurement framework is shown in Fig. 4.11.

4.2.4 No-Reference QA of Sonar Images

In the above content, we have introduced the image QA methods based on reference images, which possess better performance in assessing the quality of NSIs. However, due to the limitation of the underwater detection environment, not all reference image information can be obtained. In this case, it is more appropriate to adopt an NR image QA model to assess the underwater image effectively. Most NR image QA methods rely on a learning-based predictive model to explore the relationship between the image features and image quality. The recent NR methods have been designed based on other scenarios, which perform poorly in evaluating the acoustic lens and side-scan sonar images. In addition, the human visual perception system and brain visual cognitive mechanism also have certain defects in water acoustic transmission and transmitted image restoration. It's necessary to find an SIQA model with better performance and suitable for underwater environment detection. In this part, we mainly introduce a novel NR SIQA method.

Reference-Free QA of Sonar Image via Contour Degradation Measurement

Due to the difference between NSIs and sonar images in color change, texture structure, pixel change, and so on, many classical image QA algorithms based on reference images fail to evaluate the quality of sonar images. In order to accurately evaluate the quality of sonar images, we present an NRCDM metric [27]. We can infer whether there is a target or terrain according to the macroscopic structure in the image. In addition, contour is an important form of macroscopic structure; its integrity can determine the practical quality of sonar image to a large extent [49, 50]. The performance of the NRCDM metric is superior to other NR image QA models.

In Fig. 4.12, we depict the overall framework of the NRCDM metric. First, we extract the features reflecting contour information. Then, we compare the features between the test image I and its filtered version I' to obtain the contour degradation degree. Finally, the quality of the test image is evaluated by the degree of contour degradation in the QA model. Following the above framework, each of the parts will be presented separately.

Feature Extraction

The image quality depends on the response of HVS to spatial frequency decomposition [51, 52]. This hypothesis has been successfully applied to simple pattern recognition systems and spatial frequency-based HVS models [53]. Different components of the image correspond to different frequencies, among which image contour constitutes the intermediate frequency component. As shown in Fig. 4.13, most of the distortion types make up the rest of the low- and high-frequency components, which can destroy the contour of sonar images. As some types of distortion are introduced,

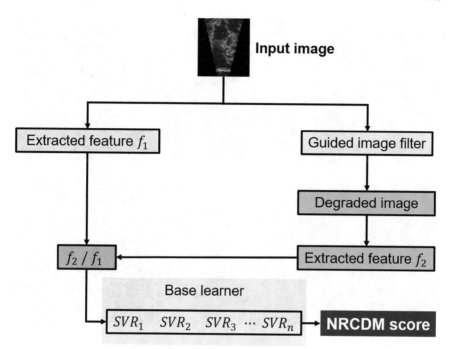

Fig. 4.12 A general framework of the proposed NRCDM metric

the high-frequency component increases and the image brightens. Instead, a decrease in the low-frequency component makes the image darker. It can be seen from the above description that the sonar image contour with low-frequency distortion usually has a low degradation rate. In this method, we adopt this theory to assess the practical quality of sonar images based on the recognition and detection of contour degradation measurement.

For obtaining the contour information, we extract features with discrete cosine transform (DCT), Cohen-Daubechies-Feauveau 9/7 wavelet transform (C-D-F 9/7), and singular value decomposition (SVD). The flowchart of the feature extraction process is shown as in Fig. 4.14. The first two transforms can collect contour information from the frequency domain, the last one can collect contour information from the spatial domain. In the process of feature extraction, we transform the sonar image I into the three domains. The coefficient matrices of DCT and C-D-F 9/7 transform are represented by D and C, respectively. S represents the diagonal matrix of the SVD transform. These three matrices are sparse, and their sparsity depends on the coefficients with large values. We use the sparsity of different transformation coefficient matrices to represent contour information. When the low-frequency or high-frequency components increase, the sparsity of the three matrices (D, C, and S) will get higher.

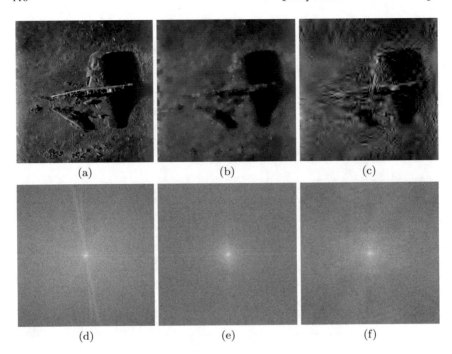

Fig. 4.13 The relationship between distortion and frequency component. When the distortion destroys the sonar image contour, the frequency spectrum will become brighter or darker. **a** Reference image; **b** Distorted sonar image with "CC"; **c** Distorted sonar image with "TS"; **d–f** Frequency spectrum of (**a**)–(**c**) (©[2021] IEEE. Reprinted, with permission, from [54].)

The sparse metric should satisfy six criteria, namely Scaling, Bill Gates, Rising Tide, Robin Hood, Babies, and Cloning. When the sparsity number is fixed, the Gini index and Hoyer measure meet all standards and perform better than other sparsity indicators (i.e., l^0, $-l^1$, and $\frac{l^2}{l^1}$). Here, we use the Gini index [55] and Hoyer measure [56] to describe contour information more comprehensively. The Hoyer measure and Gini index are calculated as follows:

$$H(\mathbf{v}) = \frac{\sqrt{N} - \left(\sum_{i=1}^{N} |\mathbf{v}_i|\right) \Big/ \sqrt{\sum_{i=1}^{N} \mathbf{v}_i^2}}{\sqrt{N} - 1}, \qquad (4.37)$$

$$G(\mathbf{v}) = 1 - 2\sum_{k=1}^{N} \frac{\mathbf{v}_{(k)}}{\|\mathbf{v}\|_1}\left(\frac{N - k + \frac{1}{2}}{N}\right), \qquad (4.38)$$

where $\mathbf{v} = [\mathbf{v}_1, \mathbf{v}_2, \ldots, \mathbf{v}_N]$ is a 1D vector transformed from a 2D transformation coefficient matrix. We rank the order of $\mathbf{v}$ from the smallest to largest, $\mathbf{v}_{(1)} \leq \mathbf{v}_{(2)} \leq \ldots \leq \mathbf{v}_{(N)}$. N represents the total number of coefficient matrices.

Fig. 4.14 The flowchart of
the feature extraction process

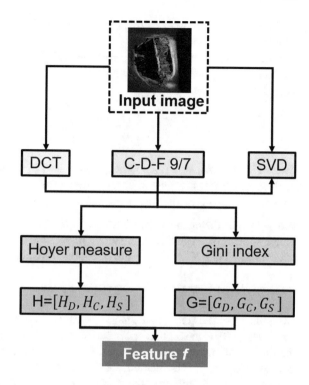

Figure 4.14 shows the feature extraction process of sonar images. The features $[H_D, H_C, H_S]$ and $[G_D, G_C, G_S]$ are Hoyer measure and Gini index of transform domain coefficient matrices D, C, and S, which contain most contour information of sonar images.

Contour Degradation Measurement

We adopt a guided image filter [57] to establish the degradation model, which degrades sonar images by smoothing. This model can measure the degree of image degradation. The kernel weight value of the filter is defined as follows:

$$W_{ij}(I) = \frac{1}{|p|^2} \sum_{k:(i,j)\in\omega_k} \left(1 + \frac{(I_i - \mu_k)(I_j - \mu_k)}{\sigma_k^2 + \epsilon}\right), \qquad (4.39)$$

where $|p|$ is the number of pixels in the window p_k, and μ_k and σ_k^2 represent the mean and variance of the guide image I in p_k, respectively. Whether the current pixel should be the average of the nearby pixels or the original average is retained is determined by the regularization parameter ϵ. The degradation intensity of the guided image filter is adjusted by ϵ, which has a positive correlation with extracted features. It is obvious that the sparsity of different transform coefficient matrices grows with the increase of ϵ. In other words, the sparsity of different transform coefficients is related to the degradation.

We set the value of ϵ to 0.01, and use a regression model to construct the connection between the degradation degree and the distortion of test images. The degree of degradation F is measured by

$$F = \frac{f_2}{f_1} = \left[\frac{H'_D}{H_D}, \frac{H'_C}{H_C}, \frac{H'_S}{H_S}, \frac{G'_D}{G_D}, \frac{G'_C}{G_C}, \frac{G'_S}{G_S} \right], \tag{4.40}$$

where H'_D, H'_C, H'_S, and G'_D, G'_C, G'_S denote the Hoyer measure and the Gini index of three transform coefficients in the filtered test sonar image I', respectively. F reflects the impact of the image distortion. Figure 4.15 shows the changes of $\frac{H'_S}{H_S}$ and $\frac{G'_S}{G_S}$ when distortion occurs in the test image. The first image is the original image without distortion. The remaining images are the distorted images, which are affected by "TC", "CC", "TS", and "CS", respectively.

Bagging-Based Support Vector Regression Module

Different from the traditional image QA model, we adopt a bagging algorithm to construct an SVR model that can describe the relationship between the features and the quality of sonar images. Besides, it can transform the features into the sonar image quality index. The method is tested on several base learners and the results are aggregated, which improves the stability and accuracy of this algorithm [58]. The NRCDM algorithm expression is given by

$$NRCDM = \frac{1}{n} \sum_{i=1}^{n} B_i(t), \tag{4.41}$$

where N denotes the size of standard training set T. Bagging generates n new training sets T_i; all of the sizes is N'. When $N = N'$, we utilize n samples to fit base learners $B_1(\cdot)$, $B_2(\cdot)$, ..., $B_n(\cdot)$ and combine the average outputs to get the final image quality index.

We conduct various experiments on the SIQD database, including 840 sonar images. Specifically, 672 images in the SIQD database are used for model training, and the remaining 168 images are test samples. The training sets and test sets are different. This method can not only improve the stability and accuracy of machine learning algorithms, but also reduce the variance and avoid overfitting caused by a small training set [59].

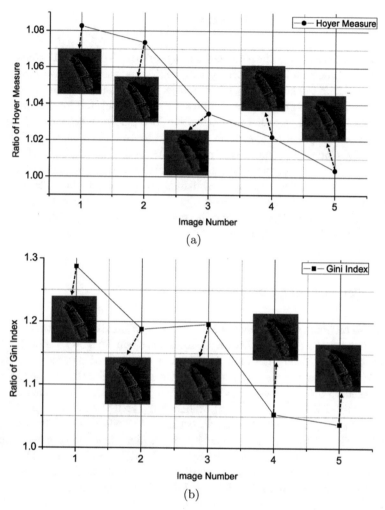

Fig. 4.15 The variation of **a** $\frac{H'_S}{H_S}$ and **b** $\frac{G'_S}{G_S}$ when distortion is added to the image (©[2021] IEEE. Reprinted, with permission, from [27])

4.3 Comparison and Analysis of Algorithm Performance

In this section, we will introduce the specific parameter settings of images in the SIQD. Then, some excellent SIQA models based on different reference information are briefly introduced. Finally, we focus on comparing and analyzing their performance with the quality evaluation model introduced in this chapter. The analysis results show that these models presented in this chapter have good performance.

4.3.1 The Sonar Image Database

First, we introduce the specific parameter settings of images in the SIQD. Considering that distorted images will be affected by compression and packet loss, we used SPIHT and ComGBR to generate compressed images with different compression ratios. Specifically, SPIHT can generate compressed images with different compression ratios by adjusting the wavelet decomposition level and parameter rate. Here, the parameter level was set to 6, and the rates were set to 0.01, 0.03, 0.1, 0.3, and 3, respectively. ComGBR compression ratios were set to 0.1, 0.2, 0.3, 0.4, and 0.5 separately. After this encoding process, we model the different situations of UAC by changing the bit errors generated in the bitstream with level 5 bit error rate (BER) to collect distorted images. Besides, we designed a random variable $c \in \{0, 1\}$, where the probability of $c = 1$ is BER, and the probability of 0 is 1-BER. Each packet contains 8 bits. When $c = 0$, the current packet is transmitted correctly.

4.3.2 Performance Comparison and Analysis

In order to reflect the effectiveness and superiority of the SIQA metrics introduced in this chapter, we compare them with some excellent image QA models. Their basic information is shown in Table 4.1. The models involved in comparison can be divided into three categories. The first category consists of 12 FR image QA measures including the SIQP measures described in this chapter. The second category consists of five RR image quality metrics including TPSIQA and PSIQP models presented in this chapter. The third category consists of 12 NR image quality indicators including NRCDM metrics introduced in this chapter. Generally, the performance of this objective image QA is verified by PLCC, SRCC, KRCC, and RMSE. The evaluation accuracy can be measured by PLCC and RMSE, while the monotonicity of the prediction can be found by SRCC and KRCC. A higher value of PLCC, SRCC, and KRCC and a lower value of RMSE represent better quality evaluation methods.

The objective assessment scores are nonlinearity obtained by PLCC, SRCC, KRCC, and RMSE, so we use a logistic function to increase the linearity. We compute the image QA scores using these four criteria by the mapping including 5 parameters as follows:

$$f(x) = \tau_1 \left(\frac{1}{2} - \frac{1}{1 + \exp^{\tau_2(x - \tau_3)}} \right) + \tau_4 x + \tau_5, \tag{4.42}$$

where $\tau_{i, i=1,2,3,4,5}$ represents the fitted parameter; $f(x)$ and x are subjective scores and their corresponding objective scores which are assessed by image QA algorithms.

To facilitate the comparison of the performance of QA metrics for the 29 competing images, we make a comparison and analysis according to four model types. By analyzing the strengths and weaknesses of these models, we can draw some important conclusions:

Table 4.1 Information of the metrics involved in the comparative experiment

Abbreviation	Category	Full Name	Refs.
SSIM	FR	Structural similarity	[5]
VSNR	FR	Visual signal-to-noise ratio	[60]
FSIM	FR	Feature similarity	[61]
VSI	FR	Visual saliency-induced index	[62]
GMSD	FR	Gradient magnitude similarity deviation	[63]
ADD-SSIM	FR	Analysis of distortion distribution-based SSIM	[64]
MAD	FR	Most apparent distortion	[65]
GMS	FR	Gradient similarity	[6]
PSIM	FR	Perceptual similarity	[66]
LTG	FR	Local-tuned-global model	[67]
LESQP	FR	Local entropy backed sonar image quality predictor	[16]
SIQP	FR	Sonar image quality predictor	[24]
QMC	RR	Quality assessment metric of contrast	[9]
RWQMS	RR	RR wavelet-domain quality measure of SCIs	[10]
OSVP	RR	Orientation selectivity-based visual pattern	[68]
RIQMC	RR	Reduced-reference image quality metric for contrast change	[8]
PSIQP	RR	Partial-reference sonar image quality predictor	[25]
TPSIQP	RR	Task- and perception-oriented sonar image quality assessment	[26]
BLINDS II	NR	Blind image integrity notator using DCT statistics	[69]
BRISQUE	NR	Blind/referenceless image spatial quality evaluator	[58]
IL-NIQE	NR	Integrated local natural image quality evaluator	[70]
ARISM	NR	AR-based image sharpness metric	[71]
NFERM	NR	NR free energy-based robust metric	[72]
SISBLM	NR	Six-step blind metric	[73]
ASIQE	NR	Accelerated screen image quality evaluator	[14]
BQMS	NR	Blind quality measure for SCIs	[74]
CourveletQA	NR	–	[75]
BPRI	NR	Blind PRI-based	[76]
HOSA	NR	High order statistics aggregation	[77]
NRCDM	NR	No-reference contour degradation measurement	[27]

(1) In the comparison of FR image QA metrics, SIQP introduced in this chapter has the best performance. Firstly, we consider the effect of four distortion types on image quality. The first is the blur damage of the sonar image caused by ComGBR compression. The second is the noneccentricity distortion brought by SPIHT and a similar blur distortion. The third is noise caused by artificial bit error distortion in ComGBR bitstream. The fourth is a messy and unnatural artifact caused by artificial bits errors distortion in the SPIHT bitstream. Except for the SIQP metric, other metrics show poor performance in the first type of distortion. This may be due to the weak ability of these image quality metrics to evaluate blur distortion. The same happens in the second distortion type. We infer that the noneccentricity distortion may confuse subjective quality prediction. In the third and fourth types of distortion, the models involved in comparison show good and reasonable performance, while SIQP is still the best. This shows that they can predict the noise in the image and evaluate the structural degradation ability in the image well. Finally, these FR image QA metrics are compared on the entire SIQD database. There is no doubt that SIQP shows the best performance in assessing the degree of blur, noneccentricity, noise, and structural degradation.

(2) In the comparison of RR image QA metrics, PSIQP introduced in this chapter has the best performance, while TPSIQA shows the suboptimal performance in SRCC, KRCC, PLCC, and RMSE. It is worth mentioning that the monotone correlation coefficient between MOS and the predicted quality of TSIQP is higher than that of PSIQA. The larger the value of this system, the better the effect of the method is. In addition, the selective ensemble learning method is added to TPSIQA, which makes the model obtain better contour information and significantly improves the model's performance.

(3) In the comparison of NR image QA metrics, the NRCDM introduced in this chapter has the best performance. Compared with blind/referenceless image spatial quality evaluator (BRISQUE) ranked second, the performance of SRCC, KRCC, PLCC, and RMSE increased by at least 14%. NRCDM has the best prediction monotonicity and accuracy for noise caused by artificial bits errors in ComGBR bitstream. It also has the best predictive consistency for noise caused by artificial bit errors in SPIHT bitstream. But when the evaluation is blur, it does not perform well in these two aspects. It is poor at predicting confusing and unnatural information. Nevertheless, it still shows a clear advantage in NR image QA metrics.

(4) In general, the four methods introduced in this chapter perform well in the test, and the PSIQP metric has the best performance. When the bit error rate is below 2×10^{-3}, the performance of the PSIQA method is almost unaffected. Since then, the performance of the PSIQA method decreases as the bit error rate increases. When the bit error rate reaches 3×10^{-3}, the performance is lower than NRCDM. In addition, although the performance of the NRCDM is superior to many traditional image QA methods, there is still much space for improvement compared with the other three methods introduced in this chapter. In order to adapt to the SIQA in the NR environment, we need to invest more energy in the design task of the NR SIQA model.

4.4 Conclusion

With the development of underwater detection and image QA technology, more and more sonar images are used to analyze underwater scene information. This chapter introduces three types of methods to assess the quality of SCIs, namely FR, RR, and NR methods. First, we present an FR SIQA approach designed from a global and detailed perspective. The similarity of local entropy map and edge map of the significant region is used as statistical information and structural information, respectively, to predict sonar image quality. Second, considering that the harsh underwater UCA environment hinders the acquisition of reference images, we introduce two RR image QA methods. One method is to take the contour information as the main representation of the overall structure, since observers pay more attention to the image content related to the global structure in the image QA based on the underwater detection task. The other method is to extract statistical information, comfort, and structural similarity to predict the sonar image quality from two aspects of quality perception and image effectiveness. Finally, considering that the reference image cannot be obtained in most cases, we introduce an NR method. It uses sparse features extracted from different domains to measure the degradation degree of sonar image contour, and obtains the relationship between contour degradation degree and sonar image quality by the learning-based method. From the analysis of the model comparison, it can be seen that these methods introduced in this chapter have good performance. In future work, we will consider more complex underwater factors and focus on the design of effective RR and NR image QA methods.

References

1. Clark D, Ruiz I, Petillot Y et al (2007) Particle PHD filter multiple target tracking in sonar image. IEEE Trans Aerosp Electron Syst 43(1):409–416
2. Lo KW, Ferguson BG (2004) Automatic detection and tracking of a small surface watercraft in shallow water using a high-frequency active sonar. IEEE Trans Aerosp Electron Syst 40(4):1377–1388
3. Stojanovic M, Freitag L (2013) Recent trends in underwater acoustic communications. Mar Technol Soc J 47(5):45–50
4. Han G, Cui J, Su Y et al (2020) Human vision system based sparse wavelet transform for underwater acoustic sonar image transmission. In: Paper presented at the global oceans 2020: Singapore-US gulf coast, 1–4 Oct 2020
5. Wang Z, Bovik AC, Sheikh H et al (2004) Image quality assessment: from error visibility to structural similarity. IEEE Trans Image Process 13(4):600–612
6. Liu A, Lin W, Narwaria M (2012) Image quality assessment based on gradient similarity. IEEE Trans Image Process 21(4):1500–1512
7. Gu K, Wang S, Yang H et al (2016) Saliency-guided quality assessment of screen content images. IEEE Trans Multimedia 18(6):1098–1110
8. Gu K, Zhai G, Lin W et al (2016) The analysis of image contrast: from quality assessment to automatic enhancement. IEEE Trans Cybern 46(1):284–297
9. Gu K, Zhai G, Yang X et al (2015) Automatic contrast enhancement technology with saliency preservation. IEEE Trans Circuits Syst Video Technol 25(9):1480–1494

10. Wang S, Gu K, Zhang X et al (2016) Subjective and objective quality assessment of compressed screen content images. IEEE J Emerg Sel Top Circuits Syst 6(4):532–543
11. Zhang Y, Zhang R (2018) No-reference image sharpness assessment based on maximum gradient and variability of gradients. IEEE Trans Multimedia 20(7):1796–1808
12. Freitas P, Akamine W, Farias M (2018) No-reference image quality assessment using orthogonal color planes patterns. IEEE Trans Multimedia 20(12):3353–3360
13. Gu K, Tao D, Qiao J et al (2018) Learning a no-reference quality assessment model of enhanced images with big data. IEEE Trans Neural Netw Learn Syst 29(4):1301–1313
14. Gu K, Zhou J, Qiao J et al (2017) No-reference quality assessment of screen content pictures. IEEE Trans Image Process 26(8):4005–4018
15. Gu K, Jakhetiya V, Qiao J et al (2018) Model-based referenceless quality metric of 3D synthesized images using local image description. IEEE Trans Image Process 27(1):394–405
16. Chen W, Yuan F, Cheng E et al (2017) Subjective and objective quality evaluation of sonar images for underwater acoustic transmission. In: Paper presented at IEEE international conference on image processing, pp 176–180, Sept 2017
17. Williams DP (2010) Image-quality prediction of synthetic aperture sonar imagery. In: Paper presented at IEEE international conference on acoustics, speech and signal processing, pp 2114–2117, March 2010
18. Debes C, Engel R, Zoubir AM et al (2009) Quality assessment of synthetic aperture sonar images. In: Paper presented at oceans 2009-Europe, 1–4 May 2009
19. Chen W, Yuan F, Cheng E et al (2018) Sonar image quality assessment based on degradation measurement. In: Paper presented at oceans - MTS/IEEE Kobe techno-oceans, 1–5 May 2018
20. Zhang H, Li D, Li S et al (2020) Using multiscale structural fusion for sonar image quality evaluation. In: Paper presented at the 5th international conference on mechanical, control and computer engineering, pp 2331–2335, Dec 2020
21. Said A, Pearlman W (1996) A new, fast, and efficient image codec based on set partitioning in hierarchical trees. IEEE Trans Circuits Syst Video Technol 6(3):243–250
22. Chen W, Yuan F, Cheng E (2016) Adaptive underwater image compression with high robust based on compressed sensing. In: Paper presented at the IEEE international conference on signal processing, communications and computing, 1–6 Aug 2016
23. BT R I R (2002) Methodology for the subjective assessment of the quality of television pictures. In: Proceedings of the international telecommunication union, 2002
24. Chen W, Gu K, Lin W et al (2020) Statistical and structural information backed full-reference quality measure of compressed sonar images. IEEE Trans Circuits Syst Video Technol 30(2):334–348
25. Chen W, Gu K, Min X et al (2018) Partial-reference sonar image quality assessment for underwater transmission. IEEE Trans Aerosp Electron Syst 54(6):2776–2787
26. Chen W, Gu K, Zhao T et al (2021) Semi-reference sonar image quality assessment based on task and visual perception. IEEE Trans Multimedia 23:1008–1020
27. Chen W, Gu K, Lin W et al (2019) Reference-free quality assessment of sonar images via contour degradation measurement. IEEE Trans Image Process 28(11):5336–5351
28. Shannon CE (1948) A mathematical theory of communication. Bell Syst Tech J 27(3):379–423
29. Fezza SA, Larabi M, Faraoun KM (2014) Stereoscopic image quality metric based on local entropy and binocular just noticeable difference. In: Paper presented at the IEEE international conference on image processing, pp 2002–2006, Oct 2014
30. Zhao M, Tu Q, Lu Y et al (2015) No-reference image quality assessment based on phase congruency and spectral entropies. In: Paper presented at the picture coding symposium, pp 302–306, May 2015
31. Zhang Y, Wu J, Shi G et al (2015) Reduced-reference image quality assessment based on entropy differences in DCT domain. In: Paper presented at the IEEE international symposium on circuits and systems, pp 2796–2799, May 2015
32. Shi W, Jiang F, Zhao D (2016) Image entropy of primitive and visual quality assessment. In: Paper presented at the IEEE international conference on image processing, pp 2087–2091, Sept 2016

33. Liu L, Liu B, Huang H et al (2014) No-reference image quality assessment based on spatial and spectral entropies. Signal Process Image Commun 29(8):856–863
34. Hochstein S, Ahissar M (2002) View from the top: hierarchies and reverse hierarchies in the visual system. Neuron 36(5):791–804
35. Pelli DG, Tillman KA (2008) The uncrowded window of object recognition. Nat Neurosci 11(10):1129–1135
36. Kalwa J, Madsen AL (2004) Sonar image quality assessment for an autonomous underwater vehicle. In: Proceedings of the world automation congress, 2004
37. Saha S, Vemuri R (2000) An analysis on the effect of image activity on lossy coding performance. In: Paper presented at the IEEE international symposium on circuits and systems, vol 3, pp 295–298, May 2000
38. Rouse DM, Hemami SS, Callet PL (2011) Estimating the usefulness of distorted natural images using an image contour degradation measure. J Opt Soc Am A 28(2):157–188
39. Rouse DM, Pepion R, Hemami SS et al (2009) Image utility assessment and a relationship with image quality assessment. In: Proceedings of the human vision and electronic imaging XIV, vol 7240, pp 724010, Feb 2009
40. Shi Z, Zhang J, Cao Q et al (2018) Full-reference image quality assessment based on image segmentation with edge feature. Signal Process 145:99–105
41. Li Q, Lin W, Fang Y (2016) BSD: blind image quality assessment based on structural degradation. Neurocomputing 236:93–103
42. Do MN, Etterli MV (2006) The contourlet transform: an efficient directional multiresolution image representation. IEEE Trans Image Process 14(12):2091–2106
43. Dong W, Bie H, Lu L et al (2019) Image quality assessment by considering multiscale and multidirectional visibility differences in shearlet domain. IEEE Access 7:78715–78728
44. Webster AA, Jones CT, Pinson MH et al (1993) An objective video quality assessment system based on human perception. In: Proceedings of the human vision, visual processing, and digital display IV, vol 1913, pp 15–26, Sept 1993
45. Hewage C, Martini M (2012) Edge-based reduced-reference quality metric for 3-D video compression and transmission. IEEE J Sel Top Signal Process 6(5):471–482
46. Abdul A, Isa M (2014) Underwater image quality enhancement through composition of dual-intensity images and Rayleigh-stretching. Springerplus 3(1):218–219
47. Lu H, Li Y, Xu X et al (2016) Underwater image descattering and quality assessment. In: IEEE international conference on image processing 1998–2002
48. Motoyoshi I, Nishida S, Sharan L et al (2007) Image statistics and the perception of surface qualities. Nature 447:206–209
49. Loffler G (2008) Perception of contours and shapes: low and intermediate stage mechanisms. Vis Res 48(20):2106–2127
50. Dumoulin DSO, Dakin SC, Hess RF (2008) Sparsely distributed contours dominate extra-striate responses to complex scenes. NeuroImage 42(2):890–901
51. Kabrisky M, Tallman O, Day CM et al (1970) A theory of pattern perception based on human physiology. Ergonomics 13(1):129–147
52. Carl JW, Hall CF (1972) The application of filtered transforms to the general classification problem. IEEE Trans Comput 100(7):785–790
53. Hall CF, Hall EL (1977) A nonlinear model for the spatial characteristics of the human visual system. IEEE Trans Syst Man Cybern 7(3):161–170
54. Zonoobi D, Kassim AA, Venkatesh YV (2011) Gini index as sparsity measure for signal reconstruction from compressive samples. IEEE J Sel Top Signal Process 5(5):927–932
55. Hurley N, Rickard S (2009) Comparing measures of sparsity. IEEE Trans Inf Theory 55(10):4723–4741
56. He K, Sun J, Tang X (2012) Guided image filtering. IEEE Trans Pattern Anal Mach Intell 35(6):1397–1409
57. Breiman L (1996) Bagging predictors. Mach Learn 24(2):123–140
58. Mittal A, Moorthy AK, Bovik AC (2012) No-reference image quality assessment in the spatial domain. IEEE Trans Image Process 21(12):4695–4708

59. Kim J, Park KC, Park J, Yoon JR (2011) Coherence bandwidth effects on underwater image transmission in multipath channel. Japan J Appl Phys 50(7S):07HG05
60. Chandler DM, Hemami SS (2007) VSNR: a wavelet-based visual signal-to-noise ratio for natural images. IEEE Trans Image Process 16(9):2284–2298
61. Zhang L, Zhang L, Mou X et al (2011) FSIM: a feature similarity index for image quality assessment. IEEE Trans Image Process 20(8):2378–2386
62. Zhang L, Shen Y, Li H (2014) VSI: a visual saliency-induced index for perceptual image quality assessment. IEEE Trans Image Process 23(10):4270–4281
63. Xue W, Zhang L, Mou X et al (2013) Gradient magnitude similarity deviation: a highly efficient perceptual image quality index. IEEE Trans Image Process 23(2):684–695
64. Gu K, Wang S, Zhai G et al (2016) Analysis of distortion distribution for pooling in image quality prediction. IEEE Trans Broadcast 62(2):446–456
65. Larson EC, Chandler DM (2010) Most apparent distortion: full-reference image quality assessment and the role of strategy. J Electron Imaging 19(1):011006
66. Gu K, Li L, Lu H et al (2017) A fast reliable image quality predictor by fusing micro-and macro-structures. IEEE Trans Ind Electron 64(5):3903–3912
67. Gu K, Zhai G, Yang X et al (2014) An efficient color image quality metric with local-tuned-global model. In: Paper presented at the IEEE international conference on image processing, pp 506–510, Oct 2014
68. Wu J, Lin W, Shi G et al (2016) Orientation selectivity based visual pattern for reduced-reference image quality assessment. Inf Sci 351:18–29
69. Saad MA, Bovik AC, Charrier C (2012) Blind image quality assessment: a natural scene statistics approach in the DCT domain. IEEE Trans Image Process 21(8):3339–3352
70. Zhang L, Zhang L, Bovik AC (2015) A feature-enriched completely blind image quality evaluator. IEEE Trans Image Process 24(8):2579–2591
71. Gu K, Zhai G, Lin W et al (2015) No-reference image sharpness assessment in autoregressive parameter space. IEEE Trans Image Process 24(10):3218–3231
72. Gu K, Zhai G, Yang X et al (2014) Using free energy principle for blind image quality assessment. IEEE Trans Multimedia 17(1):50–63
73. Gu K, Zhai G, Yang X et al (2014) Hybrid no-reference quality metric for singly and multiply distorted images. IEEE Trans Broadcast 60(3):555–567
74. Gu K, Zhai G, Lin W et al (2016) Learning a blind quality evaluation engine of screen content images. Neurocomputing 196:140–149
75. Liu L, Dong H, Huang H et al (2014) No-reference image quality assessment in curvelet domain. Signal Process Image Commun 29(4):494–505
76. Min X, Gu K, Zhai G et al (2017) Blind quality assessment based on pseudo-reference image. IEEE Trans Multimedia 20(8):2049–2062
77. Xu J, Ye P, Li Q et al (2016) Blind image quality assessment based on high order statistics aggregation. IEEE Trans Image Process 25(9):4444–4457

Chapter 5
Quality Assessment of Enhanced Images

5.1 Introduction

Images taken by digital cameras or produced by computers can convey information and help people express their thoughts and emotions. This information will be affected severely due to the incorrect manipulation, poor illumination condition, and undesirable equipment functionality, resulting in the serious degradation of image visual quality. To recover the details of degraded images, various post-processing operations have been established, such as contrast enhancement, white balance adjustment, and exposure correction. Reliable prediction of enhanced image quality can optimize post-processing enhancement methods, so it is important to construct a well-designed image quality assessment (QA).

In practical application, according to the different observation methods, the traditional image QA can be divided into subjective assessment and objective assessment. The subjective evaluation takes human observer rating as the final judgement of image visual quality, which can obtain the ultimate ground scores. The research focuses on establishing image quality databases, such as LIVE [1], MDID2013 [2], and VDID2014 [3]. Although subjective experiment is considered as the most accurate image QA method, it cannot be popularized in practical application since its high labor intensity and long time consuming.

To overcome the limitations of subjective assessment, researchers have turned their research priorities to the design of objective assessment. In the past decades, various objective image QA have played a vital role in promoting the development of fusion [8], enhancement [9, 10], and denoising [11]. In [4], Vu et al. produced an enhancement metric, which combined contrast, sharpness, and saturation variations between the pristine and corrupted photos to achieve a full-reference (FR) QA for digital photographs. In [5], an FR image QA model was designed by detecting structure and color differences. The gradient similarity between the original and modified images was adopted to measure the structure. For colorfulness and saturation changes, Fang et al. established a no-reference (NR) quality model for contrast

© The Author(s), under exclusive license to Springer Nature Singapore Pte Ltd. 2022
K. Gu et al., *Quality Assessment of Visual Content*, Advances in Computer Vision and Pattern Recognition, https://doi.org/10.1007/978-981-19-3347-9_5

changed images based on natural scene statistics (NSS) [6]. The NSS model requires to be pre-trained by utilizing fair amounts of natural images. In [7], Wang et al. presented a contrast quality index based on patch.

Despite the emergence of hundreds of objective image QA models, very few efforts have been made for the issue of contrast changed image QA. The aforementioned quality metrics are limited in application scenarios, so more general quality models for image enhancement were proposed. In [12], Li et al. constructed an enhanced image database based on five image enhancement algorithms and three image processing software. In addition, a subjective experiment has been implemented to obtain the final ground truth of enhanced images. In [13], Gu et al. built a dedicated database consisting of 655 images, which were created by five categories of contrast-oriented transfer functions. The final mean opinion score (MOS) ranked by 22 inexperienced observers, obtained from a dedicated subjective test. In [14], Gu et al. designed the first opinion-unaware blind image QA metric named blind image quality measure of enhanced images (BIQME). This metric has a novel two step framework considering five influencing factors and 17 associated features, which can effectually obtain the prediction of enhanced image quality. In [15], a new blind image QA model based on the theory of information maximization was proposed to realize the judgement of image having better contrast and quality. In [10], an automatic robust image contrast enhancement (RICE) model based on saliency preservation was designed. It combines not only the constraints from the pristine image and its histogram equalized but also the sigmoid mapping transferred versions to improve images superiorly. In [16], Wang et al. built a guided image contrast enhancement framework based on cloud images, solving the difficulty of multi-criteria optimization. This model can collectively improve the context-sensitive and context-free contrast. For evaluating the performance of those QA models, we also compared them with state-of-the-art competitors using four extensive employed standards, i.e., Spearman rank correlation coefficient (SRCC), Kendall rank correlation coefficient (KRCC), Pearson linear correlation coefficient (PLCC), and root mean square error (RMSE).

The organization of this chapter is arranged as below. Section 5.2 introduces in detail the establishment of two databases and describes the modeling process and experimental analysis of two enhanced image quality assessment and two image enhancement technology. Section 5.3 compares the performance of state-of-the-art enhanced image QA models. Section 5.4 finally draws a conclusion and provides future work.

5.2 Methodology

In this section, we first establish the contrast-changed image QA database. Second, we show the NR QA method of enhance images on the basis of feature extraction and regression and present the automatic contrast enhancement technique. Third, we introduce the NR QA methods of enhance images based on the fusion of non-structural information, sharpness, and naturalness. Finally, we illustrate the reduced-reference (RR) QA methods of enhance images that are based on phase congruency and histogram statistic and present the context-sensitive and context-independent image enhancement method. We compare and analyze their performance with the typically used indices of PLCC, SRCC, KRCC, and RMSE.

5.2.1 Database Set-Up

Nowadays, image/video enhancement is an important aspect of image processing study and practical application. Effective enhancement technology can significantly improve the visual quality of an image/video, even making them better than the original natural image. At present, there are only a few databases that can be used to evaluate image quality. In this part, we will introduce two novel enhanced image databases, namely enhanced image database (EID) [12] and contrast-changed image database (CCID2014) [13].

Creation of the CCID2014 and EID

There are some limitations in the study of enhanced images restricted by database. Photoshop is a main method used to construct typical enhanced image databases, but it cannot contain the image produced by the image enhancement algorithms. To fill this void, [12] set up a database named EID. Li et al. used 40 color images to establish the EID, which contains various content, like architectures, plants, animals, people, etc. These images in EID have typical characteristics such as low light, low contrast, underwater, foggy, as given in Fig. 5.1. To set up enhanced image database, the images with eight enhanced versions are obtained by utilizing eight approaches from the original images, including five representative image enhancement algorithms [10, 17–20] and three popular image processing software (Photoshop, digital photo professional (DPP), and ACDSee). After the above procedures, 320 enhanced images are obtained in color format. Figure 5.2 shows some examples in the database.

To get the ground truth of each image quality, a subjective experiment is conducted by adopting a single-stimulus method. In this experiment, 25 inexperienced observers are invited, containing 12 males and 13 females with the aged from 20 to 38. The subjective experiment is conducted in a lab environment with normal lighting conditions. A liquid crystal display monitor with resolution 1920×1080 is adopted to exhibit the images. During the evaluation process, the subjects are required to provide their overall perception of quality on an absolute category rating scale from 1 to 10. A GUI interface is designed based on MATLAB to facilitate rating. In order to avoid visual tiredness, all test people are required to finish the test within one hour. Then, the methods [21, 22] are used to remove an average of five outliers from the evaluation score of every image. The MOS is computed and considered as the ground truth. Figure 5.3 shows the final subjective scores and the corresponding standard deviations of the enhanced image.

Fig. 5.1 Ten original images for the establishment of EID database (©[2021] IEEE. Reprinted, with permission, from [12].)

Fig. 5.2 Examples of enhanced images in the EID database (©[2021] IEEE. Reprinted, with permission, from [12].)

In recent decades, there are few papers specializing in image QA about contrast changing and only a few image databases related to contrast (i.e., TID2008 [23], CSIQ [24], and TID2013 [25]). To fill this gap, we first present a well-designed CCID2014. We select 15 representative undamaged color images of the size 768 × 512 from the Kodak image database [26]. As shown in Fig. 5.4, the 15 natural images cover a diverse range of scenes, color, and configurations of foreground and backdrop. A total of 655 images in CCID2014 are generated by processing the 15 original images x with five methods. The five methods contain the gamma transfer, convex and concave arcs, cubic and logistic functions, the mean-shifting (intensity-shifting), and the compound function (mean-shifting followed by logistic function). In the following, these methods will be introduced respectively:

Gamma Transfer The gamma transfer is essentially equivalent to the power law function, which can be calculated by:

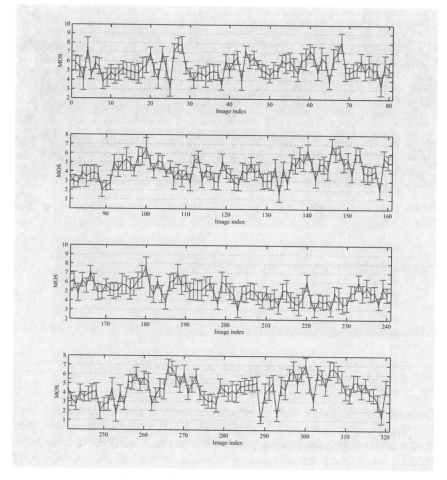

Fig. 5.3 MOS values of the enhanced images and the corresponding standard deviations (©[2021] IEEE. Reprinted, with permission, from [12].)

$$y = [x \cdot 255^{((1/n)-1)}]^n, \qquad (5.1)$$

where x is original image. $n = \{1/5, 1/3, 1/2, 1/1.5, 1.5, 2, 3, 5\}$. According to the value of n, we divide the gamma transfer into two types. When n is less than or equal to 1, it is considered as negative shown in Fig. 5.5a. And when n is greater than 1, it is considered a positive transformation shown in Fig. 5.5b.

Convex and Concave Arcs Convex and concave arcs are quite similar to the gamma transfer, except each of them is a small arc with equal derivatives everywhere. The transfer curves are exhibited in Fig. 5.5c, d.

Cubic and Logistic Functions We employ the three-order cubic function and the four-parameter logistic function for cubic and logical functions, respectively.

Fig. 5.4 15 color photographs that are lossless (©[2021] IEEE. Reprinted, with permission, from [13].)

The cubic function can be obtained by:

$$y = F_c(x, a) = a_1 \cdot x^3 + a_2 \cdot x^2 + a_3 \cdot x + a_4, \tag{5.2}$$

and the logistic function is as follows:

$$y = F_l(x, b) = \frac{b_1 - b_2}{1 + \exp(-\frac{x - b_3}{b_4})} + b_2, \tag{5.3}$$

where a_i and b_j ($i, j \in \{1, 2, 3, 4\}$) are undetermined parameters. In order to determine these parameters, we use the "nlinfit" MATLAB function to obtain the optimal transfer curves getting through four preset points. In Fig. 5.5e, f, the four color curves represent four preset points coordinates for cubic and logistic functions and R, G, B, and K in the second column.

Mean-Shifting The mean-shifted image is obtained by $y = x + \Delta$, the value of Δ comes from $\{0, 20, 40, 60, 80, 100, 120\}$. Note that y represents the original image as $\Delta = 0$.

Compound Functions The composite function appropriately combines the mean shift function and the logistic function can enhance images effectively.

After processing with the transfer functions mentioned above, we remove the boundary values in the generated images to the range of $0 \sim 255$. We conduct an experiment by adopting a single stimulus (SS) method on a continuous quality scale from 1 to 5, representing the observers' overall perception of quality. In this experiment, 22 inexperienced subjects are involved, mostly from college of different majors. We have compiled a list of the most important details regarding the testing environment in Table 5.1.

After the evaluation procedure, we clear the outliers in all subjects' scores due to inattention. Then the MOS score is calculated by $1/N_i \sum_i s_{ij}$. Where s_{ij} is the score

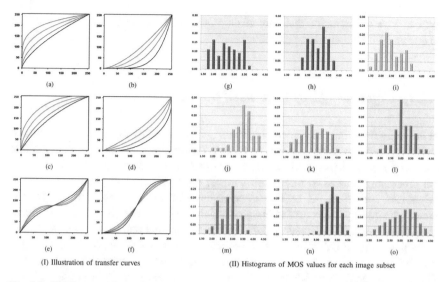

(a)   (b)   (g)   (h)   (i)

(c)   (d)   (j)   (k)   (l)

(e)   (f)   (m)   (n)   (o)

(I) Illustration of transfer curves   (II) Histograms of MOS values for each image subset

Fig. 5.5 (I) Diagram of transfer curves: **a** negative gamma transfers; **b** positive gamma transfers; **c** convex arcs; **d** concave arcs; **e** cubic functions; **f** logistic functions. (II) Histograms of MOS: **g** convex arcs; **h** concave arcs; **i** cubic functions; **j** logistic functions; **k** mean-shifting; **l** negative gamma transfer; **m** positive gamma transfer; **n** compound function; **o** entire database (©[2021] IEEE. Reprinted, with permission, from [13].)

Table 5.1 Subjective experimental conditions and parameters (©[2021] IEEE. Reprinted, with permission, from [13].)

Method	Single stimulus (SS)
Evaluation scales	Continuous quality scale from 1 to 5
Color depth	24-bits/pixel color images
Image coder	Portable network graphic (PNG)
Subjects	22 inexperienced subjects
Image resolution	768×512
Viewing distance	$3 \sim 4$ times the image height
Room illuminance	Dark

obtained from subject i to distorted image y_j; $i=\{1, ..., 22\}$, $j=\{1, ..., 655\}$; N_i is the number of observers.

Figure 5.5g–o show the distribution of MOS values for different types of contrast-changed images. Figure 5.5n indicates that the subjective quality scores of a few images processed by compound functions, which subjective quality scores is not less than 4. The MOS values of most pristine natural images are just around 3.5. This can be revealed by the truth that the logistic transfer elevates the difference of adjacent values pixels. In addition, the complementary mean-shifting adjusts the image mean luminance to be a proper value, particularly for natural images [27].

We can draw a conclusion that rational employing of compound function is valuable to design contrast enhancement methods.

5.2.2 Objective QA of Enhanced Images

In our daily lives, the post processing of images obtained by cameras, smart phones, and computer-generated is always required for obtaining better visualization and enhanced practical use, such as object recognition and detection. The image signal processing is used to improve the image quality, including visibility, contrast, brightness, and so on. An excellent performance image QA method is designed to predict the quality of processed images, which can improve and optimize enhancement algorithms. Thus, image QA is a greatly beneficial and practical task. To our knowledge, image QA models are divided into three types: FR, RR, and NR QA. It is difficult to derive the original reference information of most enhanced images. Thus, FR image QA and RR image QA are not suitable for enhanced images. In the following content, we will introduce two NR image QA metrics, namely BIQME and NIQMC.

Evaluating Quality of Enhanced Images with NR Quality Metric

In many practical applications, such as object detection or recognition, we need to enhance original images appropriately to raise the visual quality. We normally think raw images have the best visual quality. The quality of images can be improved by a suitable enhancement method, even better than original images. In this part, we will introduce two important parts. The first part takes into account 17 features of five influencing factors, including contrast, sharpness, brightness, color, and naturalness of the image. They are used to learning regression to construct an efficient NR image QA method. The second part is image enhancement using image QA mentioned above. The quality of natural images, low-contrast images, dim light images, and deblurred images are improved by the designed method. The implementation details of the proposed methods will be elaborated in the following paragraphs.

Feature Extraction

The effect of image enhancement is decided by the leading factor that is contrast. A common global measurement of image contrast is information entropy. The average amount of information included in an image is measured by entropy. In general, higher entropy indicates that pictures have more contrast, that is, better visual quality. Thus, we use a biologically plausible phase congruence (PC) model to find and recognize features in the image [28, 29] and then calculate the entropy based on PC.

According to [13], M_n^o filter implements odd-symmetric property and M_n^e filter implements even-symmetric property on scales n. At position j on scale n, we use quadrature pairs to generate a response vector $[e_n(j), o_n(j)] = [s(j) * M_n^e, s(j) * M_n^o]$. $A_n(j) = \sqrt{e_n(j)^2 + o_n(j)^2}$ is the amplitude value of the response vector. PC is defined by:

$$PC(j) = \frac{\sum_n W(j)\lfloor A_n(j) \cdot \Delta\theta_n(j) - T_n\rfloor}{\varepsilon + \sum_n A_n(j)}, \tag{5.4}$$

where $\lfloor \cdot \rfloor$ represents a threshold. If the values inside are negative, they will be deleted and equal to 0. T_n evaluates the degree of noise. $\Delta\theta_n(j) = \cos[\theta_n(j) - \overline{\theta(j)}] - |\sin[\theta_n(j) - \overline{\theta(j)}]|$ is the phase deviations. $\overline{\theta(j)}$ represents the mean values of phase at j. $W(j) = (1 + \exp[(\mu - t(j))v])^{-1}$ is the weight value. For filter parameters, μ is a cutoff value, and v is a gain variable which is used to regulate the cutoff sharpness. So, we define the PC-based entropy as:

$$E_{pc} = -\sum_{i=0}^{255} P_i(s_{pc}) \cdot \log P_i(s_{pc}), \tag{5.5}$$

where s_{pc} includes the pixels of an image signal s.

Contrast energy is the second measurement, which is used to predict local contrast of perceived images [30]. According to [31], contrast energy is calculated on three channels of s:

$$CF_f = \frac{\alpha \cdot Y(s_f)}{Y(s_f) + \alpha \cdot \theta} - \phi_f, \tag{5.6}$$

where $Y(s_f) = ((s_k * f_h)_2 + (s_k * f_v)_2)^{1/2}$. f includes three channels of s which are represented by gr, yb and rg respectively. $gr = 0.299R + 0.587G + 0.114B$, $yb = 0.5(R + G) - B$, and $rg = R - G$ [32]. For parameters in Eq. (5.23), $\alpha = \max[Y(s_f)]$, ϕ_f is a threshold which is used to control the noise. θ represents the contrast gain. The second-order derivatives of Gaussian function in the horizontal and vertical are represented by f_h and f_v respectively. Thus, contrast-related features are $F_{ct} = \{E_{pc}, CE_{gr}, CE_{yb}, CE_{rg}\}$.

Actually, sharpness assessment has been studied extensively for these years [33–35]. Similar to [34], we compute log-energy on wavelet sub-bands using an effective and efficient method. The log-energy on each wavelet sub-band is defined as:

$$LE_{k,l} = \log_{10}[1 + \frac{1}{K_l} \sum_i k_i^2(i)], \tag{5.7}$$

where i represents the pixel index; k stands for three levels LH, HL, and HH which are obtained by decomposing a grayscale image; K_l is the number of discrete wave transform coefficients. Finally, we compute the log-energy at each level as shown below:

$$LE_l = \frac{\frac{1}{2}(LE_{LH,l} + LE_{HL,l}) + w \cdot (LE_{HH,l})}{1 + w}, \tag{5.8}$$

where the parameter w set as four to improve the weights of HH sub-bands. In this part, we choose the second and third levels to obtain more sharp details. Sharpness-related features are $F_s = \{LE_2, LE_3\}$.

Brightness affects the effect of image enhancement to a great extent. On the one hand, adequate brightness can increase the dynamic range of an image. On the other hand, it may include semantic data. Following prior work on picture quality assurance for tone-mapping operators, we define image brightness using a straightforward technique [36]. According to this guide, we first produce a set of images by increasing/decreasing the original brightness of the image:

$$s_i = \max(\min(m_i \cdot s, t_u), t_l), \tag{5.9}$$

where m_i stands for the multiplier index, we will elaborate later. The image signal is restrained in range of $[t_l, t_u]$.

The variations of the luminance intensity will clear image details. In this part, the entropy of luminance changing image is used to infer whether the image has proper luminance. When selecting a multiplier index, increasing the index is beneficial to improve the performance, but not to improve computing speed. Six entropy values $\{E_{m1}, E_{m2}, \ldots, E_{m6}\}$ are used to find a good balance between efficiency and efficacy, where $m = \{n, (1/n)|n = 3.5, 5.5, 7.5\}$. It is important to note that, unlike [36], we do not contain the images itself, since we consider a similar measure E_{pc}. As mentioned earlier, brightness-related features are $F_b = \{E_{m1}, E_{m2}, E_{m3}, E_{m4}, E_{m5}, E_{m6}\}$.

Colorfulness serves a similar purpose to brightness in that it increases the dynamic range of color images. Compared with grayscale photos, it can exhibit more details and information. Color saturation, which expresses the colorfulness of a color compared to its own brightness, is used to quantify the colorfulness of a picture. In addition to considering the above factors, we then calculate the global meaning of the saturated channel and then convert the image to the HSV color space:

$$S = \frac{1}{M} \sum_{i=1}^{M} T_{X \to S}[s(k)], \tag{5.10}$$

where $T_{X \to S}$ represents a conversion function to transform an X type image into the color saturation channel. M is the sum of pixels of s.

The second measure comes from a classic study dedicated to measuring the colorfulness of natural images [32]. Hasler and Suesstrunk have provided a practical metric to predict the overall colorfulness of an image, which is highly correlated with human perceptions. More specifically, we extract four features including the mean and variance of yb and rg channel ($\mu_{yb}, \sigma_{yb}^2, \mu_{rg}$, and μ_{rg}^2). Then the metric can be derived by:

$$C = \sqrt{\sigma_{yb}^2 + \sigma_{rg}^2} + \kappa \sqrt{\mu_{yb}^2 + \mu_{rg}^2}, \tag{5.11}$$

where k is a correction for relative significance which can better match subjective opinions. As a result, colorfulness-related characteristics are characterized as $F_{cl} = \{S, C\}$.

Naturalness is the inherent property of natural images, which shows the common character of most natural images. We mainly use image naturalness to punish over-enhancement conditions, which will destroy the naturalness of visual signal seriously. We consider the classical and commonly used NSS models [11, 37, 38]. Firstly, local mean removal and segmentation normalization are preprocessed:

$$s(i)^* = \frac{s(i) - \mu(i)}{\sigma(i) + \epsilon}, \tag{5.12}$$

where $\mu(i)$ and $\sigma(i)$ represent the local mean and standard deviation of the i-th pixel respectively; ϵ denotes a positive constant. The generalized Gaussian distribution with zero mean is learned to catch the behavior of coefficients of Eq. (5.12), which are expressed by follows:

$$f(x; \nu, \sigma^2) = \frac{\nu}{2\beta\Gamma\left(\frac{1}{\alpha}\right)} \exp\left(-\left(\frac{|x|^\nu}{\beta}\right)\right), \tag{5.13}$$

where $\beta = \sigma\sqrt{\frac{\Gamma(\frac{1}{\nu})}{\Gamma(\frac{3}{\nu})}}$ and $\Gamma(a) = \int_0^\infty t^{a-1}e^{-t}$ when $a > 0$. The parameter ν controls the shape of the distribution, σ^2 denotes the variance of the distribution. ν and σ^2 as two features are collected.

The third metric of naturalness is the recently discovered dark channel prior [39]. It reveals that at least one color channel goes to zero in most nonsky parts, indicating that the scene is more natural:

$$s_{dark}(i) = \min_{q \in \{R,G,B\}} s_q(i), \tag{5.14}$$

where $q = \{R, G, B\}$ indicates the RGB channels. It was obvious that s_{dark} has definite bounds of [0, 255] or [0, 1] for normalized divided by 255. We calculate the whole meaning of the dark channel s_{dark} to determine naturalness measurement S_d. Finally, naturalness-related features are characterized as $F_n = \{\nu, \sigma^2, S_d\}$.

In summary, we carefully extracted 17 features based on the five aspects of image contrast, sharpness, brightness, colorfulness and naturalness. For the convenience of readers, all of the above features are listed in Table 5.2.

Quality Prediction

However, these features forementioned cannot directly impress the quality of the enhanced image. A regression module that translates 17 characteristics into a quality score is required in this scenario. Recently, a novel approach for locating the regression module in blind image QA designs is developed [40]. To solve the problem of

Table 5.2 Performance comparison of the most advanced frame rate algorithms based on the SIQAD database (©[2021] IEEE. Reprinted, with permission, from [15].)

Feature type	Feature symbol	Feature description	Feature ID	Computation
Contrast	E_{pc}	Phase Congruency based entropy	f_{01}	(1), (2)
	$CE_{gr}, CE_{yb}, CE_{rg}$	Contrast energy	$f_{02} - f_{04}$	(3)
Sharpness	LE_2, LE_3	Log-energy of wavelet subbands	f_{05}, f_{06}	(4), (5)
Brightness	$E_{m1}, E_{m2}, E_{m3}, E_{m4}, E_{m5}, E_{m6}$	Information entropy of luminance changing	$f_{07} - f_{12}$	(6)
Colorfulness	S	Image saturaton	f_{13}	(7)
	C	Colourfulness of natural images	f_{14}	(8)
Naturalness	θ, σ^2	Natural scene statistics	$f_{15} - f_{16}$	(9), (10)
	S_d	Dark channel prior	f_{17}	(11)

overfitting, we use more than 100,000 images as training samples to learn the regression module. We initially acquire 1642 images. They include 1242 natural scene images from the PQD database collected by Berkeley with high-quality subsets, and 400 screen content images taken with a custom snapshot technique. Then, we use 8 common global based enhancement methods to process the improved original image and get 60 enhanced images. The database finally includes 100,162 images as training data.

To avoid the concern of proposed metric does not consider the effect of colorfulness, we design the colorfulness-based PCQI (C-PCQI) metric:

$$C - PCQI = \frac{1}{M} \sum_{i=1}^{M} Q_{mi}(i) \cdot Q_{cc}(i) \cdot Q_{sd}(i) \cdot Q_{cs}(i), \qquad (5.15)$$

where Q_{mi}, Q_{cc}, and Q_{sd} indicate the resemblance between the pristine and deformed images in terms of mean intensity, contrast change, and structural distortion, respectively. M is the number of pixels. Q_{cs} measures the similarity of color saturation obtained by:

$$Q_{cs}(i) = \left(\frac{2ST_1 \cdot ST_2 + \zeta}{ST_1^2 + ST_2^2 + \zeta} \right)^{\varphi}, \qquad (5.16)$$

where ST_1 and ST_2 denote the color saturation of the pristine and corrupted images. ζ is a minor constant number to avoid division by zero. φ indicates a fixed pooling index to mark the regions which have changes of color saturation. We employ the C-PCQI scores of the 100,162 produced images to take the place of human opinion ratings.

The renowned support vector regression is utilized to learn the regression module in the designed BIQME metric once the training set is produced [41]. We can translate the basic form of support vector regression as:

$$\begin{aligned}
&\underset{\mathbf{w},\delta,\mathbf{b},\mathbf{b}'}{\text{minimize}} \frac{1}{2}\|\mathbf{w}\|_2^2 + t \sum_{i=1}^{r} \left(b_i + b_i'\right) \\
&\text{s.t. } \mathbf{w}^T \phi(x_i) + \delta - y_i \le p + b_i \\
&\quad y_i - \mathbf{w}^T \phi(x_i) - \delta \le p + b_i' \\
&\quad b_i, b_i' \ge 0, i = 1, \ldots, r
\end{aligned} \qquad (5.17)$$

Where $K(x_i, x_j) = \phi(x_i)^T \phi(x_j)$ represents the kernel function, which is set to be the radial basis function kernel defined as $K(x_i, x_j) = \exp\left(-k\|x_i - x_j\|^2\right)$. Our goal is to locate the related regression module based on the training samples and calculate t, p, and k.

Quality-Optimized Image Enhancement

Since its excellent performance and high efficiency, BIQME metrics can be used to guide image enhancement technologies. In the BOIEM algorithm, we mainly consider image brightness and contrast, especially adjusting them to an appropriate level. We constructed the framework based on RICE for two steps. In the first step, we improve two recently proposed enhancement methods, adaptive gamma correction with weighting distribution (AGCWD) [42] and RICE [10], to successively rectify image brightness and contrast. The AGCWD focuses on weighting the probability density function (PDF) of images by:

$$\text{PDF}'(z) = \text{PDF}_{\text{max}} \left(\frac{\text{PDF}(z) - \text{PDF}_{\text{min}}}{\text{PDF}_{\text{max}} - \text{PDF}_{\text{min}}}\right)^{\lambda_b}, \qquad (5.18)$$

where $z = \{z_{\text{min}}, z_{\text{min}} + 1, \ldots, z_{\text{max}}\}$, PDF_{min} and PDF_{max} denote the minimum and maximum values in pdf, and λ_b indicates a weight parameter. Then, we use the weighted PDF to calculate the cumulative distribution function:

$$\text{CDF}'(z) = \sum_{h=0}^{z} \frac{\text{PDF}'(h)}{\sum \text{PDF}'}, \qquad (5.19)$$

and access the enhanced image:

$$T(z) = 255 \left(\frac{z}{255}\right)^{1-\text{CDF}'(z)}. \qquad (5.20)$$

The RICE method is effective at improving natural photos in contrast to the AGCWD algorithm. However, it fails for other sorts of images, such as low-light images and videos, due to the RICE approach does not alter brightness. It also necessitates the use of original images in the quality-based optimization process.

During our BOIEM model design process, we first set the parameters of AGCWD and RICE. Then, to optimize these three parameters, the suggested blind BIQME algorithm is applied as:

$$\lambda_b, \lambda_s, \lambda_e = \underset{\lambda_b, \lambda_s, \lambda_e}{\text{maximize}}\, Q_B\left(T_R\left[T_A\left(\mathbf{s}, \lambda_b\right), \lambda_s, \lambda_e\right]\right), \tag{5.21}$$

where Q_B, T_R, and T_A are related to BIQME, RICE, and AGCWD respectively. After that, we use these characteristics to improve images. The BOIEM runs six times for optimization. The first three times figure out three candidates $0.3, 0.5, 0.7$ and choose the optimal λ_b for image brightness rectification. The last three times choose the λ_s and λ_e for image contrast improvement. Finally, we produce enhanced images using the parameters we've chosen.

Toward Accurate Quality Evaluation of Enhanced Images via Blind NIQMC Metric

In most cases, humans can improve the efficiency of information acquisition through specific mechanisms, such as visual saliency. It has been demonstrated to be closely related to the neural circuits of primate visual cortex [43]. Based on the basic human behavior of obtaining information, a blind NIQMC metric is designed by maximizing information. We assume that HVS associates local strategies with global strategies to perceive visual signals and judge their quality scores and significant areas. On this basis, the blind NIQMC model tries to estimate the visual appearance of contrast-altered images.

Local Quality Measure

Our method first considers the measurement of local details. According to our common sense, images with high contrast represent a lot of meaningful information. However, most images contain a large amount of residual information, such as a large area of blue sky or green grass in the background, and predictable components in the image. This information is predicted by a semi-parametric model based on autoregressive (AR) model and bilateral filtering.

AR model can simulate various natural scenes simply and effectively by adjusting parameters. Its parameters are invariant to object transformation. However, the AR model is usually unstable at the edge of the image. Similar results can also be found at the edge of the building. As a result, we adopt bilateral filtering, a nonlinear filter with high edge preservation properties that is simple to set up and compute. As shown in Fig. 5.6, compared with the input image, it can be seen that bilateral filtering can better protect the edge than AR model avoids introducing any ringing artifacts. Another example shown in Fig. 5.7 shows that bilateral filtering falls in the processing texture region, resulting in a large reduction in spatial frequency. By contrast, the AR model is suitable for texture synthesis, so it can preserve the texture part well. These two models excel at dealing with smooth regions. Therefore, it is natural to combine the advantages of AR model and bilateral filtering to obtain better results in edge, texture and smooth areas.

Fig. 5.6 **a** Original and filter processed images with **b** AR model, **c** bilateral filtering, and **d** semi-parametric model (©[2021] IEEE. Reprinted, with permission, from [15].)

Fig. 5.7 **a** Original and filter processed images with **b** AR model, **c** bilateral filtering, and **d** semi-parametric model (©[2021] IEEE. Reprinted, with permission, from [15].)

The filtered picture may be thought as an approximation of estimative data, which can be described using the free energy concept. By employing this model, the human brain can divide the input image into orderly and disorderly parts. Based on this analysis, Gu et al. identified that the internally generated model can be approximated as AR model. In contrast, by introducing bilateral filtering, a more reliable semi parametric model is developed, which has good performance in edge, texture and smooth region.

Furthermore, there is still a significant issue in determining the suitable region. If you have seen the famous portrait "Mona Lisa", do you remember what the foreground is? For most people, an elegant lady with a mysterious smile will appear in their mind. But if you ask what the background is, most people may not remember anything. In other words, although we have enough time to see the whole image, humans will pay attention to some important areas.

According to information maximization, we premise that humans want to select maximum-information regions to be perceived. In this part, visual saliency is used to select the best region. It is worth noting that visual saliency is a concept different from our application in this paper. It only provides several candidate areas that may have the largest amount of information.

More specifically, we consider the newly designed free energy excitation significance detection technology (FES) [44]. The FES model can adjust the image size to a rough 63×47 pixel representation in a small range. The FES method predicts the error map and generates its local entropy map in each color channel. Then, the three filtered and normalized local entropy maps are combined in different color channels to generate the final significance map according to the comparability of semi-parametric model. If an image has a clear foreground and background, the salient regions conveying valuable information will be concentrated. If the salient areas are scattered, the valuable information will be scattered. Therefore, valuable (unpredictable) information will be expressed by using almost the entire image.

Global Quality Measure

Our approach's second aspect is from the standpoint of global information metrics. Entropy is a key term in image contrast because it ignores the impact of pixel positions and instead evaluates the pattern of pixel values. Given two probability densities h_0 and h_1, the K-L divergence can show in:

$$D_{KL}(h_1 \| h_0) = - \int h_1(t) \log h_0(t) dt + \int h_1(t) \log h_1(t) dt,$$

$$= H(h_1, h_0) - E(h_1)$$

(5.22)

where $H(h_1, h_0)$ is the cross entropy of h_1 and h_0. By utilizing the K-L divergence, the interaction between h_1 and h_0 has been contained. However, the K-L distance is asymmetric, which might pose problems in real-world applications. Simple examples are offered by Johnson and Sinanovic to demonstrate how the sequencing of the assumptions in the K-L divergence might generate significantly different outcomes. As a result, we use the symmetric K-L divergence. We choose a symmetrized and smoothed format called the Jensen-Shannon (J-S) divergence, which is a symmetrized and smoothed format. Tests reveal that it is quite the contrary to symmetric forms, which are based on arithmetical, geometric, and harmonic means. Apart from the three functions mentioned above, the J-S divergence is a symmetrized and smoothed format:

$$D_{JS}(h_0, h_1) = \frac{D_{KL}(h_0 \| h_\triangle) + D_{KL}(h_1 \| h_\triangle)}{2}.$$

(5.23)

The tests reveal that the J-S divergence and 128-bin histogram cause approximately 2% performance improvements. Hence, given the histogram h and u of pixel values, the global quality measure is characterized by:

$$Q_G = D_{JS}(h, u).$$

(5.24)

It's worth noting that the created local and global quality measures have the opposite meanings; the higher the local Q_L (or the smaller global Q_G), the higher the contrast and quality of the picture.

Combined Quality Measure

We have presented two quality metrics according to the notion of information maximization. The former measures the relevant information from the perspective of local details by using predictable data reduction and optimum region selection. Inspired by the fundamental principle of the practical HE approach, the latter part of our blind

NIQMC metric employs the symmetrized and smoothed J-S divergence. The above operation can determine whether the input histogram is appropriately distributed in comparison to the uniform distribution or not. The two elements above serve complimentary functions in terms of working. We can also find that they are combined to mimic the HVS impression of contrast-altered image quality. We may easily combine these two metrics because they are of the same entropy. As a result, the NIQMC is characterized as a straightforward linear fusion of the two quality metrics:

$$NIQMC = \frac{Q_L + \gamma Q_G}{1 + \gamma}, \tag{5.25}$$

where γ denotes a constant weight that is utilized to control the relative significance between the local and global strategies.

Finally, we provide the fundamental architecture of the designed blind NIQMC technique to assist readers grasp how to dispose of the measure in Fig. 5.8. The symmetric and smoothed J-S divergence is used to determine the global quality metric of a picture signal. Following that, we do optimum region selection to forecast the local quality measure by adopting the semi-parametric model to analyze the pristine

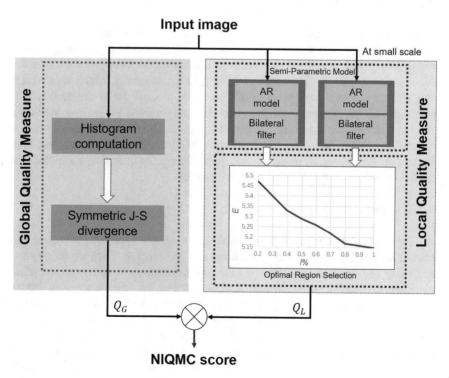

Fig. 5.8 The fundamental architecture of NIQMC metric

picture, separately. Finally, the NIQMC score is calculated using a mix of global and local estimates.

5.2.3 Enhanced Image QA Based on the Enhancement Technology

Because of operational error, low-cost imaging sensors, and undesirable equipment functions, original images may have inferior contrast and low visual quality. Contrast enhancement is the most preferred way among the different solutions to this problem since it tries to directly improve visual contrast, further improving users' experiences. However, these methods have side effects such as excessive enhancement and noise enhancement that require more attention. In this part, we introduce two methods to overcome the above problems, both of which are aimed at automatically generating visually-pleasing enhanced images.

Automatic Enhancement Technology

A good contrast enhancement method is thought to create more picture details while also suppressing motion artifacts. However, for most automatic applications or algorithms, over-enhancement and under-enhancement are such a key problem. To make higher image quality, people have to tune parameters manually, which is often difficult and consumes a lot of time. In this part, we introduce a new automatic RICE model with saliency preservation. We generate the algorithm by two steps. We firstly pose the cost function regarding the ideal histogram. Then we automatically derive the ideal histogram following the instruction of QA metric of contrast, and then improve image contrast by mapping histogram. We put the flow diagram of RICE in Fig. 5.9 in order to help understand our framework.

Ideal Histogram for Contrast Enhancement

HE [10] is a popular contrast enhancement algorithm, which targets generating distributed histograms with cumulative histograms as mapping functions to improve the quality of output images. However, HE also has many problems such as visible deterioration caused by over-enhancement. In this part, we define a novel histogram modification framework (HMF) to improve the performance of contrast enhancement. The first step of processing an input image I_i is to denote h_i by the histogram of I_i and by h_u a consistently distributed histogram. Next, we find a bicriteria optimization problem that the target histogram $\tilde{h}$ should be closer to h_u, but also make the distance $\tilde{h} - h_i$ small as a precision limit. In experiment, we find that using HE to compute the equalized histogram h_{eq} has better performance than h_u. As a result, we express the issue as a weighted average of the two goals:

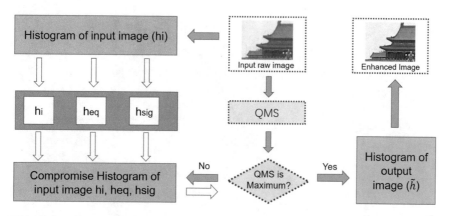

Fig. 5.9 Flowchart of the designed RICE contrast enhancement algorithm. h_i, h_{eq}, and h_{sig} respectively indicate the histograms of the input image, related histogram equalization and S-shaped transfer function based brightness preserving processed versions

$$\tilde{\mathbf{h}} = \arg \min_{\mathbf{h}} \|\mathbf{h} - \mathbf{h_i}\| + \phi \|\mathbf{h} - \mathbf{h_{eq}}\|, \tag{5.26}$$

where $\{\tilde{h}, h, h_i, h_{eq}\} \in \mathbb{R}^{256 \times 1}$ and ϕ control over $[0, \infty)$. The Eq. (5.26) discovers the balance between the original image's two histograms and their equalized version. The standard HE can be grabbed as ϕ goes to infinity, while Eq. (5.26) converges to the input image when ϕ is near to zero. However, we find that Eq. (5.26) does not include any perceptual quality associated term. We employ a four-arguments logistic function to define the sigmoid transfer mapping $T_{sig}(\cdot)$ and its linked enhanced image I_{sig} as:

$$I_{\text{sig}} = T_{\text{sig}}(I_i, \pi) = \frac{\pi_1 - \pi_2}{1 + \exp\left(-\frac{(I_i - \pi_3)}{\pi_4}\right)} + \pi_2, \tag{5.27}$$

where $\pi = \{\pi_1, \pi_2, \pi_3, \pi_4\}$ are free parameters. We hypothesis that the transfer curves through four points (β_i, α_i), $i = \{1, 2, 3, 4\}$. We use sigmoid mapping for advancing surface quality, which is rolling symmetry with regard to the straight line $y = x$. We fix seven parameters: $(\beta_1, \alpha_1) = (0, 0)$, $(\beta_2, \alpha_2) = (255, 255)$, $(\beta_3, \alpha_3) = (x, y)$, where $x = y = [mean(I_i)/32] * 32$, $\beta_4 = 25$, and let α_4 to be the unique free parameter. Then, we seek the best control parameters $\pi = \{\pi_1, \pi_2, \pi_3, \pi_4\}$ by minimizing the following objective function:

$$\pi_{\text{opt}} = \arg \min_{\pi} \sum_{i=1}^{4} |\alpha_i - T_{\text{sig}}(\beta_i, \pi)|, \tag{5.28}$$

by using the known parameters π_{opt}, we can finally access:

$$I_{\text{sig}} = \max\left(\min\left(T_{\text{sig}}(I_i, \pi_{\text{opt}}), 255\right), 0\right), \tag{5.29}$$

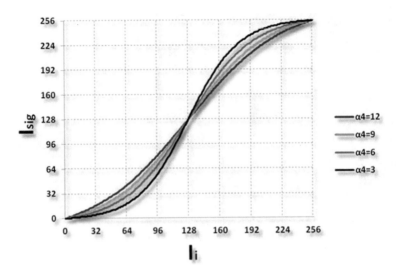

Fig. 5.10 Sigmoid curves with four different α_4 values (©[2021] IEEE. Reprinted, with permission, from [10].)

where max and min operations are utilized to confine the values of I_{sig} pixel between [0,255]. We set $\alpha_4 = 12$, which is the only control parameter to change the curvature of the transfer function. To visualize the sigmoid curve, we model four exemplary curves with the same $(\beta_3, \alpha_3) = (128, 128)$ but different α_4 in Fig. 5.10.

We use sigmoid transfer mapping to process the Matthew sculpture image, exhibited in Fig. 5.11. It is remarkable that the surface quality improves a lot compared with the original image.

Furthermore, we propose a typical natural image red door as well as its histogram equalized and sigmoid curve transferred versions in Fig. 5.11a, e, and i. We can also observe that the sigmoid mapping generates higher quality images (i) with regard to the other two (a) and (e). It is natural to combine the histogram h_{sig} into Eq. (5.26) to make the optimization objective function more integrated:

$$\tilde{\mathbf{h}} = \arg\min_{\mathbf{h}} \|\mathbf{h} - \mathbf{h_i}\| + \phi \|\mathbf{h} - \mathbf{h_{eq}}\| + \psi \|\mathbf{h} - \mathbf{h_{sig}}\|, \qquad (5.30)$$

where $h_{sig} \in \mathbb{R}^{256 \times 1}$ and ψ is a control parameter similar to ϕ. Note that a suitable selection of $\{\phi, \psi\}$ will result in the optimal tradeoff and produce optimally best images.

We use the squared number of the Euclidean norm to acquire a solution to Eq. (5.30):

$$\tilde{\mathbf{h}} = \arg\min_{\mathbf{h}} \|\mathbf{h} - \mathbf{h_i}\|_2^2 + \phi \|\mathbf{h} - \mathbf{h_{eq}}\|_2^2 + \psi \|\mathbf{h} - \mathbf{h_{sig}}\|_2^2, \qquad (5.31)$$

which leads to the quadratic optimization issue:

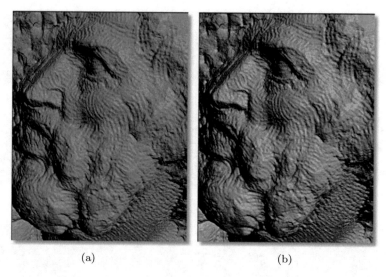

(a)   (b)

Fig. 5.11 Matthew sculpture processed by our sigmoid transfer map. **a** pristine sculpture. **b** processed sculpture (©[2021] IEEE. Reprinted, with permission, from [10].)

$$\tilde{\mathbf{h}} = \arg\min_{\mathbf{h}} \left[(\mathbf{h} - \mathbf{h_i})^T (\mathbf{h} - \mathbf{h_i}) + \phi (\mathbf{h} - \mathbf{h_{eq}})^T (\mathbf{h} - \mathbf{h_{eq}}) \\ + \psi (\mathbf{h} - \mathbf{h_{sig}})^T (\mathbf{h} - \mathbf{h_{sig}}) \right]. \tag{5.32}$$

We can derive the solution of Eq. (5.32) as:

$$\tilde{\mathbf{h}} = \frac{\mathbf{h_i} + \phi \mathbf{h_{eq}} + \psi \mathbf{h_{sig}}}{1 + \phi + \psi}. \tag{5.33}$$

Given $\tilde{h}$, the histogram matching function $T_{hm}(\cdot)$ given in [20] is utilized to generate the enhanced image:

$$\tilde{I} = T_{hm}\left(I_i, \tilde{\mathbf{h}}(\phi, \psi)\right). \tag{5.34}$$

To see the output more clearly, we exhibited the three enhanced images in Fig. 5.12c, g, and k. As expected, the enhanced output realizes considerable improvement in image quality.

Automatic Realization of Ideal Histogram

In the majority of cases, manual parameter tuning isn't convenient and operable since it is such a time-consuming job for real-time systems. We have found that suitable contrast enhancement usually reveals indistinguishable image detail while keeping the image salience unaltered (Fig. 5.12j–l). It encourages us to think about

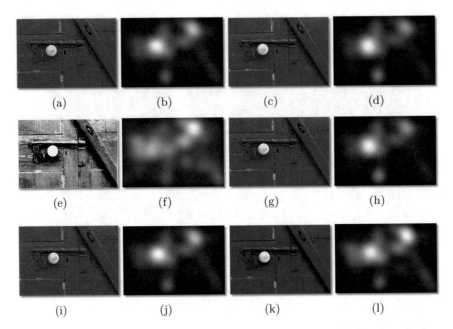

Fig. 5.12 **a** A red door image in Kodak database. **e** Output of HE. **i** Output of S-shaped transfer function based brightness preserving. **c–k** Outputs of dynamic range separate histogram equalization. **b–l** Saliency maps of (**a**)–(**k**) (©[2021] IEEE. Reprinted, with permission, from [10].)

how saliency preservation may be utilized to fine-tune the performance of contrast enhancement techniques. We develop a distance measure for the input picture I_c using the ι^0 distance of their image features as the first term of QA metric of contrast (QMC):

$$\Delta D = \left\| \mathrm{sign}\left(\mathrm{DCT2}\left(\dot{i}_i\right)\right), \mathrm{sign}\left(\mathrm{DCT2}\left(\dot{i}_c\right)\right) \right\|_0, \tag{5.35}$$

where $\dot{i}_i$ and $\dot{i}_c$ indicate downsampled images of I_i and I_c by a factor of 4 utilizing the bilateral model. This term denotes that the smaller the difference of saliency maps between I_i and I_c is, the higher the quality score of I_c will be.

Then, using a simple linear function, we combine saliency preservation with entropy increase to define the QMC as:

$$\mathrm{QMC}\left(I_i, I_c\right) = \Delta D + \gamma \Delta E, \tag{5.36}$$

where γ indicates a fixed parameter to alter the relative importance of two components. We observe that the value of γ equals to 0.2 is best, which means that saliency preservation is more important in the QA of contrast enhancement.

We also employ QMC to optimize the parameters $\{\phi, \psi\}$ for the contrast enhancement algorithm as:

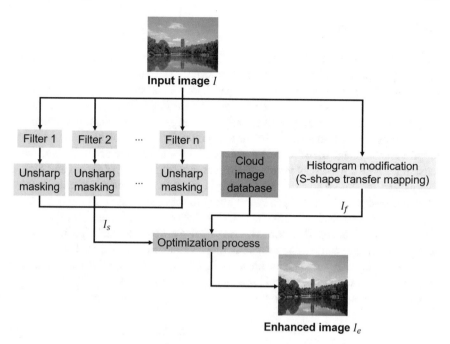

Fig. 5.13 Generalized contrast enhancement framework for unified context-free and context-sensitive methods

$$
\begin{aligned}
\{\phi_{\text{opt}}, \psi_{\text{opt}}\} \quad &= \arg \min_{\{\phi, \psi\}} \text{QMC}\left(I_i, \tilde{I}\right), \\
&= \arg \min_{\{\phi, \psi\}} \text{QMC}\left(I_i, T_{\text{hm}}\left(I_i, \frac{\mathbf{h_i} + \phi \mathbf{h}_{\text{eq}} + \psi \mathbf{h}_{\text{sig}}}{1 + \phi + \psi}\right)\right).
\end{aligned}
\tag{5.37}
$$

In this approach, we can automatically generate the properly enhanced image I_{opt} with $\{\phi_{opt}, \psi_{opt}\}$.

Unified Contrast Enhancement Framework

In this part, we introduce a general contrast enhancement framework for context-sensitive and context-free enhancement methods. In order to upgrade the context-sensitive contrast, an advanced unsharp masking is performed on images after filtering the input and edge preserving. Context-free contrast enhancement is obtained by sigmoid transfer mapping. In order to generate more ornamental images, advantages of these methods are integrated into a joint strategy. The framework is shown in Fig. 5.13. These two enhancement methods are used to process the input image, and then the obtained enhanced image is systematically fused to generate the final image.

Context-Sensitive Method

Unsharp masking can realize the function of amplifying the high-frequency part of the image signal based on linear or nonlinear filtering [45]. The filtering process can be considered as a model connected to the input. The residual signal between the original input and the low-pass filtered (such as Gaussian smoothing) image usually contains image structure and noise. However, only the image structure should be enhanced and the noise cannot be amplified in unsharp masking. Therefore, it is necessary to preprocess the image to reduce noise and maintain edges before performing unsharp masking. There are many types of edge-preserving filters, each of them can produce an unsharp version. The processed image is considered to be a context-sensitive enhanced image. For example, Bilateral filter [46] has better edge-preserving ability, and is easy to establish and compute [47], but only using edge-preserving filter will cause the loss of details. Therefore, we add impulse function to retain the information of the input image, while using a bilateral filter. Their combination can balance noise robustness and sharpness enhancement well. If you want to handle more complex scenarios, you can improve on this strategy by using more than two filters.

I is a given input image, and unsharp masking can be defined as:

$$I_s = I + \omega_1 \cdot I_{d1} + \omega_2 \cdot I_{d2}, \tag{5.38}$$

where I_{d1} represents the high-frequency signal generated by the image after the pulse function preprocessing. I_{d2} represents the high-frequency signal generated by the image after bilateral filtering. More specifically, we use Gaussian smoothing to further process the preprocessed image, which is represented as I_{d1}. We treat the residual between the input image and the smoothed image as high-frequency signal, which is replaced by I_{d2}. ω_1 and ω_2 are the control factors, and here we set $\omega_1 = \omega_2 = 0.5$.

Context-Free Approach

The context-free enhancement approach is implemented through sigmoid transfer mapping [10, 48]. When the human eye uses skewness or similar histogram asymmetry to determine surface quality, images with long positive tails in the histogram often appear darker and more glossy [49]. Sigmoid mapping can be used to improve surface quality to make the enhanced image quality more close to HVS preferences. Context-free enhanced image I_f is defined as follows:

$$I_f = f_{clip}(M_s(I, \Phi)) = f_{clip}\left(\frac{\Phi_1 - \Phi_2}{1 + exp(-\frac{(I-\Phi_3)}{\Phi_4})} + \Phi_2\right). \tag{5.39}$$

This function describes a mapping curve, where the f_{clip} action binds the pixels to the [0, 255] area, and $\Phi = \{\Phi_1, \Phi_2, \Phi_3, \Phi_4\}$ are the optional parameters. To derive these parameters, we need to determine four points (x, y) on the mapping curve before the transfer process. x represents the input intensity and y represents the transfer output. Since the sigmoid map is rolling symmetric relative to the line $y = x$, we can obtain three pairs of fixed points, namely $(x_1, y_1) = (0, 0)$, $(x_2, y_2) = (l_{max}, l_{max})$, and $(x_3, y_3) = (\frac{l_{max}}{2}, \frac{l_{max}}{2})$. l_{max} denotes the maximum density of the input image, that is, $l_{max} = 255$. The remaining (x_4, y_4) can be fixed to control the shape, where the value of x_4 is different from that of x_1, x_2, and x_3. When x_4 is determined, y_4 can be obtained. The optimal control parameter can be found by searching for the minimum value of the following objective function:

$$\Phi = \arg\min_{\Phi} \sum_{i=1}^{4} |y_i - M_s(x_i, \Phi)|. \tag{5.40}$$

Among these parameters, only y_4 can change the control parameter of the curvature of the transfer function. Here, we set $x_4 = 25$, $y_4 = 3$.

Unified Contrast Enhancement Framework

Both context-sensitive and context-free methods have advantages in terms of optimizing contrast quality. Using these two models, the contrast enhancement is described as a multi-criteria optimization issue here. The purpose is to seek image that is similar to the desired enhanced image, while retaining the structure from the input image I. Therefore, given parameters α and β that control contrast enhancement level, the generalized structure can be obtained by:

$$\min\{D(I_e, I) + \alpha \cdot D(I_e, I_f) + \beta \cdot D(I_e, I_s)\}, \tag{5.41}$$

where I_e is the enhanced image under the generalized contrast enhancement framework. I_f is an enhanced image generated by a context-free method, and I_s is an enhanced image generated by a context-sensitive method. When two vectors x and y with the same number of elements are given, the Euclidean distance D is defined as follows:

$$D(x, y) = \sum_i (x_i - y_i)^2. \tag{5.42}$$

The quadratic optimization problem can be derived from Eqs. (5.41) and (5.42):

$$\begin{aligned}
I_e &= \arg\min_{I_e}\{D(I_e, I) + \alpha \cdot D(I_e, I_f) + \beta \cdot D(I_e, I_s)\}, \\
&= \arg\min_{I_e}\{(I_e - I)^T(I_e - I) + \alpha \cdot (I_e - I_f)^T(I_e - I_f). \\
&\quad + \beta \cdot (I_e - I_s)^T(I_e - I_s)\}
\end{aligned} \tag{5.43}$$

Finally, these images (i.e., I, I_f, I_s) are fused to obtain the enhanced image I_e:

Fig. 5.14 Comparison of the context-sensitive and context-free enhanced images. **a** Input image "Lighthouse"; **b** I_s; **c** I_f; **d** I_e with $\alpha = 0.5$ and $\beta = 0.5$ (©[2021] IEEE. Reprinted, with permission, from [16].)

$$I_e = \frac{I + \alpha \cdot I_f + \beta \cdot I_s}{1 + \alpha + \beta}. \tag{5.44}$$

According to the above Eq. (5.44), α and β can construct contrast enhancement images of different levels and adjust I_e. I_e is almost a globally enhanced image as α goes to infinity. When α and β close to zero, I_e is the original input image.

Figure 5.14 shows the contrast enhancement results, where $\alpha = 0.5, \beta = 0.5$. This method combines the advantages of both context-free and context-sensitive methods, which makes the enhanced image more natural and has better visual effects. It can be seen from Fig. 5.14c, the context-free approach implemented through sigmoid transfer achieves better quality.

Guided Contrast Enhancement Scheme

In general, it is difficult to automatically enhance an image to the desired contrast level. If there is an inappropriate level of enhancement, the image will be over-enhanced, making the image unnatural. To reduce human involvement, we usually use the retrieved images to derive the level of automatic contrast enhancement. A great quantity of available images in the cloud make the realization of automatic contrast enhancement possible. Quality assessment methods based on contrast enhancement are important tasks [50] that still needs to be improved. In order to realize the automatic selection of guided images, we use the NR image QA method to reorder the images retrieved in the cloud according to the image quality. The images with the best quality are referred to as "guidance images". Subsequently, inspired by the simplified reference image quality assessment method, we extract several features that can represent the whole image for contrast enhancement, quality comparison and matching. Finally, the contrast enhancement image that best matches the guidance image is obtained. Contrast is closely related to image complexity and surface quality statistics, which also inspires us to use free-energy to explore the derivation of contrast levels.

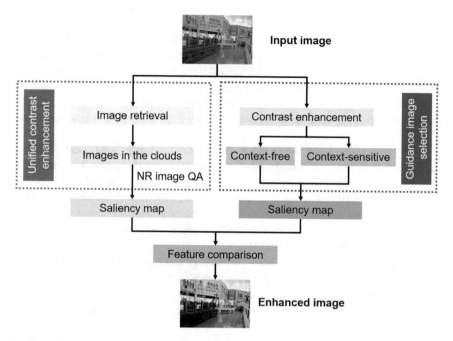

Fig. 5.15 Flowchart of the automatic contrast enhancement scheme

Guidance Image Selection with NR Image QA

Figure 5.15 shows the selection process of a guidance image. The input images are used to retrieve greatly correlated images from the cloud. In order to select the one with the best image quality, we use the recently proposed NR image QA method [37] that achieves advanced prediction accuracy to sort images with various qualities. Theoretically, any advanced NR image QA method can be applied here.

There exists an approximate linear relationship between the observed structural degradation information and the free-energy of the pristine image. On this basis, the characteristics of structural degradation $SDM_i(I)$ $(i \in \{\mu, \sigma\})$ are compared with the free-energy $F(I)$, and the difference between $NRD_1(I)$ and $NRD_2(I)$ are used to evaluate quality. $NRD_j(I) = F(I) - (\xi_j \cdot SDM_i(I) + \varphi_j)$, $j \in \{1, 2\}$. Structural degradation is assessed as follows:

$$SDM_\mu(I) = E\left(\frac{\sigma_{\mu_I \bar{\mu}_I} + C_1}{\sigma_{\mu_I} \sigma_{\bar{\mu}_I} + C_1}\right), \tag{5.45}$$

$$SDM_\sigma(I) = E\left(\frac{\sigma_{\sigma_I \bar{\sigma}_I} + C_1}{\sigma_{\sigma_I} \sigma_{\bar{\sigma}_I} + C_1}\right), \tag{5.46}$$

where $E(\cdot)$ is the operator of mathematical expectation, and C_1 is the small positive stability constant considering saturation effect. μ_I and σ_I represent the local mean and standard deviation of a 2D circularly symmetric Gaussian weight function. $\bar{\mu}_I$ and $\bar{\sigma}_I$ represent local mean and standard deviation obtained by using the impulse function rather than Gaussian weighting function. $\sigma_{\mu_I\bar{\mu}_I}$ is the local covariance between the two vectors. The structural degradation information associates with the cosine of the angle between the two mean vectors. $\sigma_{\sigma_I\bar{\sigma}_I}$ is the local covariance between vectors σ_I and $\bar{\sigma}_I$.

The $NRD_1(I)$ and $NRD_2(I)$ values of high quality images with little distortion are very close to zero, and will deviate from zero when the distortion becomes large. In addition to these characteristics, the size of the image is considered to be the criterion for excluding low resolution guidance images. This framework is suitable for single contrast enhancement using images retrieved from the cloud. In addition, it can be further extended to "photo album contrast enhancement", which is also considered as a special form of cloud storage.

Alternative strategies based on this framework can also be applied. For example, when browsing images, we can first manually select a guide image, then manually enhance an image to improve the contrast. Next, we can take this image as a guide image, and other information images can automatically enhance the guidance information.

Free-Energy-Based Brain Theory

In this work, the free-energy is used to derive the contrast enhancement level of NR image QA and feature matching. Free energy theory attempts to illustrate and unify several brain theories about human behavior, perception and learning in the biological and physical sciences [51]. The basic assumption of the free-energy-based brain theory is that cognitive processes are controlled by the internal generative mechanism (IGM).

IGM is parameterized here to explain the scene by adjusting the parameter v. In the input image I, the entropy-determined "surprise" is assessed by integrating the joint distribution $P(I, v)$ in the model parameter v space [52]:

$$- \log P(I) = - \log \int P(I, v)dv. \tag{5.47}$$

To more accurately represent the joint distribution, we add a dummy term $Q(v|I)$ to the numerator and denominator of the above formula, and rewrite it as:

$$- \log P(I) = - \log \int Q(v|I)\frac{P(I, v)}{Q(v|I)}dv, \tag{5.48}$$

where $Q(v|I)$ indicates the posterior distribution of the model parameters for a given input image signal I. Negative "surprises" can also be interpreted as log evidence of the image data given the model. In this case, the minimization of "surprise" equals the maximization of model evidence. Jensen's inequality is used to deduce from Eq. (5.49):

$$- \log P(I) \leq - \int Q(v|I) \frac{P(I,v)}{Q(v|I)} dv, \tag{5.49}$$

and the free-energy can be accessed by:

$$F(I) = - \int Q(v|I) \frac{P(I,v)}{Q(v|I)} dv. \tag{5.50}$$

The free-energy $F(I)$ defines the upper limit of input image information through $- \log P(I) \leq F(I)$. In [52], the free-energy can be proved to be expressed by the total description length of the kth order AR model.

$$F(I) = - \log P(I|v) + \frac{k}{2} \log N \quad \text{with} \ N \to \infty, \tag{5.51}$$

N is the sum of pixels in the image. The prediction residual entropy between the input image and the predicted image plus the model cost can be used to estimate the free-energy. Residuals are considered to be disordered information that cannot be well explained by the HVS.

The free-energy theory of human brain reveals that HVS cannot process sensory information entirely and tries to avoid some surprises with uncertainties. In actuality, the positive contrast changes usually highlights visibility details to get a high quality image. But this process produces extra information about the content, which makes the image more difficult to describe. The reason for the above problems is that HVS is more capable of describing low-complexity images than the higher-complexity version [53]. Prior information from guidance can estimate the proper free energy of visually pleasing images with great contrast, which is very efficient for deducing the level of contrast enhancement.

The relation between contrast enhancement level and free energy is shown in Fig. 5.16, where the enhancement level is controlled by context-sensitive parameter β. As can be seen from the figure, the free energy increases with the enhancement level.

Surface Quality Statistics

Contrast not only provides an effective clue for surface reflectance [54], but also shares higher-level attributes with gloss in the dimension of human perception. Observers usually employ skewness or histogram asymmetry to determine surface quality [49]. Skewness represents a measure of distribution asymmetry, which refers to the balance between positive and negative tails. With the increase of gloss, the skewness of image histogram tends to increase regardless of albedo.

Contrast Level Derivation from Guidance

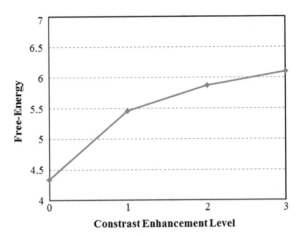

Fig. 5.16 The relationship between the contrast enhancement level (controlled by parameter) and free-energy (evaluated in terms of residual entropy) for image "Lighthouse" (©[2021] IEEE. Reprinted, with permission, from [16].)

Humans preferentially respond to high-contrast stimuli, while image saliency is sensitive to noise but immune to contrast enhancement. Hence, saliency region detection is necessary for both guided images and fused images. Firstly, the threshold is used to detect the saliency region of the salient map of guided images and fused images. Then, features such as free-energy and surface mass within the salient region are extracted. Finally, the final enhanced image is generated by using the parameters that can generate the minimum feature distance.

Various visual saliency detection methods have been successfully applied to image processing tasks [55–57]. There is a recently proposed image signature model that uses each DCT component image signature to generate saliency maps [58]. This means that the model only needs one bit per component, which makes it work efficiently at very low computational complexity costs. Image signatures are defined as follows:

$$ImgSignature(I) = sign(DCT2(I)). \tag{5.52}$$

Each input value ξ is entered through $sign(\cdot)$:

$$sign(\xi) = \begin{cases} 1, & \xi > 0 \\ 0, & \xi = 0. \\ -1, & \xi < 0 \end{cases} \tag{5.53}$$

Then, the reconstructed image can be obtained by the following way:

$$\bar{I} = IDCT2(ImgSignature(I)), \tag{5.54}$$

where DCT2 represents the discrete cosine transform of 2D image signal, and IDCT2 represents the inverse discrete cosine transform of 2D image signal. Finally, the reconstructed image is smoothed to obtain saliency mapping:

$$SaliencyMap = g * (\bar{I} \circ \bar{I}), \tag{5.55}$$

where g refers to Gaussian kernel. '$\circ$' is the entry-wise and '$*$' is the convolution operator. In the actual implementation, the saliency map can be converted to intensity images in the range of 0.0–1.0, and the salient regions can be classified by the threshold, which is determined by experience.

By analyzing free energy and surface quality statistics, we extract two features from the guided image and fused image. This method uses global features instead of pixel level or block level to compare image pairs. By doing this, it can achieve efficient dimension reduction effect and offer high accuracy in summarizing the contrast strength. So, the contrast matching problem can be transformed into an optimization problem based on the guided image and fused image:

$$(\alpha^*, \beta^*) = argmin_{\alpha^*, \beta^*} \left(|F(I_g) - F(I_e)| + \lambda |S(I_g) - S(I_e)| \right), \tag{5.56}$$

where λ balances the magnitude and importance of complexity metric and skewness metric. α^* and β^* are the optimization values that lead to an appropriate enhancement level. For facilitating comparison and reducing the computational complexity, the guided image and fused image are downsampled at the same scale, and then the feature calculation is carried out. The final enhanced image is obtained by Eq. (5.44) using I, I_f, I_s with parameters α^* and β^*.

5.3 Comparison and Analysis of Algorithm Performance

In this section, we introduce an image database named CCID 2014, and several state-of-the-art image QA methods of enhanced images. We focus on comparing and measuring the performance of the presented QA approaches in this chapter with these methods. The detailed results of the analysis will be illustrated in the following sections. It is worth mentioning that the analysis results show that the performance of these methods in this chapter perform quite well.

5.3.1 CCID 2014 Database

The CCID 2014 database is composed of 655 images derived from 15 natural images in Kodak image database [33]. It is dedicated to the distortion category of contrast altering. Based on the standard suggested by ITU-R BT.500-13 [21], 22 subjects are invited to rate these images on a suitable viewing distance and illumination condition. The final scores and the corresponding mean opinion scores (MOSs) of these viewers are recorded.

5.3.2   Performance Comparison and Analysis

In order to demonstrate the validity and superiority of the methods introduced in this chapter, we compare the proposed approaches with the state-of-the-art image QA methods. All three types of methods are listed in Table 5.3. Among them, there are 13 FR methods, 4 RR methods and 9 NR methods, respectively.

When we compare the above modern image QA methods, four commonly used metrics, namely PLCC, SRCC, KRCC, and RMSE, are used. The evaluation accuracy can be measured by PLCC and RMSE, while the monotonicity of the prediction can be found by SRCC and KRCC. A higher value of PLCC, SRCC, and KRCC and a lower value of RMSE represent a better quality evaluation methods. The objective assessment scores are nonlinearity obtained by PLCC, SRCC, KRCC, and RMSE, so we use a logistic function to increase the linearity. We compute the image QA scores using these four criteria by the mapping including 5 parameters as follows:

$$f(x) = \tau_1\left(\frac{1}{2} - \frac{1}{1 + \exp^{\tau_2(x-\tau_3)}} + \tau_4 x + \tau_5\right), \tag{5.57}$$

where $\tau_{i,i=1,2,3,4,5}$ represents the fitted parameter; $f(x)$ and x are subjective scores and its corresponding objective scores which are assessed by image QA algorithms.

It is evident that the four introduced models in this chapter have achieved encouraging results. We summarize the advantages of proposed models as follows.

(1) It is obviously found that among the tested FR image QA methods, VIF has the best performance with the highest PLCC, SRCC, KRCC, and the lowest RMSE. Compared with VIF, MS-SSIM is a bit less powerful, but it is the best performance among other methods.

(2) The performance of QMC introduced in this paper is the best. Compared with FTQM, which shows the best performance in the traditional RR method participating in the comparative experiment, QMC has increased values of PLCC, SRCC and KRCC.

(3) Among the tested NR image QA methods, BIQME obtains the superior performance than other methods. Compared with the proposed method which shows the best performance in the RR method participating in the comparative experiment, the PLCC, SRCC and KRCC values of QMC have been upgraded.

Overall, QMC performed best in this experiment. Compared to the VIF method with the best performance in the category of FR image QA model, the values of PLCC, SRCC and KRCC of QMC have been increased, respectively. Compared with FTQM, which has the optimal performance in RR methods, QMC's PLCC, SRCC and KRCC values have also increased, separately. Compared with BIQME, which has the best performance in traditional NR image QA models, the PLCC, SRCC, and KRCC values of QMC have increased too. It can be seen that among the traditional algorithms used for comparison, the FR image QA algorithm has the best performance since it has complete pristine image information. However, the semi-reference and even NR algorithms introduced in this chapter obtain opti-

Table 5.3 The proposed algorithms and modern developed QA models

Category	Abbreviation	Full Name	Refs.
FR	SSIM	Structural similarity	[59]
FR	MS-SSIM	Structural similarity	[60]
FR	VIF	Visual information fidelity	[61]
FR	MAD	Most apparent distortion	[62]
FR	IW-SSIM	Information weighted SSIM	[63]
FR	FSIM	Feature similarity	[64]
FR	GSIM	Gradient similarity index	[65]
FR	IGM	Internal generative mechanism	[66]
FR	SR-SSIM	Spectral residual SSIM	[67]
FR	VSI	VS-based index	[68]
FR	WASH	Wavelet based sharp features	[69]
FR	LTG	Local-tuned-global	[70]
RR	FEDM	Free energy based distortion metric	[52]
RR	RRED	Reduced-reference algorithms	[71]
RR	FTQM	Fourier transform based quality measure	[72]
RR	SDM	Structural degradation model	[73]
RR	RIQMC	Reduced-reference image quality metric for contrast change	[13]
RR	QMC	Quality assessment metric of contrast	[10]
NR	DIIVINE	Distortion identification-based image verity and integrity evaluation	[74]
NR	BLIINDS-II	Blind image integrity notator using DCT statistics	[75]
NR	BRISQUE	Blind/referenceless image spatial quality evaluator	[11]
NR	BIQME	Blind image quality measure of enhanced images	[14]
NR	NIQMC	No-reference image quality metric for contrast distortion	[15]
NR	NFERM	No-reference free energy-based robust metric	[37]
NR	NIQE	Natural image quality evaluator	[76]
NR	QAC	Quality-aware clustering	[77]
NR	IL-NIQE	Integrated-local NIQE	[78]
NR	BQMS	Blind quality measure for SCIs	[40]
NR	Fang et al.	–	[6]

mal performance under the condition of using less reference information, and even surpass the traditional FR algorithms.

5.4 Conclusion

Image enhancement and QA technology play a significant role in practical applications such as object detection, recognition, and so on. This chapter introduces two databases containing contrast-changed images, two NR images QA methods and one RR image QA method. First, considering that there are few databases for QA of enhanced images, we establish two novel enhanced image databases, namely EID and CCID 2014. Second, in order to improve and optimize enhancement algorithms, we design four excellent performance image QA metrics to predict the quality of processed images, including RIQMC, BIQME, NIQMC and QMC. Finally, On the basis of the better contrast and visual quality already obtained, we propose two methods, both of which target at automatically generating visually-pleasing enhanced images. One method is a new automatic RICE model with saliency preservation. The other method is a general contrast enhancement framework for context-sensitive and context-free enhancement methods. Analysis results show that the image QA models including RIQMC, BIQME, NIQMC and QMC are better than the traditional image QA models. Despite the good performance of the measures described, there is still work to be done. In future work, we will consider how to effectively assess images or videos to better improve and optimize enhancement algorithms while reducing the complexity of models.

References

1. Sheikh HR, Wang Z, Cormack L et al (2005) LIVE image quality assessment database release 2. http://live.ece.utexas.edu/research/quality
2. Gu K, Zhai G, Yang X et al (2014) Hybrid no-reference quality metric for singly and multiply distorted images. IEEE Trans Broadcast 60(3):555–567
3. Gu K, Liu M, Zhai G et al (2015) Quality assessment considering viewing distance and image resolution. IEEE Trans Broadcast 61(3):520–531
4. Vu CT, Phan TD, Banga PS et al (2012) On the quality assessment of enhanced images: a database, analysis, and strategies for augmenting existing methods. In: Paper presented at the 2012 IEEE southwest symposium on image analysis and interpretation, pp 181–184, April 2012
5. Li L, Zhou Y, Wu J et al (2016) Color-enriched gradient similarity for retouched image quality evaluation. IEICE Trans Inf Syst 99(3):773–776
6. Fang Y, Ma K, Wang Z et al (2014) No-reference quality assessment of contrast-distorted images based on natural scene statistics. IEEE Signal Process Lett 22(7):838–842
7. Wang S, Ma K, Yeganeh H et al (2015) A patch-structure representation method for quality assessment of contrast changed images. IEEE Signal Process Lett 22(12):2387–2390
8. Snidaro L, Niu R, Foresti GL et al (2007) Quality-based fusion of multiple video sensors for video surveillance. IEEE Trans Syst Man Cybern Part B 37(4):1044–1051

9. Panetta K, Agaian S, Zhou Y et al (2010) Parameterized logarithmic framework for image enhancement. IEEE Trans Syst Man Cybern Part B 41(2):460–473

10. Gu K, Zhai G, Yang X et al (2015) Automatic contrast enhancement technology with saliency preservation. IEEE Trans Circuits Syst Video Technol 25(9):1480–1494

11. Mittal A, Moorthy AK, Bovik AC (2012) No-reference image quality assessment in the spatial domain. IEEE Trans Image Process 21(12):4695–4708

12. Li L, Shen W, Gu K et al (2016) No-reference quality assessment of enhanced images. China Commun 13(9):121–130

13. Gu K, Zhai G, Lin W et al (2015) The analysis of image contrast: from quality assessment to automatic enhancement. IEEE Trans Cybern 46(1):284–297

14. Gu K, Tao D, Qiao J et al (2017) Learning a no-reference quality assessment model of enhanced images with big data. IEEE Trans Neural Netw Learn Syst 29(4):1301–1313

15. Gu K, Lin W, Zhai G et al (2016) No-reference quality metric of contrast-distorted images based on information maximization. IEEE Trans Cybern 47(12):4559–4565

16. Wang S, Gu K, Ma S et al (2015) Guided image contrast enhancement based on retrieved images in cloud. IEEE Trans Multimedia 18(2):219–232

17. Wang Y, Chen Q, Zhang B (1999) Image enhancement based on equal area dualistic sub-image histogram equalization method. IEEE Trans Consum Electron 45(1):68–75

18. Wang Q, Ward RK (2007) Fast image/video contrast enhancement based on weighted thresholded histogram equalization. IEEE Trans Consum Electron 53(2):757–764

19. Sim KS, Tso CP, Tan YY (2007) Recursive sub-image histogram equalization applied to gray scale images. Pattern Recognit Lett 28(10):1209–1221

20. Arici T, Dikbas S, Altunbasak Y (2009) A histogram modification framework and its application for image contrast enhancement. IEEE Trans Image Process 18(9):1921–1935

21. Series BT (2012) Methodology for the subjective assessment of the quality of television pictures. Recommendation ITU-R BT 500-13

22. Li L, Zhou Y, Lin W et al (2016) No-reference quality assessment of deblocked images. Neurocomputing 177:572–584

23. Ponomarenko N, Lukin V, Zelensky A et al (2009) TID2008-A database for evaluation of full-reference visual quality assessment metrics. Adv Modern Radioelectronics 10(4):30–45

24. Larson EC, Chandler DM (2010) Most apparent distortion: full reference image quality assessment and the role of strategy. J Electron Imaging 19(1):011006

25. Ponomarenko N, Jin L, Ieremeiev O et al (2015) Image database TID2013: peculiarities, results and perspectives. Signal Process Image Commun 30:57–77

26. Franzen R (2010) Kodak lossless true color image suite. http://r0k.us/graphics/kodak/

27. Mante V, Frazor RA, Bonin V et al (2005) Independence of luminance and contrast in natural scenes and in the early visual system. Nat Neurosci 8(12):1690–1697

28. Li C, Bovik AC, Wu X (2011) Blind image quality assessment using a general regression neural network. IEEE Trans Neural Netw 22(5):793–799

29. Kovesi P (1999) Image features from phase congruency. Videre: J Comput Vis Res 69(3):1–26

30. Groen IIA, Ghebreab S, Prins H et al (2013) From image statistics to scene gist: evoked neural activity reveals transition from low-level natural image structure to scene category. J Neurosci 33(48):18814–18824

31. Choi LK, You J, Bovik AC (2015) Referenceless prediction of perceptual fog density and perceptual image defogging. IEEE Trans Image Process 24(11):3888–3901

32. Hasler D (2003) Suesstrunk S E (2003) Measuring colorfulness in natural images. In: Paper presented at the International Society for Optics and Photonics, vol 5007, pp 87–95, June 2003

33. Vu CT, Phan TD, Chandler DM (2012) S3: a spectral and spatial measure of local perceived sharpness in natural images. IEEE Trans Image Process 21(3):934–945

34. Vu PV, Chandler DM (2012) A fast wavelet-based algorithm for global and local image sharpness estimation. IEEE Signal Process Lett 19(7):423–426

35. Gu K, Zhai G, Lin W et al (2015) No-reference image sharpness assessment in autoregressive parameter space. IEEE Trans Image Process 24(10):3218–3231

36. Gu K, Wang S, Zhai G et al (2016) Blind quality assessment of tone-mapped images via analysis of information, naturalness, and structure. IEEE Trans Multimedia 18(3):432–443
37. Gu K, Zhai G, Yang X et al (2015) Using free energy principle for blind image quality assessment. IEEE Trans Multimedia 17(1):50–63
38. Ruderman DL (1994) The statistics of natural images. Netw Comput Neural Syst 5(4):517–548
39. He K, Sun J, Tang X (2011) Single image haze removal using dark channel prior. IEEE Trans Pattern Anal Mach Intell 33(12):2341–2353
40. Gu K, Zhai G, Lin W et al (2016) Learning a blind quality evaluation engine of screen content images. Neurocomputing 196:140–149
41. Chang C, Lin J (2011). LIBSVM: a library for support vector machines. ACM Trans Intell Syst Technol 2(3):1-27
42. Huang SC, Cheng FC, Chiu YS (2013) Efficient contrast enhancement using adaptive gamma correction with weighting distribution. IEEE Trans Image Process 22(3):1032–1041
43. Bruce N, Tsotsos J (2005) Saliency based on information maximization. Adv Neural Inf Process Syst 155–162
44. Gu K, Zhai G, Lin W et al (2015) Visual saliency detection with free energy theory. IEEE Signal Process Lett 22(10):1552–1555
45. Deng G (2010) A generalized unsharp masking algorithm. IEEE Trans Image Process 20(5):1249–1261
46. Tomasi C, Manduchi R (1998) Bilateral filtering for gray and color images. In: Paper presented at the 6th international conference on computer vision, pp 839–846, Jan 1998
47. Milanfar P (2013) A Tour of modern image filtering: new insights and methods, both practical and theoretical. IEEE Signal Process Mag 30(1):106–128
48. Gu K, Zhai G, Liu M et al (2013) Brightness preserving video contrast enhancement using S-shaped transfer function. In: Paper presented at the 2013 visual communications and image processing, 1–6 Nov 2013
49. Motoyoshi I, Nishida SY, Sharan L et al (2007) Image statistics and the perception of surface qualities. Nature 447(7141):206–209
50. Gu K, Zhai G, Yang X et al (2013) Subjective and objective quality assessment for images with contrast change. In: Paper presented at the 2013 IEEE international conference on image processing, pp 383–387, Sept 2013
51. Friston K (2010) The free-energy principle: a unified brain theory? Nat Rev Neurosci 11(2):127–138
52. Zhai G, Wu X, Yang X et al (2011) A psychovisual quality metric in free-energy principle. IEEE Trans Image Process 21(1):41–52
53. Ma S, Zhang X, Wang S et al (2015) Entropy of primitive: from sparse representation to visual information evaluation. IEEE Trans Circuits Syst Video Technol 27(2):249–260
54. Allred SR, Brainard DH (2009) Contrast, constancy, and measurements of perceived lightness under parametric manipulation of surface slant and surface reflectance. J Opt Soc Am A 26(4):949–961
55. Liu H, Heynderickx I (2011) Visual attention in objective image quality assessment: based on eye-tracking data. IEEE Trans Circuits Syst Video Technol 21(7):971–982
56. Min X, Zhai G, Gao Z et al (2014) Visual attention data for image quality assessment databases. In: Paper presented at the 2014 IEEE international symposium on circuits and systems, pp 894–897, June 2014
57. Hadizadeh H, Bajic IV (2013) Saliency-aware video compression. IEEE Trans Image Process 23(1):19–33
58. Hou X, Harel J, Koch C (2011) Image signature: highlighting sparse salient regions. IEEE Trans Pattern Anal Mach Intell 34(1):194–201
59. Wang Z, Bovik AC, Sheikh HR et al (2004) Image quality assessment: from error visibility to structural similarity. IEEE Trans Image Process 13(4):600–612
60. Wang Z, Simoncelli EP, Bovik AC (2003) Multi-scale structural similarity for image quality assessment. In: Paper presented at thrity-seventh asilomar conference on signals, systems and computers, pp 1398–1402, Nov 2003

61. Sheikh HR, Bovik AC (2006) Image information and visual quality. IEEE Trans Image Process 15(2):430–444

62. Larson EC, Chandler DM (2010) Most apparent distortion: full-reference image quality assessment and the role of strategy. J Electron Imaging 19(1):6–21

63. Wang Z, Li Q (2011) Information content weighting for perceptual image quality assessment. IEEE Trans Image Process 20(5):1185–1198

64. Zhang L, Zhang L, Mou X et al (2011) FSIM: a feature similarity index for image quality assessment. IEEE Trans Image Process 20(8):2378–2386

65. Liu A, Lin W, Narwaria M (2012) Image quality assessment based on gradient similarity. IEEE Trans Image Process 21(4):1500–1512

66. Wu J, Lin W, Shi G et al (2013) Perceptual quality metric with internal generative mechanism. IEEE Trans Image Process 22(1):43–54

67. Zhang L, Li H (2012) SR-SIM: a fast and high performance IQA index based on spectral residual. In: Paper presented at the 19th IEEE international conference on image processing, pp 1473–1476, Sept 2012

68. Zhang L, Shen Y, Li H (2014) VSI: a visual saliency induced index for perceptual image quality assessment. IEEE Trans Image Process 23(10):4270–4281

69. Reenu M, Dayana D, Raj SSA et al (2013) Wavelet based sharp features (WASH): an image quality assessment metric based on HVS. In: Paper presented at the 2nd international conference on advanced computing, networking and security, pp 79–83, Dec 2013

70. Gu K, Zhai G, Yang X et al (2014) An efficient color image quality metric with local-tuned-global model. In: Paper presented at the 2014 IEEE international conference on image processing, pp 506–510, Oct 2014

71. Soundararajan R, Bovik AC (2012) RRED indices: reduced-reference entropic differencing for image quality assessment. IEEE Trans Image Process 21(2):517–526

72. Narwaria M, Lin W, McLoughlin IV et al (2012) Fourier transform-based scalable image quality measure. IEEE Trans Image Process 21(8):3364–3377

73. Gu K, Zhai G, Yang X et al (2013) A new reduced-reference image quality assessment using structural degradation model. In: Paper presented at the IEEE international symposium on circuits and systems, pp 1095–1098, May 2013

74. Moorthy AK, Bovik AC (2011) Blind image quality assessment: from scene statistics to perceptual quality. IEEE Trans Image Process 20(12):3350–3364

75. Saad MA, Bovik AC, Charrier C (2012) Blind image quality assessment: a natural scene statistics approach in the DCT domain. IEEE Trans Image Process 21(8):3339–3352

76. Mittal A, Soundararajan R, Bovik AC (2013) Making a 'completely blind' image quality analyzer. IEEE Signal Process Lett 22(3):209–212

77. Xue W, Zhang L, Mou X (2013) Learning without human scores for blind image quality assessment. In: Proceedings of the IEEE conference on computer vision and pattern recognition, pp 995–1002

78. Zhang L, Zhang L, Bovik AC (2015) A feature-enriched completely blind image quality evaluator. IEEE Trans Image Process 24(8):2579–2591

79. Final report from the video quality experts group on the validation of objective models of video quality assessment. VQEG, http://www.vqeg.org/

Chapter 6
Quality Assessment of Light-Field Image

6.1 Introduction

Nowadays, with the increasing demand for immersive media applications, light-field (LF) imaging has widespread applications such as 3D reconstruction, virtual reality, and image-based rendering [1–6]. As a type of digital visual signal, LF images are inevitably prone to loss of visual details during the various stages of acquisition, encoding, denoising, transmission, and rendering to display. The perceived quality and the system processing ability of the LF images will be affected by distortion. Therefore, it is necessary to obtain the LF image quality and design the corresponding image processing system to improve the performance of practical applications of LF images.

From the perspective of the presence or absence of participants, these methods are divided into subjective image QA method and objective image QA method. The subjective image quality evaluation method aims to obtain the image quality through observers' subjective evaluation, then acquire the final score through the mean opinion score (MOS). But this method is laborious, which is unsuitable for practical applications such as dynamically monitoring, adjustment of image quality, and so on. Thus, the objective image QA method has become the mainstream QA method. On the basis of the accessibility of reference information, these image QA methods can be divided into three types, namely full-reference (FR) image QA methods, reduced-reference (RR) image QA methods, and no-reference (NR) image QA methods. The FR image QA methods exploit complete information about reference images and compute the discrepancy between the original images and the corrupted images. The RR image QA approaches only refer to part of the original image information. The NR image QA models assess the image quality without any information of the original image, which makes it more usable in most real-world applications. In [9], Yang et al. designed a 3D FR image QA method by using the average peak signal-to-noise ratio and the absolute difference between left and right views. In [10], Chen et al. presented a 3D NR image QA algorithm by combining the features obtained from cyclopean images, disparity maps, and uncertainty maps.

K. Gu et al., *Quality Assessment of Visual Content*, Advances in Computer Vision and Pattern Recognition, https://doi.org/10.1007/978-981-19-3347-9_6

In [11], Gu et al. put forward an NR multi-view image QA method named AR-plus thresholding, which can employ the autoregression-based local image description.

While there have been many efforts for researching the image QA, the advanced QA approaches are unsuitable for the LF images. Unlike traditional imaging techniques that directly record the light intensity of the camera sensor, the images generated by the LF imaging technology contain fundamental depth information. Specifically, LF images contain not only radiation intensity information, but also the direction information of light rays in the free space [7, 8].

To achieve a better quality evaluation result of LF images, a large number of researchers have done a lot of work to design different LF image QA approaches. For example, in [15], Tian et al. designed an FR image QA model, which measures the light-field coherence (LFC) between the pristine LF image and the corrupted LF image to evaluate the image quality. In [12], Paudyal et al. put forward a RR image QA model that investigates the association between the perceptual quality of LF images and the distortion of the estimated depth map. In [13], Shi et al. designed a NR LF image QA scheme named NR-LFQA, which derives the quality degradation of LF images by assessing the spatial quality and the angular consistency. In [14], Zhou et al. put forward a new tensor-oriented no-reference light-field image quality evaluator (Tensor-NLFQ) based on tensor theory. In order to evaluate the performance of these image QA models, we compared them with state-of-the-art competitors using four typically used metrics, namely Pearson linear correlation coefficient (PLCC), Spearman rank correlation coefficient (SRCC), root mean square error (RMSE), outlier ratio (OR).

The remainder of this chapter is arranged as follows. Section 6.2 introduces in detail the modeling process and comparison and analysis of three types of LF image QA models, namely the FR LF image QA, the RR LF image QA, and the NR LF image QA. Section 6.3 compares several advanced image QA methods of LF images with the introduced approaches. Section 6.4 finally draws the conclusion and provides future work.

6.2 Methodology

In this section, we mainly introduce various LF image QA methods. These approaches can be divided into three types according to the accessibility of original information, namely FR, RR, and NR LF image QA method. To be specific, we first introduce the FR LF image QA method from different feature extraction methods, i.e., multi-scale Gabor feature extraction and single-scale Gabor feature extraction. Second, we illustrate a RR LF image QA method, which is based on the selected feature information. Third, the NR LF image QA methods based on spatial-angular measurement and tensor are shown. We validate the performance of the above-mentioned methods with the typically used indices of PLCC, SRCC, RMSE, and OR.

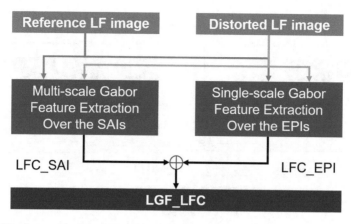

Fig. 6.1 The framework of the LGF-LFC model

6.2.1   FR QA of LF Images

Different from the traditional two-dimension (2D) natural images, LF images record both the color information of the scene and the depth information of the bottom layer. The various image distortions caused by tasks based on LF image will affect the above two characteristics. Changes in the first characteristic can be reflected by sub-aperture images (SAIs), while changes in the latter can be reflected by epi-polar images (EPIs). Hoping to utilize these features to evaluate LF images, we introduce an FR image QA model based on log-Gabor feature-based light-field coherence (LGF-LFC). This model measures the light-field coherence (LFC) between the pristine LF image and the corrupted LF image to evaluate the image quality [15]. The framework of this method is exhibited in Fig. 6.1. It includes the following two stages: (1) multi-scale Gabor feature extraction for reference and distorted SAIs; (2) single-scale Gabor feature extraction for reference and distorted EPIs.

Multi-Scale Gabor Feature Extraction Based on Sub-Aperture Images

When the human visual system (HVS) receives visual information, the multi-channel mechanism of the human brain processes the information during the transmission from retina to the visual cortex. Each channel needs to be adjusted to a specific direction and scale [16, 17]. Direction information of visual stimuli in the receptive field can be reflected and processed by simple cells and complex cells in the visual cortex, respectively [18, 19]. Moreover, the details of the image can be better described in multi-scale, that is, this method can explain the image content from coarse to fine levels [20–22]. Notably, the log-Gabor filter is used in [23, 24], which basically represents a multi-channel representation that can be adjusted for multi-directional and multi-scale cellular responses to visual stimuli. This is consistent with the perceptual

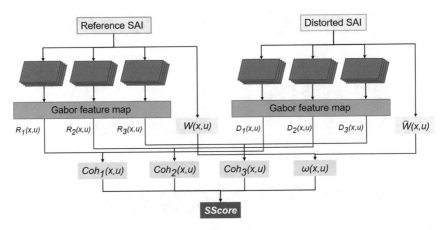

Fig. 6.2 Multi-scale log-Gabor feature extraction framework of SAIs

information mechanism of HVS. According to the above analysis, we will introduce a SAIs-based multi-scale Gabor feature extraction scheme, which can evaluate the image details from the perspective of HVS.

The proposed method's framework is shown in Fig. 6.2. Firstly, each reference and distorted version of the SAI are screened using the Log-Gabor filter to obtain representations with three scales, where each scale contains four directions. Then, LFC measures (or the similarity of the two LFs) at each scale are calculated separately, the results are weighted and aggregated to calculate the score for each SAI. Finally, the average of these scores is taken as the SAI final evaluation score SS_{core}.

The log-Gabor filter can be defined as:

$$G_{m,n}(r, \theta) = exp\left\{\frac{-[log(r/r_m)]^2}{2[log\sigma_m]^2}\right\} exp\left[\frac{-(\theta - \mu_n)^2}{2\sigma_n^2}\right], \qquad (6.1)$$

where m indicates the spatial scale index, and n indicates the orientation index. $r_m = 2/3m$ represents the filter's center frequency. u_n represents the various directions used in the filter, σ_m is the radial bandwidth and σ_n is the angular width. They are defined as $u_n = (n - 1)\pi/4$, $\sigma_m = 1.1$, and $\sigma_n = \pi/6$, respectively. Gabor feature maps are obtained from superposition of feature maps in this scale's four directions. The Gabor feature map $R_m(x, y)$ of pristine SAI $S(x, y)$ and the Gabor feature map $D_m(x, y)$ of distortion SAI $\widehat{S}(x, y)$ are defined as follows:

$$R_m(x, y) = \left(\sum_{n=1}^{4} R_{m,n}^2(x, y)\right)^{1/2}, \qquad (6.2)$$

$$D_m(x, y) = \left(\sum_{n=1}^{4} D_{m,n}^2(x, y)\right)^{1/2}. \qquad (6.3)$$

Each feature map is generated under the scale m, where $m \in \{1, 2, 3\}$. After the decomposition of each SAI for the reference and distorted versions, the corresponding filtering results, namely $R_{m,n}$ and $D_{m,n}$, can be obtained by the Log-Gabor filter. They are defined as follows:

$$R_m(x, y) = F^{-1}(G_{m,n}(r, \theta) \cdot F(S(x, y))), \tag{6.4}$$

$$D_m(x, y) = F^{-1}(G_{m,n}(r, \theta) \cdot F(\widehat{S}(x, y))), \tag{6.5}$$

where F represents for Fourier transform and F^{-1} represents for inverse Fourier transform.

Studies have shown that Gabor filters with different scales can reflect the distortion of SAI. Gabor feature maps with small scale have more detailed information, while Gabor feature maps with large scale have more contour information. By using the Gabor features extracted at each scale, the coherence map $Coh_m(x, y)$ between the $S(x, y)$ and the $\widehat{S}(x, y)$ can be calculated with the following expression:

$$Coh_m(x, y) = \frac{2R_m(x, y)D_m(x, y) + \lambda_m}{R_m^2(x, y) + D_m^2(x, y) + \lambda_m}, \tag{6.6}$$

where $m \in \{1, 2, 3\}$, λ_m is a positive constant defined to avoid potential numerical instability.

Simply averaging the coherent map $Coh_m(x, y)$ can obtain the Gabor feature score easily, but that does not take into account the different contributions of different regions to the overall perception. Considering this, weight strategy is added into the process of calculating feature scores below.

In HVS, visual resolution decays spatially from a point in the human retina [25]. The points in the images are usually very different from the points around them, which makes HVS more sensitive to the pixels in the object contour [26].

In [27] and [28], they mentioned a Hession matrix that can accurately locate the feature points in scale points. These feature points can be utilized as the key point of the object contour. Based on the above considerations, the Hessian matrix feature pool is developed here. Hessian matrix can be obtained by

$$H(x, y) = \begin{bmatrix} \frac{d^2y}{dx^2} & \frac{d^2y}{dxdy} \\ \frac{d^2y}{dxdy} & \frac{d^2y}{dy^2} \end{bmatrix}, \tag{6.7}$$

where $\frac{d^2y}{dx^2}$, $\frac{d^2y}{dxdy}$, and $\frac{d^2y}{dy^2}$ are the second-order derivatives of the input image along the x and/or y directions. They can be calculated by a Gaussian function with standard deviation $\sigma_H = 2$. Then, the Hessian feature map $W(x, y)$ can be defined as

$$W(x, y) = \frac{d^2y}{dx^2}\frac{d^2y}{dy^2} - (\frac{d^2y}{dxdy})^2. \tag{6.8}$$

Through Eq. (6.8), the Hessian feature maps $W(x, y)$ and $\widehat{W}(x, y)$ corresponding to the pristine SAI $S(x, y)$ and the distortion SAI $\widehat{S}(x, y)$ can be obtained, separately. HVS is more sensitive to pixel position (x, y) that produces larger Hessian feature response. Based on this, the maximum value is selected from the Hessian feature map to generate the weight map $w(x, y)$:

$$w(x, y) = max\{W(x, y), \widehat{W}(x, y)\}. \tag{6.9}$$

Therefore, the weighted Gabor feature score on m scale can be calculated by

$$W\_Coh_m = \frac{\sum_{(x,y)\epsilon\Omega} Coh_m(x, y) \cdot w(x, y)}{\sum_{(x,y)\epsilon\Omega} w(x, y)}. \tag{6.10}$$

The final score of distorted SAI can be derived by

$$SSore = (W\_Coh_1)^\alpha \cdot (W\_Coh_2)^\beta \cdot (W\_Coh_3)^\gamma, \tag{6.11}$$

where α, β, and γ are three positive integers, which are utilized to control the relative importance of the three terms. Here they are set to 1, which means they have the same importance.

The weighted consistency score of each SAI is calculated separately. The weighted coherence scores are then averaged as the final quality score of the distorted LF image. The calculation is carried out as follows:

$$LFC\_SAI = \frac{1}{U} \sum_{u=1}^{U} SScore(u), \tag{6.12}$$

where $u = \{1, 2, \ldots, U\}$, and U is the total number of SAIs in an LF image.

Single Scale Gabor Feature Extraction Based on Epi-Polar Images

EPI is a special 2D data, which can be constructed from the 2D slicing of 3D LF images. The moving 2D slice window across all SAIs, which is the same as projecting each scenic spot onto a straight line. Therefore, the oblique line is an important part of EPI, and the slope of the oblique line reflects the depth information of the scene [1, 29].

When distortion happened in LF image, the nature of the oblique line is affected. More importantly, the rapid change of content in EPI image usually corresponds to the target boundary. The method introduced in this part only needs the single-scale Gabor features of EPI, and the slash can be checked with lower computational complexity to calculate the quality change. Specifically, the response in horizontal direction $(H(x, u), \widehat{H}(x, u))$ and in vertical direction $(V(x, u), \widehat{V}(x, u))$ are obtained by using the reference EPI $E(x, u)$ and distortion EPI $\widehat{E}(x, u)$. The value r_m of logarithmic Gabor filter is set to 2/9, and the corresponding Gabor features can be generated by using these responses.

$$F(x, u) = (H^2(x, u) + V^2(x, u))^{1/2}, \tag{6.13}$$

$$\widehat{F}(x, u) = (\widehat{H}^2(x, u) + \widehat{V}^2(x, u))^{1/2}, \tag{6.14}$$

where $F(x, u)$ is Gabor feature of reference EPIs, $\widehat{F}(x, u)$ is Gabor feature of distorted EPIs.

Then the Gabor characteristic coherence $Coh_{EPI}(x, u)$ between the reference EPI and the corrupted EPI is calculated by the following equation:

$$Coh_{EPI}(x, u) = \frac{2F(x, u)\widehat{F}(x, u) + \lambda_E}{F^2(x, u) + \widehat{F}^2(x, u) + \lambda_E}. \tag{6.15}$$

In order to avoid potential numerical instability, a positive constant λ_E is used. The distortion EPI score can be calculated as follows:

$$EScore = \frac{1}{X \times U}\left(\sum_{x=1}^{X}\sum_{u=1}^{U} Coh_{EPI}(x, u)\right), \tag{6.16}$$

where X refers to the width of an SAI or EPI. After considering all the EPIs, the final score can be obtained by

$$LFC\_EPI = \frac{\sum_{y=1}^{Y}(EScore(y) - \bar{E})^2}{Y - 1}, \tag{6.17}$$

where $y = \{1, 2, 3, \ldots, Y\}$. Y is the height of an SAI and is same as the total number of EPI in an LF diagram. $\bar{E}$ is the average value of all $EScore(y)$.

Finally, after acquiring the SAI and EPI of the pristine image and the corresponding distorted LF image, the LGF-LFC model can be obtained according to Eq. (8.12) and Eq. (6.17).

$$LGF - LFC = (LFC_SAI)^{\rho}(LFC_E PI)^{1-\rho}, \tag{6.18}$$

where ρ is employed to balance the importance of the LFC_SAI and LFC_EPI.

6.2.2 RR QA of LF Images

The LF imaging has been considered as the next generation imaging technology that offers the possibility of providing novel services, containing six degree-of-freedom videos. This technique requires the development of new compression systems and ad-hoc perceptual quality evaluation methods. Among three different image QA categories, the FR metric is rarely applicable in an image communication environment. In addition, its applicability is further confined in LF imaging technology due to the size of the reference LF image. In RR methods, only partial information is required, which is suitable for QA of LF images.

Evaluating Quality of LF Images with Selected Feature Information

This part will introduce a RR LF image QA metric, which is called LF image QA metric (LF-IQM). This method firstly estimates the pristine and corrupted depth maps from the pristine and corrupted LF images. Then the perceptual quality of LF images is evaluated utilizing the distortion on the depth map. It is essential to point out that depth information is an important feature of many LF applications, such as refocused view synthesis and 3D visualization. Since even minor errors in depth can lead to significant differences in rendering views, this method uses depth mapping to predict the overall quality of LF images.

Proposed RR QA Framework

A. *Background*

Depth Map as a Reduced Information of LF Images In order to study the perceptual QA method of 2D/3D images, different image features such as natural scene statistics (NSS) [30], visual saliency map [31], depth/disparity map [32] are developed. To estimate the LF images' perceptual quality, the depth map information is used as the reduction information feature of LF content. With more views of a scene recorded by an LF camera, it is possible to better estimate the depth map. This choice is made for the following causes. (1) Compared to 2D or 3D images, LF content provides many view point images, which has the ability to employ the features of each image results in a greater amount of information. It is important to recognize that dimensional reduction is part of the process of extracting a grayscale depth map from a color image. The size of the predicted depth map is 576 KB, which is obviously below the size of the original LF image 46656 KB. Obviously, the depth map is much smaller than a single view point image of the LF content. (2) By choosing different view points in LF images, many depth maps can be obtained, however, only one depth map is sufficient to estimate the quality. (3) The pristine depth map can be adopted for many applications such as refocused view synthesis, 3D visualization, and so on. It can also be utilized to reconstruct the LF at the sink or receiver terminal. The accuracy of the most advanced 2D and 3D image/video measurement relies on the accuracy of the feature estimation used. Similarly, the accuracy may also be related to the depth map estimation system in the introduced measurement.

Depth Map Quality and Overall Image Quality of Experience In the past decades, people have made a lot of efforts to develop 3D technology. Perceptual dimensions such as picture quality, depth quality, and visual comfort are considered to be the most important factors contributing to the quality of experience (QoE) provided by stereoscopic systems. Some recent studies show the depth quality is an indispensable part of QoE of stereoscopic 3D images. According to the fact that the depth map quality is highly associated with the overall QoE of 3D image/video, a conclusion can be drawn. The conclusion is that there is a semblable trend in the relationship between LF image depth map quality and QoE of LF image. The designed QA framework of LF images relied on the hypothesis that distortion in the depth map is highly associated with QoE in LF images. That is

$$QoE_{LF} = f(Dist), \tag{6.19}$$

where QoE_{LF} is the predicted LF image's QoE. $Dist$ denotes the measure of the distortion between the depth maps. $f(\cdot)$ indicates the proposed function reflecting the correlation between QoE and $Dist$.

B. *QA Framework*

In this part, we introduce a LF image QA framework named LF_{IQM}. This method is based on the correlation between the depth map quality of a pristine LF image and a distorted image (e.g., distorted by transmission or coding problems).

It can be divided into four steps. Firstly, we can estimate the reference depth map (DM_{ref}) from the reference LF image. Then, we compute the distorted depth map (DM_{dist}) from the distorted LF image. After that, we can compute the level of distortion in depth map as

$$Dist = f\left(DM_{ref}, DM_{dist}\right), \tag{6.20}$$

where $Dist$ measures the distortion on the depth map and $f(\cdot)$ is the function representing the selected FR image quality metric such as SSIM. Finally, a mapping model is employed to predict the perceptual quality of test LF image from $Dist$.

Depth Map Estimation For assessing the designed framework, DM_{ref} and DM_{dis} need to be computed. Various methods for estimating depth maps have been developed. In order to checkout the null hypothesis ($H0$) and the established QA method, three specially introduced depth map prediction models are picked out. They respectively are multi-resolution depth map (MRDM) [33], stereo-like taxonomy depth map (SLTDM) [34], and accurate depth map (ADM) [35].

MRDM uses multiple views of a scenario to predict the depth map. A random function without employing the depth of field divides the conditional joint probability from a pair of sub-aperture views (center view and other views) for the given field depth. Maximum likelihood (ML) is used for estimating the depth of the functional, and a weighted median filter is adopted to refine the predicted depth map.

SLTDM employs the taxonomy of stereo algorithms. A pair of stereo cameras is used to find the distance to a point such as seeking for the disparity between the images obtained from two reflected cameras. By making comparison between every pixel in a sub-aperture image and every pixel in other sub-apertures, the cost volume is computed. After aggregating the costs, disparity is picked out according to the minimum cost per pixel.

ADM proposes stereo matching between sub-aperture images. By using the phase shift theorem in the Fourier domain, the pixel shifts of sub-aperture images are predicted. A cost volume is calculated to assess the matching cost of disparity levels by utilizing sub-aperture images and central view sub-aperture images shifted at different sub-pixel locations. The gradient matching costs are adaptively aggregated. Then, a weighted median filter is used to clear noise out of the cost volume, and multi-label optimization is used to predict disparity in weak texture regions. In the final, iterative polynomial interpolation is implemented to improve the predicted depth map.

Distortion Measure in Depth Maps The distortion measure of $Dist$ on DM_{dist} is measured by adopting DM_{ref}. The target is to make a comparison between the two depth maps, DM_{ref} and DM_{dist}, and to estimate the degree of similarity between them. In the following, DM_{ref} is hypothesized as the reference depth map and DM_{dist} represents distorted depth map, which is corrupted by noise. A primary test shows that SSIM is a related measurement, since structural information plays a vital role in the depth map. SSIM contains three elements, that are luminance, contrast, and structure. In addition, SSIM relies on the hypothesis that the HVS collects structural information from the region of images' text. With regard to 2D images, SSIM is highly correlated with subjective scores compared with other algorithms, like mean square error (MSE) and PSNR. Hence, the distortion of depth maps can be predicted by calculating the SSIM between DM_{ref} and DM_{dist}:

$$Dist = SSIM\left(DM_{ref}, DM_{dist}\right), \tag{6.21}$$

$$Dist = \frac{\left(2\mu_x\mu_y + c1\right)\left(2\sigma_{xy}\right) + c2\right)}{\left(\mu_x^2 + \mu_y^2 + c1\right)\left(\sigma_x^2 + \sigma_y^2 + c2\right)}, \tag{6.22}$$

where $c1$ and $c2$ represent two variables employed to achieve the stabilization of division with weak denominator. μ_x, μ_y and σ_x, σ_y denote the mean and standard deviation, and σ_{xy} indicates the covariance of DM_{ref} and DM_{dist}.

6.2.3 NR LF Image QA Based on Spatial-Angular Measurement

Most methods proposed recently use the pristine LF image information showing good performance, but their application scenarios are confined. In practical applications, it may be more practical to use the NR LF image QA method considering various influential factors. In [13], Shi et al. designed an NR LF image QA method named NR-LFQA. It qualities the quality degradation of LF images by assessing the spatial quality and the angular consistency. In [14], Zhou et al. put forward a new

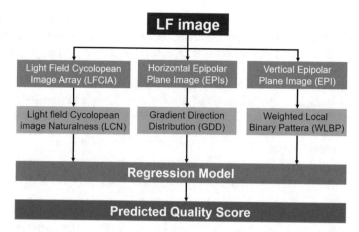

Fig. 6.3 The functional diagram of NR-LFQA method

tensor-oriented NR LF image quality evaluator named Tensor-NLFQ based on tensor theory. In this part, these two image quality schemes will be introduced in detail.

Spatial-Angular Measurement-Based NR LF Image QA

The functional diagram of NR-LFQA method is exhibited in Fig. 6.3. First, the binocular fusion and competition are simulated to produce light-field cyclopean image array (LFCIA), and then its naturalness is analyzed. Besides spatial quality, angle consistency is also significant to LF image perception. Based on EPI containing LF image angle information, the degradation degree of angle consistency on EPI can be measured by extracting features. There are two key points, one is to construct a novel gradient direction distribution that can represent the global distribution to estimate the distribution of EPI gradient direction map. The other one is to describe the correlation between different SAIs with a weighted local binary pattern descriptor. Finally, the extracted features can be utilized to reflect the change of angle consistency.

LF Panoramic Image Array Naturalness

Generally speaking, HVS determines LF image perceptual quality. On this basis, LF image quality can be quantified by simulating the human perception procedure. This method uses the binocular fusion and binocular competition theory to assess the spatial quality of the LF image. Most scenes are observed in the comfort zone where binocular fusion occurs due to the small disparity between the left and right views of the LF image [36]. However, a failure of binocular fusion can lead to binocular competition when there is a significant difference between the perception of the left and right eyes [37].

This method uses human perceptual theory to effectively simulate the visual perceptual process. When an observer sees a stereoscopic image, it is formed in the brain accordingly. The image includes both the information of the left view and the right view, and it considers the characteristics of binocular fusion and binocular competition. On this basis, it can effectively represent the perceptive image quality [37, 38].

The horizontally adjacent SAIs in the LF image are considered as the left and right viewing angles. The left angle of view is $v(s, t)$, which indicates the spatial coordinates of SAI located at (s, t). (u, v) represents the angular coordinates of the LF image. The central eye image array of the LF image can be synthesized according to the following equation:

$$C_{u,v}(s, t) = W_{u,v}(s, t) \times I_{u,v}(s, t) + W_{u+1,v}(s, t) \times I_{u+1,v}\left((s, t) + d_{s,t}\right), \quad (6.23)$$

where $C_{u,v}$ is the sub-ring image located at angular coordinates (u, v). $d_{s,t}$ is the horizontal disparity between $I_{u,v}$ and $I_{u+1,v}$ located at (s, t). The disparity map d is produced by utilizing a simple stereo disparity prediction algorithm, in which SSIM is regarded as the matching standard [38]. The weights $W_{u,v}$ and $W_{u+1,v}$ can be calculated by

$$W_{u,v}(s, t) = \frac{\varepsilon\left[S_{u,v}(s, t)\right] + \alpha_1}{\varepsilon\left[S_{u,v}(s, t)\right] + \varepsilon\left[S_{u+1,v}\left((s, t) + d_{s,t}\right)\right] + \alpha_1}, \quad (6.24)$$

$$W_{u+1,v}(s, t) = \frac{\varepsilon\left[S_{u+1,v}\left((s, t) + d_{s,t}\right)\right] + \alpha_1}{\varepsilon\left[S_{u,v}(s, t)\right] + \varepsilon\left[S_{u,v+1}\left((s, t) + d_{s,t}\right)\right] + \alpha_1}, \quad (6.25)$$

where α_1 is a small value set to ensure stability. $\varepsilon[S_{u,v}(s, t)]$ denotes the spatial activation value in $S_{u,v}(s, t)$. The spatial activation map can be obtained according to the following formula:

$$\varepsilon\left[S_{u,v}(s, t)\right] = \log_2\left[var_{u,v}^2(s, t) + \alpha_2\right], \quad (6.26)$$

where $var_{u,v}(s, t)$ represents the variance of the unit item to prevent non-positive activities. Commonly, it is necessary to ensure the quantities of $S_{u+1,v}(s, t)$, $var_{u+1,v}(s, t)$, and $[S_{u,v}(s, t)]$ on the $I_{u+1,v}(s, t)$.

After deriving LFCIA, local mean subtracted and contrast normalized (MSCN) coefficients can be used to estimate their naturalness. For each sub-cyclopean image, the MSCN coefficients can be computed as follows:

$$\widehat{I}_{u,v}(s, t) = \frac{I_{u,v}(s, t) - \mu_{u,v}(s, t)}{\sigma_{u,v}(s, t) + 1}, \quad (6.27)$$

where Iu,v(s,t) and Iu,v(s,t) denote the MSCN coefficient and sub-cyclopean value of the image located at the spatial position (s,t), separately. $\mu_{u,v}(s, t)$ and $\sigma_{u,v}(s, t)$, respectively, represent the local mean and standard deviation of the local patch centered at (s, t). They can be obtained by

$$\mu_{u,v}(s,t) = \sum_{k=-K}^{K} \sum_{l=-L}^{L} z_{k,l} I_{k,l}(s,t), \tag{6.28}$$

$$\sigma(s,t) = \sqrt{\sum_{k=-K}^{K} \sum_{l=-L}^{L} z_{k,l} \left(I_{k,l}(s,t) - \mu(s,t)\right)^2}, \tag{6.29}$$

where $z = \{z_{k,l} | K = -K, ..., K, L = -L, ..., L\}$ represents a 2D circularly-symmetric Gaussian weighting function. The values of K and L are 3.

In order to estimate the spatial quality of LF images, the naturalness distribution of LFCIA and MSCN coefficients of all images are considered. Then, a zero-mean asymmetric generalized Gaussian distribution model (AGGD) model is used to fit the distribution of MASVN coefficient. The distribution can be produced by

$$f\left(\chi; \alpha, \sigma_l^2, \sigma_r^2\right) = \begin{cases} \dfrac{\alpha}{(\beta_l + \beta_r)\Gamma\left(\frac{1}{\alpha}\right)} \exp(-(\dfrac{-x}{\beta_l})^\alpha)\chi & <0 \\[4mm] \dfrac{\alpha}{(\beta_l + \beta_r)\Gamma\left(\frac{1}{\alpha}\right)} \exp(-(\dfrac{-x}{\beta_r})^\alpha)\chi & \geq 0 \end{cases}, \tag{6.30}$$

where $\beta_l = \sigma_l \sqrt{\dfrac{\Gamma\left(\frac{1}{\alpha}\right)}{\Gamma\left(\frac{3}{\alpha}\right)}}$ and $\beta_r = \sigma_r \sqrt{\dfrac{\Gamma\left(\frac{1}{\alpha}\right)}{\Gamma\left(\frac{3}{\alpha}\right)}}$, in which α is a shape parameter that controls the shape of the statistical distribution. σ_l and σ_r represent scale parameters on the left and right sides, separately. In addition, the above three parameters are used to calculate another feature η, which can be generated by the following equation:

$$\eta = (\beta_r - \beta_l) / \dfrac{\Gamma\left(\frac{2}{\alpha}\right)}{\Gamma\left(\frac{1}{\alpha}\right)}. \tag{6.31}$$

The kurtosis and skewness characteristics are further supplemented. Besides, a down-sampling factor of 2 is used on SAIs, which indicates that the relationship between model estimation and subjective evaluation can be improved [39]. Eventually, LFCIA naturalness F_{LCN} is derived.

Global Direction Distribution

Spatial quality and angular consistency affect the LF image's quality. In general, angular reconstruction operations destroy angle consistency. Feature extraction from EPI can obtain the angle information of LF image, so it is an executable method to measure the deterioration of angle consistency.

Generally, the depth information of the scene can be captured from the slope of the line in EPI. Based on this special property, a lot of LF image processing missions have been done, such as super-resolution and depth map prediction [1, 40]. The feature is also found in [13], in which angular deformation destroys the existing structure and significantly changes the distribution of linear slope in EPI. In other words, the EPI with the unified distortion category has similar distribution, which indicates angular distortion is insensitive to the depth and content of the pristine LF image. Hence, the degradation degree of LF image angle distortion can be measured by the slope of the line in the distortion EPI.

Firstly, the gradient direction map of EPIs is calculated, and next its distribution is analyzed to obtain the gradient direction distribution (GDD) characteristics. Here, the vertical EPI is defined as $E_{u^*,s^*}(v, t)$, and the horizontal EPI is defined as $E_{v^*,s^*}(u, s)$, where u^*, s^* and v^*, t^* denote determined coordinates. The EPI direction distribution can be obtained by computing the EPI gradient map:

$$G_{v^*,s^*} = atan2(-Ey_{u^*,s^*}, Ex_{u^*,s^*}) * \frac{180}{\pi}, \tag{6.32}$$

where

$$Ex_{u^*,s^*} = E_{u^*,s^*} \otimes h_x, \tag{6.33}$$

and

$$Ey_{u^*,s^*} = E_{u^*,s^*} \otimes h_y, \tag{6.34}$$

$$h_x = \begin{bmatrix} -1 & 0 & 1 \\ -2 & 0 & 2 \\ -1 & 0 & 1 \end{bmatrix}, \tag{6.35}$$

$$h_y = \begin{bmatrix} -1 & -2 & -1 \\ 0 & 0 & 0 \\ 1 & 2 & 1 \end{bmatrix}. \tag{6.36}$$

Like the calculation procedure of $G_{u*,s*}$, $G_{v*,t*}$ can be obtained for the gradient pattern of horizontal projection. Then, the gradient pattern is quantified into 360 panels, that is, from $-180°$ to $179°$. Different types of distortion have different effects on EPIs. To be specifical, the nearest neighbor (NN) and LINEAR interpolation distortion lead EPI to present a ladder shape, and its direction is primarily concerned at $-180°$ and $0°$. The optical flow estimation (OPT) and quantitative depth map (DQ) distortions have high peaks at $-150°$ and $30°$. On the whole, the GDD can effectively measure angle consistency degradation. In the final, the mean, entropy, skewness, and kurtosis of G_{u^*,s^*} and G_{v^*,t^*} are calculated separately. Then averaging the above values yields the characteristic F_{GDD}.

Weighted Local Binary Pattern

The relationship between SAIs can be reflected by the correlation between pixel rows from different SAIs. Based on this property, the change of angle consistency can be measured by analyzing the relative relationship of pixels in EPI. In addition, local angle consistency information can be measured by pixel relations of different distances. Therefore, a weighted local binary pattern (WLBP) is described to capture the relationship between different SAIs. LBP is very useful for extracting the information of local distribution, and has good performance in evaluating the QA task of 2D image [41–46]. The local rotation-invariant uniform LBP operator $L_{u^*,s^*}^{R,P}$ of vertical EPI is calculated as

$$
L_{u^*,s^*}^{R,P}(E_{u^*,s^*}^c) =
\begin{cases}
\displaystyle\sum_{p=0}^{p-1} \theta(E_{u^*,s^*}^p - E_{u^*,s^*}^c) & \psi(\hat{L}_{u^*,s^*}^{R,P}) \le 2 \\[2ex]
P+1 & otherwise
\end{cases},
\tag{6.37}
$$

where R represents the value of radius, and P is the sum of adjacent points. E_{u^*,s^*}^c is a central pixel corresponding to the position (x_c, y_c) in EPIs, and E_{u^*,s^*}^p is the adjacent pixel around E_{u^*,s^*}^c.

$$
x_p = x_c + Rcos(2\pi\frac{p}{P}),
\tag{6.38}
$$

and

$$
y_p = y_c + Rsin(2\pi\frac{p}{P}),
\tag{6.39}
$$

where p is the sum of adjacent pixels sampled from E_{u^*,s^*}^c to E_{u^*,s^*}^p distance R, $p \in \{1, 2, ...\}$. At this time, $\theta(z)$ is a step function that can be expressed by

$$
\theta(z) =
\begin{cases}
1 & z \ge T \\
0 & otherwise
\end{cases},
\tag{6.40}
$$

where T denotes the threshold. ψ indicates the sum of bitwise transformations:

$$
\begin{aligned}
\psi() =& ||\theta(E_{u^*,s^*}^{P-1} - E_{u^*,s^*}^c) - \theta(E_{u^*,s^*}^0 - E_{u^*,s^*}^c)|| \\
&+ \sum_{p=0}^{p-1} ||\theta(E_{u^*,s^*}^p - E_{u^*,s^*}^c) - \theta(E_{u^*,s^*}^p - E_{u^*,s^*}^c)||.
\end{aligned}
\tag{6.41}
$$

where $\hat{L}_{u^*,s^*}^{R,P}$ is rotation-invariant operator:

$$
\hat{L}_{u^*,s^*}^{R,P}(E_{u^*,s^*}^c) = min\{ROR(\sum_{p=0}^{P-1} \theta(E_{u^*,s^*}^p - E_{u^*,s^*}^c)2^P, k)\},
\tag{6.42}
$$

where $ROR(\beta, k)$ represents a circular bit-wise right shift operator, which shifts the tuple β by k position, $k \in \{0, 1, 2..., P-1\}$. After that, $L_{u^*,s^*}^{R,P}(E_{u^*,s^*}^c)$ of length $P + 2$ can be obtained.

For LF images, there are a lot of EPIs in vertical and horizontal directions. If each EPI-derived LBP feature is derived, this can lead to dimension disaster. Reducing feature dimension is always necessary. Considering that the LBP features of some EPIs with less information are mainly focused on the statistical directions, entropy weighting is used here. That is, these EPIs include less angle consistency information, and their entropy value is extremely close to zero. So, the vertical EPI WLBP can be obtained by

$$
Lver_{R,P} = \frac{\sum\limits_{u=1}^{U} \sum\limits_{s=1}^{S} \omega_{u,s}^{R,P} . * L_{u,s}^{R,P}}{\sum\limits_{u=1}^{U} \sum\limits_{s=1}^{S} \omega_{u,s}^{R,P}}. \tag{6.43}
$$

The entropy of $L_{u,s}^{R,P}$ is regarded as the weight $\omega_{u,s}^{R,P}$. Using the same operation, the WLBP feature $Lhor_{R,P}$ of EPI E_{v^*,t^*} is obtained.

In the implementation, $R = 1, 2, 3$, $P = 3 \times R$, $T = \frac{R}{2}$. Finally, all features are combined to obtain FWLBP as

$$
FWLBP = \{Lver_{R,P}, Lhor_{R,P}\}. \tag{6.44}
$$

6.2.4   Tensor Oriented NR LF Image QA

Due to the high-dimensional characteristics of the LF image, LF image QA has become a multi-dimensional problem. LF image quality is influenced by the spatial-angle resolution, spatial quality, and angular consistency. On the basis of tensor theory, a new tensor-oriented image QA device without reference information is proposed. We consider the influence of brightness and chroma, and the effect of angular consistency in different directions on the LF image quality using the proposed device.

The details of the framework of the tensor-nonlinear finite difference algorithm are as follows. First, the SAI color space in RGB is converted to CIELAB color space. Second, the Tucker decomposition is utilized to produce the main elements of the view stack in different directions. Third, principal component spatial characteristics (PCSC) features, tensor angular variation index (TAVI) metric space quality degradation, and angle consistency are all extracted, respectively. Finally, the regression model is employed to estimate the sensing LF image quality.

Color Space Conversion

Color information is an important and dense natural visual cue, without which the human brain would not be able to achieve visual perception. In order to know what effect the brightness and chroma have on the image quality, a lot of research work has been done before [47–49]. These works have proved that color information has a definite role in determining image quality. On this basis, using color spatial information to assess the spatial quality of the LF image is reasonable. The color difference of different SAI may destroy the angular consistency of LF image, and color information can estimate the deterioration of the LF image angle consistency [14].

In order to better approach the color perception of the HVS, the color SAI of each LF image is converted to the CIELAB-related color space, which is more in line with human perception [50].

View the Stack

The light in nature is continuous. In practical applications, according to the hypothesis of the angular resolution $(S \times T)$ of the LF image, each SAI has four-direction angular consistency, namely $0°, 45°, 90°$, and $135°$. Then, SAI is stacked along these four directions to generate the following view stack:

$$C_{n,s}^{0°} = \{C_n(s, 1, :, :), C_n(s, 2, :, :), \ldots, C_n(s, T, :, :)\}, \quad (6.45)$$

$$C_{n,t}^{90°} = \{C_n(1, t, :, :), C_n(2, t, :, :), \ldots, C_n(S, t, :, :)\}, \quad (6.46)$$

$$\begin{aligned} C_{n,s+t-1}^{45°} = &\{C_n(s, t, :, :), C_n(s+1, t+1, :, :), \ldots, \\ &C_n(s + \min\{S-s, T-t\}, t + \{\min\{S-s, T-t\}, :, :)\}, \end{aligned} \quad (6.47)$$

$$\begin{aligned} C_{n,s+t-1}^{45°} = &\{C_n(s, t, :, :), C_n(s+1, t-1, :, :), \ldots, \\ &C_n(s + \min\{S-s, T-t\}, t - \{\min\{S-s, T-t\}, :, :)\}, \end{aligned} \quad (6.48)$$

where $s = \{1, 2, \ldots, S\}$ and $t = \{1, 2, \ldots, T\}$ represent angular coordinates. $n = \{1, 2, 3\}$ represents the luminance and two chroma channels. For the LF image with angle resolution of $S \times T$, the view stack can be extracted in four directions. The first two of these four directions are a horizontal stack with S angular resolution T and T vertical stacks with resolution S. The latter two are $(S + T - 1)$ left and right diagonal stacks with angular resolution raised from 1 to $\min\{S, T\}$, respectively.

Tucker Decomposition

The different images in the view stack have high structural similarity (SSIM), which indicates that there is a lot of information redundancy in the angle dimension. In order to solve this issue, tensor decomposition is used to clear redundant information out of the angle dimension [51]. The Tucker decomposition factorizes a tensor into a core tensor multiplied by a matrix on each dimension. That is to say, the three dimension LF signal is decomposed into the core tensor and the principal elements of spatial dimension and angular dimension. For the horizontal view stack $C_n^{0°}$, it can be defined as:

$$C_n^{0°} \approx CT \times_1 U_1 \times_2 U_2 \times_3 U_3, \quad (6.49)$$

where $CT \in J^{J_1 \times J_2 \times J_3}$ represents the core tensor, indicating the level of interaction between different elements. When $i = 1, 2, U_i \in J^{k_i \times J_i}$ represent the factor matrices in the spatial dimension. When $i = 3$, $U_i \in J^{k_i \times J_i}$ represents the angular dimension factor matrix.

For $C_n^{0°}$, the angle decomposition component can be obtained by multiplying the kernel tensor with each mode of the factor matrices U_1 and U_2 along the spatial dimension.

$$\mathbf{A}_n^{0°} = CT \times_1 U_1 \times_2 U_2, \tag{6.50}$$

where $C_n^{0°} \approx \mathbf{A}_n^{0°} \times_3 U_3$. To reconstruct spatial information and get the decomposition vector of angular dimension, U_3 must be removed. In a similar process, the corner decomposition components of the view stack in other directions can be obtained. Besides, the angular decoupling position components of view stack in other directions can be obtained using same methods, such as $\mathbf{A}_n^{45°}$, $\mathbf{A}_n^{90°}$, $\mathbf{A}_n^{135°}$.

In addition, the factor matrix here can be seen as a principal component representing the stack of the decomposed 3D tensors on the angular dimension [51]. The first principal component is the highest energy component, which includes basic texture information.

Feature Extraction and Quality Regression

It can be seen from the previous part that the first principal component includes the most basic information of each view stack. Based on this, the features extracted from principal components can be used to estimate the degradation degree of LF image spatial quality. To be specific, PCSC is extracted from the first principal component, which uses the global naturalness and local frequency distribution characteristics to assess the distortion of spatial quality. Besides spatial quality, angle consistency also influences LF image quality. The TAVI captures angle consistency distortion by calculating the SSIM between the first principal component in the view stack and each view.

Principal Component Spatial Characteristics In order to effectively measure the naturalness of the image, the local MSCN coefficient can be modeled. Generally speaking, local MSCN coefficients can be modeled to effectively measure the naturalness of images, and the calculation method can refer to Eqs. (6.27)–(6.29). Subsequently, the distribution of MSCN coefficients is quantified by using the zero-mean AGGD model according to Eq. (6.30). The another feature η is calculated by Eq. (6.31).

After combining the above conditions, the multivariate generalized Gaussian distribution (MGGD) [53, 54] is used to fit the joint distribution. It can be expressed as follows:

$$f(\mathbf{x} \mid \mathbf{M}, \gamma, \varphi) = \frac{1}{|\mathbf{M}|^{\frac{1}{2}}} g_{\gamma,\varphi} \left(\mathbf{x}^T \mathbf{M}^{-1} \mathbf{x} \right), \tag{6.51}$$

where $x \in J^N$ and $\mathbf{M}$ indicate an $N \times N$ symmetric scattering matrix. γ and φ denote scale and shape parameters, separately. $g_{\gamma,\varphi} ()$ represents the density generator:

$$g_{\gamma,\varphi}(\chi) = \frac{\varphi\Gamma\left(\frac{N}{2}\right)}{\left(2^{\frac{1}{\varphi}}\pi\gamma\right)^{\frac{N}{2}}\Gamma\left(\frac{N}{2\varphi}\right)}e^{-\frac{1}{2}\left(\frac{\chi}{\gamma}\right)^{\varphi}},\tag{6.52}$$

where $x \in J^+$ and Γ are dual gamma functions. The parameters of MGGD model are estimated by [52]. The local distribution of principal components changes due to the degradation of LF image space quality. The entropy E of DCT coefficients without DC component is used to extract the local features of each color channel principal component. The calculation process of E is as follows:

$$E = -\sum_{l}^{L}\sum_{h}^{H}(p_{lh}log(p_{lh})),\tag{6.53}$$

where L indicates the width of the DCT block, H represents the height of the DCT block. p_lh represents the DCT coefficients located in (l, h). Entropy is calculated from three aspects, that is the overall DCT block, three frequency bands and three directions. So, the fitting parameters of AGGD and MGD, and three average entropy features are fused to obtain $\mathbf{f}_{PCSC}$. In addition, the feature dimension of PCSC is set to 57, and the entropy feature includes 15 dimensions. The characteristic dimensions of AGGD parameters and MGGD parameters based on MSCN are 36 and 6, respectively. Apart from the brightness information, the distribution of chromaticity space is also calculated.

Tensor Angle Variation Index (TAVI) In addition to spatial quality, there is also angle consistency that affects LF image quality. Angle reconstruction operations (such as interpolation) usually break the angle consistency. Here, the tensor angle change index is used to estimate the degradation degree of angle consistency. Firstly, the SSIM between each view and its corresponding first principal component in the view stack is calculated as

$$ss_n^d(i) = F\left(C_n^d(i), M_n^d\right).\tag{6.54}$$

Among them, C_n^d represents the input view stack. M_n^d indicates the corresponding first principal component. i represents the angular coordinate of C, $n \in \{1, 2, 3\}$ and $d \in \{0°, 45°, 90°, 135°\}$. F represents a function to compute the SSIM between $C_n^d(i)$ and M_n^d. SSIM distribution has good ability to measure various types and degrees of distortion.

A second-order polynomial is then used to fit the SSIM distribution, as shown below

$$ss_n^d(i) = f_1i^2 + f_2i + f_3,\tag{6.55}$$

where i indicates the angular coordinate. f_1, f_2, and f_3 are fitting parameters for simulating consistent changes in angle. Several complementary features including contrast, angular second moment, entropy, and inverse different moments are extracted [55] to reflect the degradation information. The size of the feature TAVI is set to 30 by connecting the fitting parameters (f_1, f_2, f_3) and complementary features. After combining the above conditions, the final features are modeled in the following ways:

$$\mathbf{f}_{final} = w_1 \mathbf{f}_{0°} + w_2 \mathbf{f}_{45°} + w_3 \mathbf{f}_{90°} + w_4 \mathbf{f}_{135°}, \tag{6.56}$$

where w_i $i \in \{1, 2, 3, 4\}$ represents the corresponding weights in the four directions. Let $w_1 = w_2 = w_3 = w_4 = \frac{1}{4}$. The final result is trained with the average features of each stack in the uniform direction, and next all directions are weighted. In the final, a regression model is trained to map the final feature vector to the quality score. Support vector regression (SVR) is employed to achieve this. To be specific, the LIBSVM package is adopted to implement a SVR machine with a radial basis function kernel.

6.3   Comparison and Analysis of Algorithm Performance

In this section, we introduce an image database for LF image QA and some modern reference-free and reference-based image QA methods. We concentrate on comparing and measuring the performance of the QA models introduced in this chapter with these methods. The analysis results show that the performance of these models in this chapter performs quite well.

6.3.1   Elaborated SMART Database

The database includes 16 pristine LF images obtained by the Lytro Illum. It contains 256 contaminated LF images which are generated by introducing four different categories of distortion with four distortion levels to each pristine LF image. The distortion types consist of HEVC Intra, JPEG, JPEG2000 and system-sparse set and disparity coding (SSDC). Similar to MPI-LFA, the PC approach is utilized to obtain the subjective scores and offer the Bradley-Terry scores.

6.3.2   Performance Comparison and Analysis

In order to reflect the models introduced in this chapter validity and superiority, we compare the introduced models (LGF-LFC [15], LF-IQM [12], NR-LFQA [13], and Tensor-NLFQ [14]) with the 22 classical image QA models. They can be divided into three categories in Table 6.1. All the 26 models include 17 full-reference image QA models and 8 free reference image QA models. Only the introduced LF-IQM utilizes partial information from original reference.

Table 6.1 The introduced algorithms with modern developed QA models for LF images

Category	Abbreviation	Full Name	Refs.
FR	PSNR	Peak signal-to-noise ratio	[9]
FR	IFC	Information fidelity criterion	[56]
FR	NQM	Noise quality measure	[57]
FR	VSNR	Visual signal-to-noise ratio	[21]
FR	HDR-VDP2	Visual difference predictor for high dynamic range images	[58]
FR	Chen et al	–	[38]
FR	SSIM	Structural similarity	[59]
FR	MS-SSIM	Multi-scale SSIM	[60]
FR	VIF	Visual information fidelity	[61]
FR	IW-SSIM	Information content weighting SSIM	[20]
FR	FSIM	Feature similarity	[62]
FR	LGF-LFC	Log-Gabor feature-based light-field coherence	[15]
FR	MP-PSNR Full	Morphological pyramid PSNR Full	[63]
FR	MP-PSNR Reduc	Morphological wavelet peak signal-to-noise ratio Reduc	[64]
FR	MW-PSNR Full	Morphological wavelet peak signal-to-noise ratio Full	[63]
FR	MW-PSNR Reduc	Morphological wavelet peak signal-to-noise ratio Reduc	[63]
FR	3DSWIM	3D synthesized view image quality metric	[65]
RR	LF-IQM	Light-field image quality assessment metric	[12]
NR	BRISQUE	Blind/referenceless image spatial quality evaluator	[39]
NR	FRIQUEE	Feature maps-based referenceless image quality evaluation engine	[47]
NR	NIQE	Natural image quality evaluator	[66]
NR	SINQ	S3D integrated quality	[36]
NR	BSVQE	Binocular vision theory	[67]
NR	BELIF	Blind quality evaluator of light-field image	[68]
NR	NR-LFQA	No-reference light-field image quality assessment	[13]
NR	Tensor-NLFQ	Tensor oriented no-reference light-field image quality evaluator	[14]

To assess these models' performance on the SMART database described above, we select 4 evaluation criteria, SRCC, PLCC, RMSE, and OR. The SRCC reflects the monotonicity, PLCC reflects the linear relationship. The RMSE and OR, respectively, denote the prediction accuracy and consistency. The higher the SRCC and PLCC values, the better the model performance is. On the contrary, the lower values of RMSE and OR indicate the model has better performance. Before computing the values of SRCC, PLCC, RMSE, and OR, a nonlinear function is applied as below

$$f_1 = \alpha_1 \{\frac{1}{2} - \frac{1}{1 + \exp[\alpha_2(p - \alpha_3)]} + \alpha_4 p + \alpha_5\}, \qquad (6.57)$$

where p is the predicted score. The parameter α_j, $j \in \{1, 2, 3, 4, 5\}$ are optimized to minimize the number of squared errors between p and the subjective score. After mapping, we split each image database into two parts, 80% images for training, the remaining 20% for testing. Cross validation with 1000 iterations is conducted on the SMART database.

From the experiment, we obtain the final performance of the introduced models on the SMART database by using four quality performance metrics including SRCC, PLCC, RMSE, and OR. We find the best-performing model in each category. By analyzing the superiority of these models, we are able to derive some important conclusions as follows.

(1) For FR image QA metrics, we employ four widely employed evaluation criterion to assess the performance of these methods. By analyzing the results of the experiment, we observe that the typical MP-PSNR Full is the best FR image QA model among all the FR QA models, which has the largest SRCC, PLCC, and lowest values of RMSE. The performance of the introduced LGF-LFC model is in second place. In addition, the semi-reference algorithm LF-IQM proposed also achieves good performance.

(2) Across four NR image QA metrics, the introduced NR-LFQA has the best performance on all SRCC, PLCC, RMSE and the introduced Tensor-NLFQ is ranked second place. The NR image QA model has more obvious performance disadvantages than FR and RR image QA models, since it doesn't utilize any reference image information. But there are still exceptions. The SRCC, PLCC, RMSE value of the introduced NR image QA model named NR-LFQA and Tensor-NLFQ is significantly superior than MP-PSNR Full.

In these algorithms, all the FR QA models are established by the process of equations modeling, whereas most of the free reference models are obtained by supervised learning methods. Furthermore, we use the uniformed percentages to train these learning-based models, same as the introduced models on the SMART database. Based on the procedure above mentioned, we derive accurate statistics. All the results indicate the proposed models have excellent ability in accuracy, monotonicity, and linear correlation.

6.4 Conclusion

To better realize the guidance of the acquisition, processing, and application of immersive media, LF image QA is becoming more and more significant. This chapter researches the QA approaches for LF images from three perspectives: FR, RR, and NR QA methods.

First, considering that Gabor feature can well represent the perception of HVS, an FR LF image QA method based on multi-scale and single-scale Gabor feature extraction is introduced. Second, we describe a RR LF image QA based on the relationship between the quality of LF image depth map and the overall quality. Finally, considering the spatial quality and angle consistency quality, two NR LF image QA methods are presented. One of them uses image naturalness to predict degradation of spatial-dimensional quality and utilizes the slope of a line contained in the EPI to reflect angular information. The other one uses global inherent and local frequency characteristics to measure the spatial dimension quality of LF image, while the angle consistency quality is measured by analyzing the structural similarity distribution among the views of the first principal component in the view stack. Extensive results of comparison experiments demonstrate that the RR image QA method based on spatial-angular measurement and tensor outperforms the state-of-the-art LF image QA approaches. In the future work, it is believed that the LF image QA methods with better performance can come up with through the joint effort of researchers.

References

1. Wu G, Masia B, Jarabo A et al (2017) Light field image processing: an overview. IEEE J Sel Top Signal Process 11(7):926–954
2. Yu J (2017) A light-field journey to virtual reality. IEEE MultiMedia 24(2):104–112
3. Ni Y, Chen J, Chau L (2018) Reflection removal on single light field capture using focus manipulation. IEEE Trans Comput Imaging 4(4):562–572
4. Zhu K, Xue Y, Fu Q et al (2019) Hyperspectral light field stereo matching. IEEE Trans Pattern Anal Mach Intell 41(5):1131–1143
5. Wang Y, Yang J, Guo Y et al (2019) Selective light field refocusing for camera arrays using bokeh rendering and superresolution. IEEE Signal Process Lett 26(1):204–208
6. Chen J, Hou J, Ni Y et al (2018) Accurate light field depth estimation with superpixel regularization over partially occluded regions. IEEE Trans Image Process 27(10):4889–4900
7. Levoy M (2016) Light fields and computational imaging. Computer 39(8):46–55
8. Ihrke I, Restrepo J, Mignard-Debise L (2016) Principles of light field imaging: briefly revisiting 25 years of research. IEEE Signal Process Mag 33(5):59–69
9. Yang J, Hou C, Zhou Y et al (2009) Objective quality assessment method of stereo images. In: Paper presented at the 2009 3DTV conference: the true vision-capture, transmission and display of 3D video, 1–4 May 2009
10. Chen M, Cormack L, Bovik A (2013) No-reference quality assessment of natural stereopairs. IEEE Trans Image Process 22(9):3379–3391
11. Gu K, Jakhetiya V, Qiao J et al (2018) Model based referenceless quality metric of 3D synthesized images using local image description. IEEE Trans Image Process 27(1):394–405

12. Paudyal P, Battisti F, Carli M (2019) Reduced reference quality assessment of light field images. IEEE Trans Broadcast 65(1):152–165
13. Shi L, Zhou W, Chen Z et al (2020) No-reference light field image quality assessment based on spatial-angular measurement. IEEE Trans Circuits Syst Video Technol 30(11):4114–4128
14. Zhou W, Shi L, Chen Z et al (2020) Tensor oriented no-reference light field image quality assessment. IEEE Trans Image Process 29:4070–4084
15. Tian Y, Zeng H, Hou J (2020) Light field image quality assessment via the light field coherence. IEEE Trans Image Process 29:7945–7956
16. Daugman JG (1985) Uncertainty relation for resolution in space, spatial frequency, and orientation optimized by two-dimensional visual cortical filters. J Opt Soc Am A 2(7):1160–1169
17. Daugman JG (1980) Two-dimensional spectral analysis of cortical receptive field profiles. Vis Res 20(10):847–856
18. Simoncelli EP, Heeger DJ (1998) A model of neuronal responses in visual area MT. Vis Res 38(5):743–761
19. Hegde J, Van Essen DC (2000) Selectivity for complex shapes in primate visual area V2. J Neurosc 20(5):RC61-RC61
20. Wang Z, Li Q (2010) Information content weighting for perceptual image quality assessment. IEEE Trans Image Process 20(5):1185–1198
21. Chandler DM, Hemami SS (2007) VSNR: a wavelet-based visual signal-to-noise ratio for natural images. IEEE Trans Image Process 16(9):2284–2298
22. Gao X, Lu W, Tao D et al (2009) Image quality assessment based on multiscale geometric analysis. IEEE Trans Image Process 18(7):1409–1423
23. Field DJ (1987) Relations between the statistics of natural images and the response properties of cortical cells. J Opt Soc Am A 4(12):2379–2394
24. Fischer S, Cristobal G, Redondo R (2006) Sparse overcomplete Gabor wavelet representation based on local competitions. IEEE Trans Image Process 15(2):265–272
25. Da Costa ALNT, Do MN (2014) A retina-based perceptually lossless limit and a Gaussian foveation scheme with loss control. IEEE J Sel Top Signal Process 8(3):438–453
26. Fang Y, Lin W, Lee BS et al (2011) Bottom-up saliency detection model based on human visual sensitivity and amplitude spectrum. IEEE Trans Multimedia 14(1):187–198
27. Liu J, White JM, Summers RM (2010) Automated detection of blob structures by Hessian analysis and object scale. In: Paper presented at the 2010 IEEE international conference on image processing, pp 841–844, Sept 2010
28. Hassaballah M, Abdelmgeid AA, Alshazly HA (2016) Image features detection, description and matching. In: Image Feature Detectors and Descriptors, pp 11–45
29. Neri A, Carli M, Battisti F (2018) A maximum likelihood approach for depth field estimation based on epipolar plane images. IEEE Trans Image Process 28(2):827–840
30. Saad MA, Bovik AC, Charrier C (2012) Blind image quality assessment: a natural scene statistics approach in the DCT domain. IEEE Trans Image Process 21(8):3339–3352
31. Zhang L, Shen Y, Li H (2014) VSI: a visual saliency-induced index for perceptual image quality assessment. IEEE Trans Image Process 23(10):4270–4281
32. Benoit A, Le Callet P, Campisi P et al (2009) Quality assessment of stereoscopic images. EURASIP J Image Video Process 2008:1–13
33. Neri A, Carli M, Battisti F (2015) A multi-resolution approach to depth field estimation in dense image arrays. In: Paper presented at the 2015 IEEE international conference on image processing, pp 3358–3362, Sept 2015
34. Calderon FC, Parra CA, Nino CL (2014) Depth map estimation in light fields using an stereo-like taxonomy. In: Paper presented at the 2014 XIX symposium on image, signal processing and artificial vision, 1–5 Sept 2014
35. Jeon HG, Park J, Choe G et al (2015) Accurate depth map estimation from a lenslet light field camera. In: Proceedings of the IEEE conference on computer vision and pattern recognition, pp 1547–1555
36. Liu L, Liu B, Su CC et al (2017) Binocular spatial activity and reverse saliency driven no-reference stereopair quality assessment. Signal Process Image Commun 58:287–299

37. Steinman BA, Garzia RP (2000) Foundations of binocular vision: a clinical perspective. McGraw-Hill Education/Medical
38. Chen MJ, Su CC, Kwon DK (2013) Full-reference quality assessment of stereopairs accounting for rivalry. Signal Process Image Commun 28(9):1143–1155
39. Mittal A, Moorthy AK, Bovik AC (2012) No-reference image quality assessment in the spatial domain. IEEE Trans Image Process 21(12):4695–4708
40. Wu G, Zhao M, Wang L et al (2017) Light field reconstruction using deep convolutional network on EPI. In: Proceedings of the IEEE conference on computer vision and pattern recognition, pp 6319–6327
41. Ojala T, Pietikainen M, Maenpaa T (2002) Multiresolution gray-scale and rotation invariant texture classification with local binary patterns. IEEE Trans Pattern Anal Mach Intell 24(7):971–987
42. Satpathy A, Jiang X, Eng HL (2014) LBP-based edge-texture features for object recognition. IEEE Trans Image Process 23(5):1953–1964
43. Nanni L, Lumini A, Brahnam S (2012) Survey on LBP based texture descriptors for image classification. Expert Syst Appl 39(3):3634–3641
44. Freitas PG, Akamine WY, Farias MC (2016) Blind image quality assessment using multiscale local binary patterns. J Imaging Sci Technol 60(6):60405-1
45. Zhang M, Muramatsu C, Zhou X et al (2014) Blind image quality assessment using the joint statistics of generalized local binary pattern. IEEE Signal Process Lett 22(2):207–210
46. Zhang M, Xie J, Zhou X et al (2013) No reference image quality assessment based on local binary pattern statistics. In: Paper presented at the 2013 visual communications and image processing, 1–6 Nov 2013
47. Deepti G, Bovik AC (2017) Perceptual quality prediction on authentically distorted images using a bag of features approach. J Vis 17(1):32–32
48. Lee D, Plataniotis KN (2015) Towards a full reference quality assessment for color images using directional statistics. IEEE Trans Image Process 24(11):3950–3965
49. Lee D, Plataniotis KN (2016) Toward a no-reference image quality assessment using statistics of perceptual color descriptors. IEEE Trans Image Process 25(8):3875–3889
50. Rajashekar U, Wang Z, Simoncelli EP (2010) Perceptual quality assessment of color images using adaptive signal representation. In: Paper presented at the international society for optics and photonics
51. Kolda TG, Bader BW (2009) Tensor decompositions and applications. Soc Ind Appl Math 51(3):455–500
52. Pascal F, Bombrun L, Tourneret JY et al (2013) Parameter estimation for multivariate generalized Gaussian distributions. IEEE Trans Signal Process 61(23):5960–5971
53. Su CC, Cormack LK, Bovik AC (2014) Bivariate statistical modeling of color and range in natural scenes. In: Paper presented at the international society for optics and photonics, 9014:90141G, Feb 2014
54. Sinno Z, Caramanis C, Bovik AC (2018) Towards a closed form second-order natural scene statistics model. IEEE Trans Image Process 27(7):3194–3209
55. Kim HG, Chung YE, Lee YH et al (2015) Quantitative analysis of the effect of iterative reconstruction using a phantom: determining the appropriate blending percentage. Yonsei Med J 56(1):253–261
56. Sheikh HR, Bovik AC, De Veciana G (2005) An information fidelity criterion for image quality assessment using natural scene statistics. IEEE Trans Image Process 14(12):2117–2128
57. Damera-Venkata N, Kite TD, Geisler WS et al (2000) Image quality assessment based on a degradation model. IEEE Trans Image Process 9(4):636–650
58. Mantiuk R, Kim KJ, Rempel AG et al (2011) HDR-VDP-2: a calibrated visual metric for visibility and quality predictions in all luminance conditions. ACM Trans Graph 30(4):1–14
59. Wang Z, Bovik AC, Sheikh HR et al (2004) Image quality assessment: from error visibility to structural similarity. IEEE Trans Image Process 13(4):600–612
60. Wang Z, Simoncelli EP, Bovik AC (2003) Multiscale structural similarity for image quality assessment. In: Paper presented at the thrity-seventh asilomar conference on signals, systems and computers, vol 2, pp 1398–1402

61. Sheikh HR, Bovik AC (2006) Image information and visual quality. IEEE Trans Image Process 15(2):430–444
62. Zhang L, Zhang L, Mou X et al (2011) FSIM: a feature similarity index for image quality assessment. IEEE Trans Image Process 20(8):2378–2386
63. Sandic-Stankovica D, Kukolj D, Calletc PL (2015) DIBR synthesized image quality assessment based on morphological pyramids. In: Paper presented at the 2015 seventh international workshop on quality of multimedia experience, 1–6 May 2015
64. Sandic-Stankovic D, Kukolj D, Le Callet P (2016) Multi-scale synthesized view assessment based on morphological pyramids. J Electr Eng 67(1):3
65. Battisti F, Bosc E, Carli M et al (2015) Objective image quality assessment of 3D synthesized views. Signal Process Image Commun 30:78–88
66. Mittal A, Soundararajan R, Bovik AC (2012) Making a "completely blind" image quality analyzer. IEEE Signal Process Lett 20(3):209–212
67. Chen Z, Zhou W, Li W (2017) Blind stereoscopic video quality assessment: from depth perception to overall experience. IEEE Trans Image Process 27(2):721–734
68. Shi L, Zhao S, Chen Z (2019) BELIF: blind quality evaluator of light field image with tensor structure variation index. In: Paper presented at the 2019 IEEE international conference on image processing, pp 3781–3785, Sept 2019

Chapter 7
Quality Assessment of Virtual Reality Images

7.1 Introduction

Recently, with the rapid evolution of multimedia technology, virtual reality (VR) technique has attracted great interest from audiences and researchers because of its enormous application range, likely gaming, 360-degree images, video viewing, and so on [1]. As the significant form of VR content, 360-degree images can be presented to viewers in the format of spherical images through VR devices such as a head-mounted display (HMD), enhancing the immersive and realistic viewing experience for people [2]. For this purpose, full range of content needs high spatial resolution (such as 4K or 8K), huge storage space and wide bandwidth [3]. The VR images that present the content are inevitably distorted during acquisition, transmission, and preservation, which affects the visual quality of these images [4]. Therefore, it is crucial to assess the perceptual quality of immersive VR images before image processing such as image restoration and enhancement, which has significant implication in leading the development of VR image applications.

In the past decades, there have been a tremendous number of research scholars who have designed numerous QA approaches, which are divided into subjective image quality assessment (QA) methods and objective image QA methods. Subjective VR image QA is the process in which the VR images perceived quality is evaluated by human subjects. To be specific, in the subjective QA methods, various experiments are carried out to obtain the mean opinion scores (MOSs) from observers. According to ITU-R BT50011 [11], the subjective testing methodologies proposed to assess the quality of VR images include single-stimulus (SS), double-stimulus impairment scale (DSIS), and paired comparison (PC). Based on the accessibility of reference information, the objective VR image QA methods are classified into full-reference (FR), reduced-reference (RR), and no-reference (NR). The FR VR image QA methods require all the information of the pristine images. The RR VR image QA methods need some information of the original images. The NR VR image QA methods can directly assess the perceived quality of VR images with no need for any pristine reference images. Unlike the traditional planar images that are displayed on computer or TV screens, the 3D VR images are much larger and need substantially greater computing power. Besides, the pixels of images in the 2D projection domain do not correspond linearly to the pixels in the spherical domain [5]. By this token, the existing 2D image QA methods are difficult to accurately evaluate the 3D VR images' visual quality since they do not take the characteristics of the 3D VR images into account. Therefore, it is necessary to study the QA method of 3D VR images.

As far as we know, there are a large number of VR databases that contain subjective measurements. Most of them contain traditional image distortions and VR-specific stitching distortions, such as image compression artifacts, GN, and Gaussian blur. In [12], Upenik et al. constructed an immersive image database with JPEG compression and proposed a mobile testbed for assessing immersive images. In [3], Sun et al. established a compressed VR image quality database, which includes five pristine images and corresponding compressed images generated by adopting three coding techniques, namely JPEG, H.264/AVC, and H.265/HEVC. In [13], Duan et al. constructed an omnidirectional image QA database that contains four distortion categories (i.e., JPEG compression, JPEG2000 compression, Gaussian blur, and GN) and head and eye tracking data. On the basis of the databases mentioned above, many researchers have proposed various subjective VR image QA approaches [6–10]. In [14], Yu et al. presented the spherical peak signal-to-noise ratio (PSNR) model named spherical peak signal-to-noise ratio (S-PSNR), which can average the observed quality in all directions. In [15], Zakharchenko et al. proposed a craster parabolic projection based PSNR (CPP-PSNR) VR image QA method. In [9], Xu et al. introduced two types of perceptual video QA (P-VQA) models, which are a non-content-based PSNR (NCP-PSNR) model and a content-based PSNR (CP-PSNR) model, respectively.

Except these researches mentioned above, more dedicated and deep research for 3D VR images are introduced in this chapter. In [19], Chen et al. studied the immersive 3D subjective image QA. They invited 42 observers to rate the 450 corrupted images in a controlled VR setting and recorded these data and eye tracking data. In [22], Yu et al. established an omnidirectional image dataset composing stitched images, which can be considered as ground-truth for VR images' stitching regions. In [28], Sun et al. designed blind 360-degree image quality assessment by employing multi-channel CNN. In [27], Hak Gu Kim et al. proposed a deep learning-based VR image QA method that can quantify omnidirectional images by adopting positional and visual information. For evaluating the performance of those QA models, we compared them with state-of-the-art competitors using four extensive employed standards, i.e., Spearman rank correlation coefficient (SRCC), Kendall rank correlation coefficient (KRCC), Pearson linear correlation coefficient (PLCC), and root mean square error (RMSE).

The remainder of this chapter is arranged as follows. Section 7.2 introduces in detail the modeling process of four types of VR image QA approaches, namely subjective VR image QA method, objective VR image QA method, subjective-objective VR image QA method, and cross-reference stitching QA method. Section 7.3 finally draws the conclusion and provides future work.

7.2 Methodology

In this section, we mainly introduce several VR image QA models. These models can be separated into two types, namely subjective VR image QA model and objective VR image QA model from the perspective of the presence or absence of participants. Specifically, we first introduce the subjective VR image QA approaches on the basis of different databases that contain various types of distortion. Second, we introduce the objective VR image QA approaches according to the accessibility of original reference information. Third, an approach that combines the above two methods together is introduced.

7.2.1 Subjective QA of VR Images

During transmission, compression, and storage, the resolution of VR images/videos is usually reduced and the various distortions (such as projection distortion and compression distortion) are introduced. They often make viewers uncomfortable and even suffer from VR diseases [17]. In order to assess the quality of VR images, it is necessary to conduct a subjective QA before designing objective image/video QA metrics. The obtained MOSs reflect human subjective feelings and provide a criterion for the design of objective QA metrics. This part first introduces a more comprehensive 3D immersed image database constructed by Chen et al, which is called LIVE VR IQA database [18]. It is the first database used to assess gaze-tracked quality of stereoscopic 3D VR images. A detailed description of the subjective testing, design, and training based on this database will be illustrated [19].

Creation of Database

The LIVE VR IQA database includes 15 immersive 3D 360° pristine images with high quality captured by Insta360 Pro cameras. These images contain a variety of scenes, such as sunny/cloudy, daytime/night, and indoor/outdoor, rather than simply capturing colorful and highly saturated images. In order to ensure that an image with the fewest motion blur and stitching errors can be selected, four or five raw images were captured for each scene. In addition, a 3D image of over-under equirectangular was generated for each scene. From the perspective of spatial information and color information, these selected images have a wide range of space and rich colors. Figure 7.1 shows some examples from the LIVE VR IQA database.

The selected 15 pristine VR content was processed by using six distortions (i.e., Gaussian noise, Gaussian blur, downsampling, stitching distortion, VP9 compression, and H.265 compression). These distortions were mainly divided into three categories, namely traditional distortion, VR-specific distortion, and compression processing. Each distortion processing is set to a different degree of distortion to

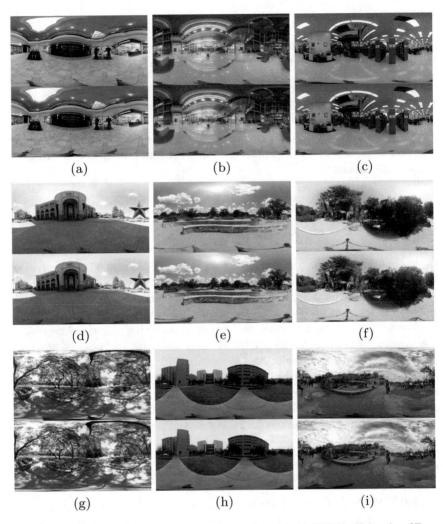

Fig. 7.1 Examples from the LIVE VR IQA database (Copyright (c) 2019 The University of Texas at Austin. Reprinted, with permission, from [18].)

distinguish perceptual differences. 360° images were produced through Insta360 Stitcher. In order to match the resolution of VR headset, the original resolution of 7680×3840 was reduced to 4096×2048. Next the six distortion settings are described in detail.

Gaussian Noise The Gaussian noise was used for unit normalized RGB channel. It is standard deviation $\mu \in [0.002 \sim 0.03]$.

Gaussian Blur The left and right images were separated. Then the standard deviation in the [0.7–3.1] pixel range was used to blur the RGB channel of the separated image using the circular symmetric two-dimensional Gaussian kernel.

Downsampling After separating the left and right images, bicubic interpolation was used to down sample each original immersed image to one of five reduced spatial resolutions. According to [20, 21], the maximum total resolution is 4096×2048 and the minimum resolution is 820×820, which covers an extensive range of quality.

Stitching Distortion Similar to the above process, the left and right images should be divided before other operations. MATLAB was utilized to capture 14 perspective images from each image and let them spread over the complete spherical image. This can simulate the 14 panoramic cameras put in the central part of each scene [16]. After deriving a set of images taken with the virtual lens, they were sewn together with the stitching tool Nuke. Each spliced image was aligned in the direction of the reference image. Finally, stitching parameters such as convergence distance and error threshold were adjusted to produce different degrees of distortion. It is worth noting that the stitching distortion of the left and right images should be at the same position to avoid further discomfort caused by binocular competition.

VP9 Compression VP9 compression was implemented by using FFmpeg and libvpxvp9 encoders. Here, the constant quality score factor in the range of [50, 63] is changed. The lower their value represents the better their quality.

H.265 Compression H. 265 (HEVC) compression distortion was adopted by utilizing FFmpeg libx265 encoder which QP value ranges from 38 to 50. If this value is higher, the degree of compression is greater, which means worse quality.

Subject Testing Design, Display, and Training

Subject Testing Design

The single stimulus continuous QA method described in [23] was used in subjective tests. The rating scale ranges from 0 to 100. Subjects can adjust the quality by entering scores. A higher score indicates higher quality.

To guarantee the reliability of data, the adaptability of 3D environment, visual acuity, pupil spacing, and depth perception of subjects should be tested before the subjective test. Subjects who are uncomfortable with virtual reality or 3D environments will be excluded. The subjects' visual acuity was tested by the Snellen test, and they were required to wear corrective eyeglasses to obtain normal vision while taking the subjective test. Limited by the HTC Vive's pupil spacing, subjects may feel uncomfortable if their pupil spacing exceeds the range of 60.3–73.7 mm. These subjects were permitted to undergo the HMD trial for a period of time. They will be advised not to undergo the test if the subjects feel uncomfortable. Deep perception and stereoscopic vision were tested using the RanDot Stereoscopic test. If the test shows impairment, the subject will also be advised to abandon the test and their results will be discarded even if they continue to take the test. In addition, the data will be abandoned when the subjects do not follow the instructions.

Each subject was required to participate in three sessions, each spaced at least 24 h apart. The average observing time per session was 27 min, and the average observing time and rating time per image was 23 s. Each round of testing randomly selected 9 contents and 60 distorted images. In order to avoid the influence of memory, there should be at least 5 different images of the same content.

Subject Testing Display

To track the direction of gaze, it uses a corneal reflex technique at the center of the pupil. Its tracking accuracy is 0.5°, with a delay of about 10 ms and a sampling frequency of 120 Hz. Image playback is performed by dedicated high-performance servers. Device and system timestamps, fixation starting point, fixation orientation, pupil location, and absolute pupil size are all data outputs for testing the human eye. The detailed process of subjective testing is presented as follows.

Eye tracking is performed at the beginning of each stage. Five red dots will flash in sequence at different locations in the HMD, which are located at the four corners and the center of the rectangle. Mapping these points to normalized coordinates, the upper left and lower right corners of the front viewport were represented by (0, 0) and (1, 1), respectively. Each observer was required to gaze at every dot until the last dot departure. This system uses the obtained point fixation to standardize the eye tracker. If the standardization is unsuccessful, the process is repeated. And if standardization is still fails after 5 tests, subjects will be required to participate in the experiment next time.

In order to unify the viewing time, the interface will automatically pop up the quality scale after the subjects watch the image for 20 s. In addition, the background is set to gray, which could prevent the subjects from continuing to view the image when filling out the quality scale. The quality scale was marked with five labels, "Bad", "Poor", "Fair", "Good", and "Excellent", as the rating range. Subjects can make choices using a hand-held controller. Click "Submit Next" to view the next picture, and the submitted score will be written into the file with the picture name. The other function of the submission time is confirming the correspondence between gaze data and images. Subsequent images were selected at random from the entire images during the session, in the order in which they are displayed as described above. Tobii Pro output detailed gaze data at the end time of experiment.

Subjects and Training

The whole 40 subjects are undergraduates from the University of Texas at Austin who had little experience in image QA. About 15 students were assigned to grade each image.

In addition to oral presentations on research objectives, detailed procedures were described in writing for subjects. The subjects also signed consent forms. Each subject was asked to look at as many images as possible and rate them based on image quality without considering the attractiveness of content. Before the actual test, the subjects looked at 10 images that were not included in the database that had the same distortion pattern and quality range. At the same time, they were asked to use the same test process to familiarize themselves with controllers and virtual headsets.

7.2.2 Objective QA of VR Images

With the progress of science and technique, VR has been widely studied by many image and video processing researchers. But recently proposed QA models for VR video are poor in efficiency and performance due to the lack of suitable databases. For improving the above mentioned limitation, an VR QA method with high efficiency was designed in [22]. 21 subjects were invited to establish the VR video QA database, and two projection formats were introduced to the obtained database. Subsequently, a 3D convolutional neural network (CNN) was proposed to estimate the quality of VR videos without pristine videos. The preprocessed video blocks are input to this network, and various quality rate strategies are adopted to derive the final score value. The 3D-CNN achieves an excellent performance, which can be improved by calculating weights via the combination of the two projection formats.

The Panoramic Video Database Set-Up

Database Set-Up

For establishing this database, seven typical panoramic videos were selected from the recommendation of IEEE1857.9M1053 proposal [23], which have been set as pristine sequences. All these standard panoramic videos' resolution is 4096×2048, with the 30 fps frame rate and yuv420p format.

To construct the VR video database, these pristine sequences are primarily processed by the following two steps. First, the pristine sequences' equirectangular projection (ERP) projection format is transformed into the equal-area projection (EAP) projection format by utilizing the 360lib official software. Second, the pristine videos of two formats (ERP and EAP) are compressed by two kinds of encoding methods, which are H.264/AVC [24] and H.265/HEVC [25]. The quantization parameters QP are set from 30 to 50 with an interval of 5. Finally, the VR video database was obtained, which is composed of a total of 147 panoramic videos.

For assessing the derived database, a subjective experiment was conducted. Considering the brain's viewing behavior for video, every test only focuses on one sequence using the HTC-VIVE helmet. A single stimulus suggested by the ITU-R BT500-13 [26] was adopted in this experiment. Unlike traditional subjective image QA experiments, the test requires an empty and silent environment. It is not affected by external conditions such as viewing distance, luminance, the resolution of displayed screen, and so on. 21 observers with an average age of 24.2 years (eleven boys and ten girls with normal or corrected vision) were invited to this subjective test that lasted fourteen days.

From this experiment, all the values of observers' MOSs were gathered. According to the recommendation of the international telecommunication union [11], many parameters are computed, including individual mean, standard deviation, kurtosis coefficient, and so on. The final results show that the excessive deviation of individual value was cleaned. For each distortion a, the MOS can be derived by:

$$MOS_a = \frac{1}{M} \sum_{b=1}^{M} m_{ab}, \tag{7.1}$$

where M denotes the number of observers and m_{ab} represents the score given by observer b under the distortion condition a.

After calculating the MOS values for all video sequences, it can be concluded that the 5 levels of scores are comparatively specific. More specifically, the subjective experience of ERP projection format resembles that of EAP projection format.

Neural Network-Based Objective QA Algorithm

3D Convolutional Neural Network (3D-CNN)

A novel 3D-CNN network is proposed to implement objective QA. Compared with the 2D convolutional neural network (2D-CNN) methods, this method can retain the input time information, indicating that this network can derive better video analysis performance. The network's input is defined as $(X^{(t)}, q^{(t)}, w^{(t)})_{t=1}^{T}$, in which $X^{(t)}$ denotes the tth block's data of the tested video. The block is split into 10 frames drawn in equal parts of the video. After merging them, a non-overlapping and non-interval approach was adopted to segment them into 128×128 blocks. Since the video consists of three channels, that is RGB channels, a block's size is $3 \times 10 \times 128 \times 128$. $q^{(t)}$ denotes the objective MOS values of video's tth block. $w^{(t)}$ means the discrepancy between the central Y-axis of the tth block and the Y-axis of the video central spot. Figure 7.2 exhibits the frame of this network. The input block gets through the network with 6 layers, including 3 convolutional layers and 2 fully connected layers. There exists a combination of ReLU activation function and a maximum pooling layer after every 3 convolutional layers. After the block across 3 convolutional layers, the feature map is derived. Passing the first fully connected layer, the feature map accesses a 256 dimensional vector. Then the dropout strategy is adopted to pass the second fully connected layer. After passing all these layers, a fractional output is obtained. When estimating the values and the mean squared error (MSE) of the MOS, the loss function can be expressed as follows:

$$l = \frac{1}{N} \sum_{t=1}^{N} (q^{(t)} - \widehat{q}^{(t)})^2, \tag{7.2}$$

where $q^{(t)}$ indicates the MOS value of the video at the location of the block. $\widehat{q}^{(t)}$ denotes the output block's estimated score obtained from the network. The stochastic gradient descent (SGD) is utilized to assign the training parameters of the network.

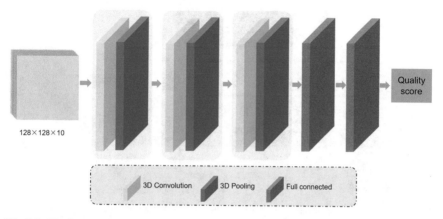

Fig. 7.2 The framework of 3D-CNN

Specifically, the primal learning rate is set to 0.001, the momentum factor is set to 0.9, and the size of block is set to 128.

In the projecting process, the VR video's spatial distribution is non-uniformed. Different projection formats have their weights calculated in different ways. The weight of the ERP projection format can be derived as follows:

$$S_f = \frac{(\sum_x \sum_y S_{sy} W_{xy})}{\sum_x \sum_y W_{xy}}, \tag{7.3}$$

$$W = cos(\pi \frac{h'}{h}), \tag{7.4}$$

where S_f means the final score value. S_{xy} indicates the total VR video blocks' objective fraction. h' is the distance in the vertical direction between the video patch's central location and the entire video center point. h is the VR video's height in the vertical direction. In addition, the EAP is an equal domain projection format with video blocks assigned a weight of 1.

7.2.3 Subjective-Objective QA of VR Images

A deep network is used to assess the visual quality of omnidirectional images. The network is composed of VR quality predictor and perception guide. The designed VR quality predictor encodes the position and visual features of the upper slice of omnidirectional images to learn the location and visual features. The designed perception guider assesses the obtained score by using adversarial learning with reference to human subjective scores. There are both subjective and objective QA in

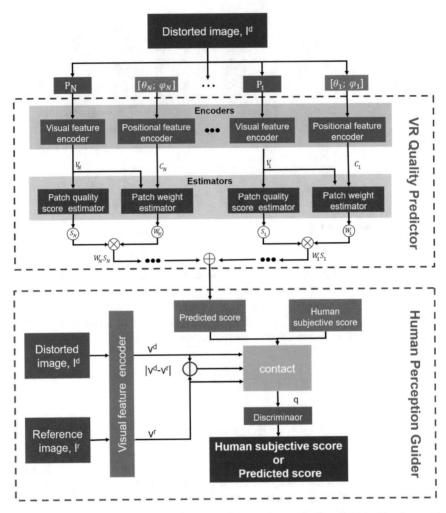

Fig. 7.3 The overall framework of the proposed Deep VR image QA method with adversarial learning

the network which is sufficient to understand the characteristics of omnidirectional images that affect visual quality.

VR Image QA with Human Perception Guider for VR Image

As shown in Fig. 7.3, the whole process of omnidirectional image QA in training is based on deep networks, which consists of VR quality predictor and human perception guider [27].

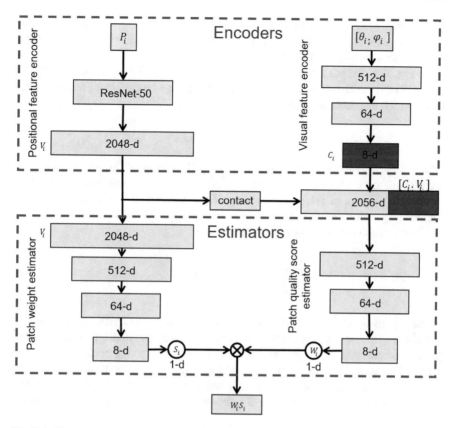

Fig. 7.4 The architecture of the proposed VR quality score predictor for the ith patch, pi

As illustrated in the Fig. 7.3, the input of VR quality predictor is the patches divided by the distorted image I^d. Each patch includes the positional feature and visual feature. The $[\theta_i, \phi_i]$ denotes the central point of p_i. The positional feature c_i and visual feature v_i are obtained respectively after the patches pass through the positional feature encoder and visual feature encoder. The patch weight and patch quality score estimators are set after the positional feature encoder and visual feature encoder. They can be used to obtain the weight w_i and score s_i of each patch. Finally, all patches' weights and scores are aggregated and the predicted quality score $\hat{s}$ is derived.

One input of human perception guider is the MOS value s^h accessed by observers. Other outputs are distorted images I^d and reference image I^r. The visual V^d and V^r can be acquired after processing the I^d and I^r by visual feature encoder. The proposed guider feeds back the prediction score to the predictor according to the subjective score. Based on the visual characteristics of corrupted image and pristine image, a comprehensive QA system can achieve more accurate performance evaluation.

According to above analysis, the distorted omnidirectional I^d is divided into 256 × 256 N patches ($N = 32$). The whole structure of designed VR quality predictor for ith path p_i is shown in Fig. 7.4.

In Fig. 7.4, the positional feature encoder consists of 3 fully connected layers, that is, 512-d, 64-d, and 8-d fully connected layers. c_i is a positional feature vector of p_i, which can be obtained by:

$$c_i = fc_{pos}([\theta_i; \phi_i]), \tag{7.5}$$

where $fc_{pos}(.)$ denotes the function of the fully connected layers for encoding the position information. The architecture of visual feature encoder on the basis of ResNet50 is shown in Table 7.1. Conv a_x ($a = 1, 2, 3, 4, 5$) represent five convolutional stages in visual feature encoder.

V_i can be calculated in following formulation:

$$v_i(d) = \sum_{m=1}^{8} \sum_{n=1}^{8} f_i^5(m, n, d), d \in \{1, \ldots, 2048\}, \tag{7.6}$$

where f_i^5 represents the last convolutional layer's feature map. After processing the encoder, positional features and visual features can be obtained. The weight of the patch is determined by the positional and visual features, so the position and visual information is the input of the patch weight estimator. However, visual information is the only input to the patch quality estimator to obtain the predicted patch quality score $\hat{s}$. The predicted quality score of omnidirectional image can be calculated by:

$$\hat{s} = P(I^d) = \frac{\sum_{i=1}^{N} W_i S_i}{\sum_{i=1}^{N} W_i}. \tag{7.7}$$

The detailed architecture of perception guider is exhibited in Fig. 7.5.

Human subjective score S^h and predicted score $\hat{s}$ are two inputs of human perception guider. The other input is $|v^d - v^r|$ obtained from source input distorted image I^d and reference image I^r, respectively. The total input of human perception guider is defined as $q = [s; v^d; v^r; |v^d - v^r|]$. The perception guider contains 4 fully connected layers, that is 512-d, 64-d, 8-d, and 1-d fully connected layers. In addition, there is a sigmoid function in this model. The final output of the guider can be accessed by:

$$G(s|I^d, I^r) = \frac{1}{1 + e^{-q}}, \tag{7.8}$$

where $G(\cdot)$ indicates the perception guider, and q represents the last fully connected layer's value of the perception guider. The objective function of the predictor E_P can be defined as:

$$E_p = (P(I^d) - S^h)^2 + \gamma J(G(P(I^d)|I^d, I^r), 1), \tag{7.9}$$

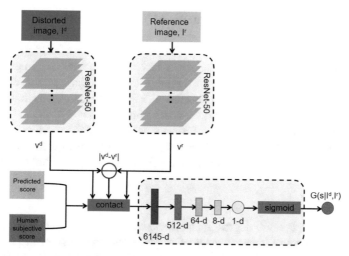

Fig. 7.5 The architecture of the proposed human perception guider

Table 7.1 Visual feature encoder architecture

Layer name	conv1	conv2_x	conv3_x	conv4_x	conv5_x	
Output size	128×128	64×64	32×32	16×16	8×8	2048×1
visual feature encoder	7×7, 64, stride 2	1×1×64 3×3×64 ×3 1×1×256	1×1×128 3×3×128 ×4 1×1×512	1×1×256 3×3×256 ×6 1×1×1024	1×1×512 3×3×512 ×3 1×1×2048	Global average pooling

$$J(x, y) = -y \ln x - (1 - y) \ln(1 - x), \tag{7.10}$$

where $J(x, y)$ represents cross entropy loss. $P(I^d)$ indicates the predicted score, which is treated as the subjective score. The objective function of perception guider E_G can be written as:

$$E_G = -J(G(S^h|I^d, I^r), 1) - J(G(P(I^d)|I^d, I^r), 0). \tag{7.11}$$

By minimizing the objective function of the predictor E_P, the prediction accuracy and efficiency of the VR quality predictor can be further improved.

Evaluating Subjective-Objective Quality of VR Images via VR QA System

To assess the 360-degree image quality, a new multi-channel CNN-based model named multi-channel neural network for blind 360-degree image quality assessment (MC360IQA) is established [28]. In this model, a 360-degree image is first projected into six viewport images, and then the six viewport images and itself are transferred to the CNN. The model extracts and fuses the features via the multi-channel CNN from input images. By regressing these features, the objective quality score can be attained. The projection and QA procedure will be described in detail as follows.

Projection Method

In the VR device, the 360-degree image is shown as a sphere in 3D spherical coordinates. The content of image is rendered as plane segment tangential to the sphere, determined by the observing angle and the field of view (FoV) of the device. When the observers view the 360-degree image by utilizing the VR device, they should rotate their head to look at all the angles of image to watch the entire image.

On this basis, viewport-based images are designed to implement the omnidirectional image QA. To obtain the best predict pixel, the mapping backward procedure [14] is used to compute pixel value in the spherical image. In the above processing, the FoV is set to 90 degree, which is the same protocol as for typical VR devices (i.e., HTC VIVE, Gear VR and so on). To convey all the visual content, an omnidirectional image presents six viewport images covering the entire 360-degree image. The six view port images are derived from front, back, right, left, top and down views, which can be represented by V_{front}, V_{back}, V_{right}, V_{left}, V_{top}, and V_{down}. In addition, different observers view the image from different angles, which inspires us to consider different starting viewing angles in the training process. Hence, the longitude of the observing angle is rotated from 0 degree to 360 degree on the front view and its interval is set to α degree. The omnidirectional images are then projected to six viewport images at each front viewing angle. Finally, the one omnidirectional image generates N sets of viewport images, which are defined as $V_{viewport}^n$, where the $viewport = \{front, back, right, left, top, down\}$, $n = \{1, 2,..., N\}$, and $N = \frac{360}{\alpha}$. This method can effectively prevent the overfitting of the constructed model.

MC360IQA

The ResNet [29] as the most famous CNN has the strong ability to realize generalization without too much memory consumption. Hence, the introduced MC360IQA model chooses it as the base CNN-channel. These features extracted from center layers are fused to achieve image QA. The structure of the MC360IQA can be introduced in detail as follows.

This MC360IQA model is composed of multi-channel CNN and image QA regressor. Its structure is presented in Fig. 7.6. The multi-channel CNN adopts 6 parallel ResNet to extract useful features from corresponding six viewport images. Further-

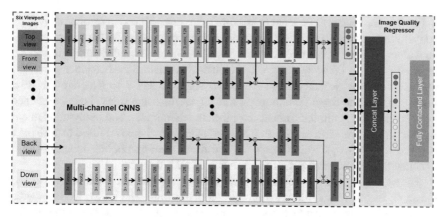

Fig. 7.6 The network structure of the MC360IQA

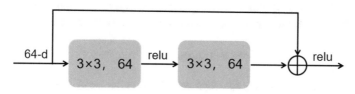

Fig. 7.7 A building block for ResNet34 on the 56 × 56 feature maps

more, the ResNet employs residual learning to deepen the CNN network, which is normally shown in the format of several deeper building blocks. Depending on the sum of layers, ResNet can be classified into ResNet18, ResNet34, ResNet50, and ResNet101. To improve the accuracy of the model and reduce the time consumed, the ResNet34 is considered as the base CNN-channel. All the building blocks of ResNet34 contain two convolution layers, where the kernels' dimension is 3 × 3. The identity short cut connection is inserted from the building block's input to the output. The Fig. 7.7 shows the building block. The ResNet34 can be expressed by five parts ($conv1$, $conv2_i$, $conv3_i$, $conv4_i$, and $conv5_i$). In the $conv1$, convolution kernels's dimension is 7 × 7 and 64 channels are implemented by using stride 2. The $conv2_{i,i=1,2,3}$ denote three repeated building blocks. In $conv2_i$, there exists a 3 × 3 max pooling with stride 2. The $conv3_i$, $conv4_i$ and $conv5_i$ have four, six and three repeated building blocks, respectively. The only difference between building blocks in these parts is the kernel channels. From $conv3_i$ to $conv5_i$, the kernel channels are 128, 256, and 512 separately. The designer takes place the last layer of each baseline ResNet34 with ten output features via average pooling.

After acquiring the feature maps from low layers, the hyper-ResNet architecture with hierarchical element-wise addition is used to fuse these valuable features from $conv2_i$, $conv3_i$, $conv4_i$, and $conv5_i$. Since the feature maps obtained from different stages have different channels and dimensions, this model adopts two convolution operations to downscale the dimension and supplement the channels. As described in Fig. 7.7, the features extracted from $conv2_i$ are first reduced in resolution by 3×3 convolution kernel with stride 2. Then the number of channels is increased by 1×1 convolution layers with stride 1. Hence, the dimension size and channel number can match the $conv3_i$ in the next stage. The element-wise addition is conducted between the feature maps extracted from these two stages 2 and 3 to generate the fused feature maps. The fused feature maps will repeat the same steps above mentioned, downscaling its resolution, increasing its channels number, and applying element-wise addition. The same steps are conducted to emerge the novel fused feature maps and the feature maps from $conv5_i$. In the final, average pooling is employed to generate the feature vector with a dimension of 10×1.

The six hyper-ResNet34 channels have uniform weights and are trained to extract the same features for different compression distortions. The image quality regressor first obtains the fused features maps by connecting the outputs of multi-channel CNNs. Then, it allocates weights to images from different viewport. Finally, the image quality regressor utilizes a fully connected layer to compute the quality prediction. For end-to-end training, the loss function can be defined as:

$$Loss = (Q_{estimate} - Q_{lable})^2, \tag{7.12}$$

where $Q_{estimate}$ is the estimated value, and Q_{lable} is the MOS value.

Two metrics are designed for predicting the 360-degree images' quality. The $MC360IQA_{prestine}$ metric utilizes the score computed by the MC360IQA using viewport images without longitude rotating. The $MC360IQA_{average}$ metric utilizes the mean score of N groups of viewport images computed by the MC360IQA

The two metrics can be defined as follows:

$$MC360IQA_{prestine} = MC360IQA(V_{viewport}^1), \tag{7.13}$$

$$MC360IQA_{average} = \sum_{n=1}^{N} MC360IQA(V_{viewport}^n), \tag{7.14}$$

where $viewport = \{front, back, right, left, top, down\}$ and $n = \{1,2,...,N\}, N = \frac{360}{\alpha}$.

7.2.4 Cross-Reference Stitching QA

Due to the rapid growth of immersive multimedia content in VR, the omnidirectional images with high quality are necessary to create a natural immersion of real-world settings in head-mounted displays. A considerable requirement for stitched omnidirectional images QA has arisen as a result of the advancement of stitching methods. To obtain a high-quality ground-truth pristine information for the connected areas, a novel cross-reference omnidirectional stitching dataset (CROSS) firstly established. Second, an omnidirectional stitching images QA algorithm is suggested to properly measure sewing regions quality as well as the image global experience of environmental absorption.

The Cross-Reference Database

The cross-reference omnidirectional image database is constructed first contains 292 quaternions of fisheye images as well as the stitched images created by seven methods. To improve the robustness, a series of fisheye cameras are utilized to record data in diverse situations.

Omnidirectional Database Collection

The CROSS database is made up of photos from ten different scenarios that may be divided into two groups. The indoor groups include photos of the meeting room, reading room, staircase, and so on. The outdoor groups include streets, wilderness, housing estates, and basketball grounds. Because each scene is made up of photos recorded at different angles, the composite areas contain real ground observation data for assessment. It is significant to ensure that the image content does not alter in time of the obtaining process.

Cross-Reference Grouping

For acquiring omnidirectional photos of high quality, a series of fisheye cameras are used to gather data in the form of image groups. Each group consists of four photographs taken at the same camera position from different orthogonal types ($0°$, $90°$, $180°$, $270°$) degrees. When stitching two photos in opposing orientations, there are always two images that may serve as reference information without any damage. The fisheye photos in orthogonal degrees are referred to as the cross-reference for stitched image QA at a given degree.

The Quality Assessment Algorithm

Based on the cross-reference database, a novel omnidirectional stitching images QA algorithm has been designed. This QA algorithm considers three stitching regions including histogram statistics, perceptual hash, and sparse representation. Apart from that, two global factors are introduced as well, which are global color difference and blind zone. After weighting the above five factors, a linear regressor is employed to match the weighted value with the human subjective judgment.

Stitching Region Attentive Sampling

The major distortions in stitching photographs are most likely near stitching areas, whereas areas remote from stitching areas normally have less distortions and other optical errors. On this basis, a simple but effective attentive sampling technique has been devised to place a premium on stitching areas during the QA procedure.

The Gaussian criterion is adopted to sample more patches around the stitching area, which can be expressed by:

$$At(x) = \frac{1}{\sqrt{2\pi}\sigma} \exp\left(-\frac{(x-\mu)^2}{2\sigma^2}\right), \tag{7.15}$$

where x and $At(x)$ are the coordinates of where the stitching line and where the sampled patches are. As an example, the region indicators μ for stitching areas and reference areas are determined to 0.5 times their width. The region indicators σ for stitching areas are fixed to be 220 and 350, respectively. In particular, the reference information is sampled more often than the stitching area in order to lower the chance of misregistration.

Stitching Region Assessment Metrics

Three local indicators have been established to implement the stitching area QA, where distortions are most likely to arise in omnidirectional pictures. **Histogram Feature** The histogram of oriented gradient (HOG) features are the most common metrics for assessing picture similarity. The histogram between the stitching area and the reference area is used to determine the gray level divergence. The N represents the sum of observations. The gray level divergence between two histogram vectors $\mathbf{m_i}, \mathbf{m_j}$ can be expressed by:

$$\mathcal{L}_h = \sum_i \sum_j \cos\left(\mathbf{m}_i, \mathbf{m}_j\right) \|\mathbf{m}_i\|_F^2 \|\mathbf{m}_j\|_F^2. \tag{7.16}$$

The gray value range is divided into N bins, and the sum of gray values in each bin is counted on the picture area. In this way, a vector denotes stitching area and reference area are obtained, which computes the cosine similarity of sampled blocks between $\mathbf{m_i}$ and $\mathbf{m_j}$.

Perceptual Hash Although the texture information is lost in stitching zones, the gamma correction may have a significant impact on the histogram feature. As a result, disparities in the picture's pixel level estimated by using the perceptual hash technique concerning image details are erased, and only structure and shading are left.

The size of stitching and reference areas are altered to 64 × 64 followed with the discrete cosine transform (DCT). The hash fingerprint is computed after filtering the high-frequency elements to provide a 4096-dimensional vector for stitching and reference areas, separately. The hash distance $\mathcal{L}_{ha}$ between the stitching area and reference area is considered as the final similarity metrics.

Sparse Reconstruction The sparse reconstruction errors are utilized to reliably quantify region similarity at various degrees of detail. In particular, the visual weight processing module obtains the matching stitching area and sample area. The Gaussian sampling result of reference area is then employed as a dictionary, and the stitching results are used as the transmission data. The ground-truth picture is represented by minimum vectors from the lexicon. The finest stitching photos should have the most information in common. Based on this, sparse reconstruction is employed to discover the best stitched pictures with the fewest pieces.

The D is a super-completed dictionary which is composed of stitching patches of the cross-referenced omnidirectional image. The stitched images are represented as R and the process of the minimal $\mathbf{X}^*$ can be expressed as follows:

$$\mathbf{X}^* = \operatorname{argmin}_X \frac{1}{2}\|R - DX\|_F^2 + \lambda\|X\|_1. \tag{7.17}$$

Then SVD decomposition is used to get the principal element. The final score can be obtained by:

$$\mathbf{X}^* = \sum_{i=1}^{r} \mathbf{U}_i \, \Sigma_i \, \mathbf{V}_i^T,$$
$$\mathcal{L}_s = -\sum_{i=1}^{r} \|\mathcal{F}_{PCA}\,(\Sigma_i)\|_1 . \tag{7.18}$$

By using the principal element analysis $\mathcal{F}_{PCA}$, the summarization of the sum of vectors for sparse reconstruction is adopted to represent the final score.

Global Assessment Metrics

To improve stitching performance, several stitching models are employed to modify the optical parameters of the pictures, which normally introduces some chromatic aberrations. Furthermore, these systems frequently overlook blind areas. Hence, two global measures are created to assess the global experience of stitching omnidirectional photos, which can evaluate the environmental immersion appropriately.

Color Difference To explore the difference of image color, scale invariant feature transform (SIFT) [30] matching is adopted to seek out pixel correspondences between the stitching area and the reference area. Then K nearest neighbors are computed for each matched point pair to remove mismatches. S and R are indicate the sampled block of stitching areas and reference areas, separately. The following is a formula for the sift matching procedure:

$$R^* = \operatorname{argmin}_R \|S - \mathcal{H}_{sift}\,(R_i)\|_F^2 , i = 1 \dots K. \tag{7.19}$$

After matching every S and R, the color difference can be computed as:

$$\mathcal{L}_c = -\sum_{i=1}^{N}\sum_{k=1}^{C} \lambda \frac{S_{ik} - R_{ik}^*}{N \times C}, \tag{7.20}$$

where N represents the sum of sampled patches, C denotes the sum of channels and the λ is set to 100 for balancing score.

Blind Zone The stitched areas below the image without any information are named blind zones, and they have a significant impact on the visual comfort of the immersive experience. A subjective review is undertaken to determine the impact of blind zones. The observers are invited to rate from 1 to 10, representing the influence of the blind zone on the performance of omnidirectional stitching measures. Standardization will immediately assign a relative score to the average value.

Considering the human visual saliency of omnidirectional pictures, the following options are set. Since most stitching methods produce blind areas that are rectangular in shape, the fraction of blind areas in the pictures may be calculated by integrating the subjective visual saliency values. To be specific, the integration $D(x, y)$ indicates human gaze region in I image, ranging from the rectangles region. The final blind zone assessing value $\mathcal{L}_b$ can be calculated by:

$$\mathcal{L}_b = 1 - \frac{\iint_{D(x,y)} P(x, y) dxdy}{\iint_I P(x, y) dxdy}, \tag{7.21}$$

where $P(x, y)$ is the integral function on the basis of visual-times distribution.

Human Guided Classifier Learning

The next step is incorporating human subjective assessments to oversee classifier after obtaining the local and global evaluation metrics in the preceding part. It is difficult for participants to judge the quality of single images without making comparisons. When comparing two photos, a specific method is utilized, in which participants chose the superior quality image based on perception, and the timings during the experiment are recorded. The classifier aspires to be as close to human observation as feasible. To this goal, the human subjective ground-truth is fitted by using multiple linear regression (MLR) [31]. The human assessing values are set as the ground-truth $\mathcal{G}$. The weight-balance parameters α can be learned by generalized least squares predicting:

$$\mathcal{G} = \alpha \cdot \mathbf{y},$$
$$\alpha^* = \operatorname{argmin}_{\alpha} \left(\mathbf{y}^T \gamma^{-1} \mathbf{y}\right)^{-1} \mathbf{y}^T \gamma^{-1} \mathcal{G}, \tag{7.22}$$

where γ represents the covariance matrix of residual error. The final QA result can be obtained via $\hat{\mathcal{R}} = \alpha^* \cdot \mathbf{y}$, which can rank different stitching results.

7.3 Comparison and Analysis of Algorithm Performance

In this section, we introduce several state-of-the-art image QA methods of VR images. We focus on comparing and measuring the performance of the presented QA approaches in this chapter with these methods. The detailed results of the analysis will be illustrated in the following sections. It is worth mentioning that the analysis results show that the performance of these methods in this chapter perform quite well.

7.3.1 Performance Comparison and Analysis

In order to demonstrate the validity and superiority of the methods introduced in this chapter, we compare the proposed approaches with the state-of-the-art image QA methods. All methods are listed in Table 7.2. Among them, there are 12 FR methods and 10 NR methods, respectively.

When we compare the above modern image QA methods, three commonly used metrics are utilized, namely PLCC, SRCC and RMSE. The evaluation accuracy can be measured by PLCC and RMSE, while the monotonicity of the prediction can be found by SRCC. A higher value of PLCC and SRCC, and a lower value of RMSE represent the QA method with the better performance. The objective assessment scores are nonlinearity obtained by PLCC, SRCC and RMSE, so a logistic function is utilized to increase the linearity. We compute the image QA scores using these three criteria by the mapping including 5 parameters as follows:

$$f(a) = \delta_1 \left(\frac{1}{2} - \frac{1}{1 + \exp^{\delta_2(a-\delta_3)}} + \delta_4 a + \delta_5 \right), \tag{7.23}$$

where $\delta_{i,i=1,2,3,4,5}$ represents the fitted parameter. $f(a)$ and a are subjective scores and its corresponding objective scores which are assessed by image QA approaches. It is apparent that the models presented in this chapter have achieved encouraging results. We summarize the advantages of proposed models as follows.

(1) It can be seen that the OS-IQA metric has the best performance compared to other methods, which is more sensitive to evaluate the quality of stitching regions. To be specific, the OS-IQA metric is more sensitive to the local distortions and global color difference even under the complicated lightness conditions and various scenarios.

(2) For the ERP projection format, the performance of the 3D-CNN with added weight calculation is better than other approaches.

(3) The $MC360IQA_{origin}$ and $MC360IQA_{mean}$ outperform the state-of-the-art FR and NR QA models of VR images. The $MC360IQA_{mean}$ is slightly worse than the $MC360IQA_{origin}$ due to the reason that the mean score of viewport images

Table 7.2 The proposed algorithms and modern developed QA models

Category	Abbreviation	Full Name	Refs.
FR	S-PSNR	Spherical peak signal-to-noise ratio	[14]
FR	CPP-PSNR	Craster parabolic projection based peak signal-to-noise ratio	[15]
FR	NCP-PSNR	Non-content-based peak signal-to-noise ratio	[9]
FR	CP-PSNR	Content-based peak signal-to-noise ratio	[9]
FR	SSIM	Structural similarity index	[32]
FR	MS-SSIM	Multiscale-structural similarity	[33]
FR	S-SSIM	Spherical SSIM	[34]
FR	VSI	Visual saliency-induced Index	[35]
FR	GMSD	Gradient magnitude similarity deviation	[36]
FR	FSIM	Feature similarity	[37]
FR	MDSI	Mean deviation similarity index	[38]
FR	OS-IQA	Omnidirectional stitching image quality assessment	[39]
NR	BRISQUE	Blind/referenceless image spatial quality evaluator	[40]
NR	QAC	Quality-aware clustering	[41]
NR	GMLF	The gradient magnitude and laplacian of gaussian	[42]
NR	SISBLIM	Six-step blind metric	[43]
NR	NIQE	Natural image quality evaluator	[44]
NR	3D-CNN	3D convolutional neural network	[22]
NR	3D-CNN (ERP)	3D-CNN Equirectangular	[22]
NR	$MC360IQA_{origin}$	Multi-channel CNN for blind 360-degree image quality assessment origin	[28]
NR	$MC360IQA_{mean}$	MC360IQA mean	[28]
NR	DeepVR-IQA	Deep virtual reality image quality assessment	[27]

is more stable and less susceptible to abnormal predictive scores. In short, the $MC360IQA_{origin}$ is more generalizable and accomplishes tasks more efficiently.

(4) The DeepVR-IQA provides good prediction performance compared to the conventional omnidirectional image quality metrics, which are S-PSNR and CPP-PSNR. Specifically, it has the highest values of PLCC and SRCC.

7.4 Conclusion

Along with the development of virtual reality, omnidirectional images play a significant role in the production of multimedia content with immersive experiences. That is to say, the better the quality of VR images, the better the user experience will be. In this chapter, we introduce two QA methods for VR images from the perspective of the presence or absence of participants, namely subjective VR image QA method and the objective VR image QA method. The subjective image QA method on the basis of LIVE VR IQA database that contains various types of distortion. The subjective QA can obtain more accurate results, but it is time consuming, expensive, and unsuitable for practical applications such as 3D positioning tracking, etc. In contrast, the objective image QA method is based on a mathematical model of the subjective visual system. One model is a blind 360-degree image quality assessment by employing multi-channel CNN. The other one is a deep learning-based VR image QA method that can quantify omnidirectional images by adopting positional and visual information. Despite the good performance of the models introduced, there is still work to be done. In the future, it is believed that the VR image QA methods with better performance can be put forward through the joint effort of researchers.

References

1. Diemer J, Alpers W, Peperkorn H (2015) The impact of perception and presence on emotional reactions: a review of research in virtual reality. Front Psychol 6:26
2. Upenik E, Rerabek M, Ebrahimi T (2017) On the performance of objective metrics for omnidirectional visual content. In: Paper presented at the 2017 ninth international conference on quality of multimedia experience, 1–6 July 2017
3. Sun W, Gu K, Zhai G et al (2018) CVIQD: subjective quality evaluation of compressed virtual reality images. In: Paper presented at the 2017 IEEE international conference on image processing, pp 3450–3454, Feb 2018
4. Ng K, Chan S, Shum H (2005) Data compression and transmission aspects of panoramic videos. IEEE Trans Circuits Syst Video Technol 15(1):82–95
5. Sun Y, Lu A, Yu L (2017) Weighted-to-spherically-uniform quality evaluation for omnidirectional video. IEEE Signal Process Lett 24(9):1408–1412
6. Xu M, Li C, Liu Y et al (2017) A subjective visual quality assessment method of panoramic videos. In: Paper presented at the IEEE international conference on multimedia and expo, 10–14 July 2017
7. Tran H, Ngoc N, Bui C et al (2017) An evaluation of quality metrics for 360 videos. In: Paper presented at the ninth international conference on ubiquitous and future networks, 7–11 July 2017
8. Xiu X, He Y, Ye Y et al (2017) An evaluation framework for 360-degree video compression. In: Paper presented at the IEEE visual communications and image processing, 1–4 Dec 2017
9. Xu M, Li C, Chen Z et al (2019) Assessing visual quality of omnidirectional videos. IEEE Trans Circuits Syst Video Technol 29(12):3516–3530
10. Li C, Xu M, Du X et al (2018) Bridge the gap between VQA and human behavior on omnidirectional video: a large-scale dataset and a deep learning model. In: Paper presented at the 26th ACM international conference on multimedia, pp 932–940

11. ITU-R BT Recommendation 500-11 (2002) Methodology for the subjective assessment of the quality of television. https://www.itu.int/rec/R-REC-BT.500-11-200206-S/en
12. Upenik E, Rerabek M, Ebrahimi T (2017) A testbed for subjective evaluation of omnidirectional visual content. In: Paper presented at the picture coding symposium, April 2017
13. Duan H, Zhai G, Min X et al (2018) Perceptual quality assessment of omnidirectional images. In: Paper presented at the IEEE international symposium on circuits and systems, 27–30 May 2018
14. Yu M, Lakshman H, Girod B (2015) A framework to evaluate omnidirectional video coding schemes. In: Paper presented at the IEEE international symposium on mixed and augmented reality, pp 31–36, Nov 2015
15. Zakharchenko V, Choi K, Park J (2016) Quality metric for spherical panoramic video. In: Paper presented at the SPIE optical engineering and applications, pp 57–65, Sept 2016
16. Cheung G, Yang L, Tan Z et al (2017) A content-aware metric for stitched panoramic image quality assessment. In: Paper presented at the IEEE international conference on computer vision workshops, pp 2487–2494, Oct 2017
17. Kim J, Kim W, Ahn S et al (2018) Virtual reality sickness predictor: Analysis of visual-vestibular conflict and vr contents. In: Paper presented at the 10th international conference on quality of multimedia experience, 1–6 May 2018
18. Chen M, Jin Y, Goodall T et al (2019) LIVE 3D VR IQA Database. http://live.ece.utexas.edu/research/VR3D/index.html
19. Chen M, Jin Y, Goodall T et al (2020) Study of 3D virtual reality picture quality. IEEE J Sel Top Signal Process 14(1):89–102
20. Guo P, Shen Q, Ma Z et al (2018) Perceptual quality assessment of immersive images considering peripheral vision impact. arXiv preprint arXiv: 1802.09065
21. Zhou R, Huang M, Tan S et al (2016) Modeling the impact of spatial resolutions on perceptual quality of immersive image/video. In: Paper presented at the international conference on 3D Imaging, 1–6 Dec 2016
22. Wu P, Ding W, You Z et al (2019) Virtual reality video quality assessment based on 3d convolutional neural networks. In: Paper presented at the IEEE international conference on image processing, pp 3187–3191, Aug 2019
23. Beijing Institute of Technology (2016) Study of a subjective quality evaluation methodology on panoramic video based on samviq. IEEE 1857:9
24. Wiegand T, Sullivan GJ, Bjontegaard G et al (2003) Overview of the h.264/avc video coding standard. IEEE Trans Circuits Syst Video Technol 13(7):560–576
25. Sullivan GJ, Ohm JR, Han WJ et al (2012) Overview of the high efficiency video coding (HEVC) standard. IEEE Trans Circuits Syst Video Technol 22(12):1649–1668
26. ITU-R BT Recommendation (2012) The subjective evaluation method of television image quality. https://www.itu.int/rec/R-REC-BT.500-13-201201-S/en
27. Kim HG, Lim H, Ro YM (2020) Deep virtual reality image quality assessment with human perception guider for omnidirectional image. IEEE Trans Circuits Syst Video Technol 30(4):917–928
28. Sun W, Min X, Zhai G et al (2020) MC360IQA: a multi-channel CNN for blind 360-degree image quality assessment. IEEE J Sel Top Signal Process 14(1):64–77
29. He K, Zhang X, Ren S et al(2016) Deep residual learning for image recognition. In: Paper presented at the conference of IEEE conference on computer vision and pattern recognition, pp 770–778, Dec 2016
30. Lowe DG, et al (1999) Object recognition from local scale-invariant features. In: Paper presented at the 7th IEEE international conference on computer vision, pp 1150–1157, Sept 1999
31. Li C, Bovik AC, Wu XJ (2011) Blind image quality assessment using a general regression neural network. IEEE Trans Neural Netw 22(5):793–799
32. Wang Z, Bovik AC, Sheikh HR, Simoncelli EP (2004) Image quality assessment: from error visibility to structural similarity. IEEE Trans Image Process 13(4):600–612
33. Wang Z, Simoncelli EP, Bovik AC (2003) Multiscale structural similarity for image quality assessment. In: IEEE Asilomar Conference on Signals, vol 2, pp 1398–1402

34. Chen S, Zhang Y, Li Y et al (2018) Spherical structural similarity index for objective omni-directional video quality assessment. In: Paper presented at the IEEE international conference on multimedia and expo, 1–6 July 2018
35. Zhang L, Shen Y, Li H (2014) VSI: a visual saliency-induced index for perceptual image quality assessment. IEEE Trans Image Process 23(10):4270–4281
36. Xue W, Zhang L, Mou X et al (2014) Gradient magnitude similarity deviation: a highly efficient perceptual image quality index. IEEE Trans Image Process 23(2):684–695
37. Zhang L, Zhang L, Mou X et al (2011) FSIM: a feature similarity index for image quality assessment. IEEE Trans Image Process 20(8):2378–2386
38. Nafchi HZ, Shahkolaei A, Hedjam R et al (2016) Mean deviation similarity index: efficient and reliable full-reference image quality evaluator. IEEE Access 4:5579–5590
39. Li J, Yu K, Zhao Y et al (2019) Cross-reference stitching quality assessment for 360° omni-directional images. In: Proceedings of the 27th ACM international conference on multimedia, pp 2360–2368
40. Mittal A, Moorthy AK, Bovik AC (2012) No-reference image quality assessment in the spatial domain. IEEE Trans Image Process 21(12):4695–4708
41. Xue W, Zhang L, Mou X (2013) Learning without human scores for blind image quality assessment. In: Paper presented at the 2013 IEEE conference on computer vision and pattern recognition, pp 995–1002, June 2013
42. Xue W, Mou X, Zhang L et al (2014) Blind image quality assessment using joint statistics of gradient magnitude and Laplacian features. IEEE Trans Image Process 23(11):4850–4862
43. Gu K, Zhai G, Yang X et al (2014) Hybrid no-reference quality metric for singly and multiply distorted images. IEEE Trans Broadcast 60(3):555–567
44. Mittal A, Soundararajan R, Bovik AC (2013) Making a "Completely blind" image quality analyzer. IEEE Signal Process Lett 20(3):209–212

Chapter 8
Quality Assessment of Super-Resolution Images

8.1 Introduction

Image super-resolution (SR) has extensively been utilized in a wide variety of applications, which contain infrared imaging, medical image processing, face recognition, and so on. This technology intends to generate a high-resolution (HR) image from one or several given low-resolution (LR) images. Many image SR algorithms have been presented in the past decades [1–6]. These SR algorithms can be divided into two categories based on the availability of LR images, namely multi-frame SR method and the single-frame SR method. Until now, there have been several single-image SR approaches proposed from different perspectives. Bilinear interpolation, bicubic interpolation, and Lanczos resampling [7] are the representative approaches that intend to simply utilize the information of LR images to acquire HR images. In general, the methods mentioned above are simple and efficient. However, there exist severe blending artifacts and blurring distortion in the edge and high-frequency areas due to pixel interpolation operations. They will reduce the image perception quality and affect image processing such as image enhancement and restoration. Hence, it is necessary to use the image quality assessment (QA) method to assess the SR image perceptual quality.

Recently, image QA has attracted extensive researchers' interest. The image QA approaches can be divided into subjective image QA method and objective image QA method based on whether humans are involved in quality evaluation. To the best of our knowledge, subjective QA approaches are expensive and time-consuming since they set human spectators as the ultimate recipient of images. This design has a weak ability to evaluate the system and optimize related parameters. Objective image QA methods utilize computational models to automatically assess the perceived quality of images. This kind of method is preferred by a wide range of researchers because of its high accuracy and strong robustness. The objective QA approaches can be categorized into three kinds, which are the full-reference (FR) approach, reduced-reference (RR) approach, and no-reference (NR) approach, separately. The FR image QA method needs the full information of the original reference image. The NR image QA method predicts the perceived quality of the distorted image when the original image is unavailable. The RR image QA method [8, 9] provides a balance between the FR and NR methods, which requires only a few features

© The Author(s), under exclusive license to Springer Nature Singapore Pte Ltd. 2022   217
K. Gu et al., *Quality Assessment of Visual Content*, Advances in Computer Vision
and Pattern Recognition, https://doi.org/10.1007/978-981-19-3347-9_8

or a lot of information from the original reference image. For example, in [10], the visual signal-to-noise-ratio takes advantage of the near-threshold and supra-threshold properties of human vision. In [11], Larson et al. proposed a method called most apparent distortion, which autonomously utilized Fourier transformation and log-Gabor filtering to extract visual features on the basis of distortion visibility. In [12], Mittal et al. presented a completely blind image quality analyzer by employing natural scene statistics (NSS) features.

Unlike the traditional images, the details in SR images are more important. In addition, existing image QA methods do not take into account several artifacts that may occur in SR images. Therefore, it is imperative to propose some image QA approaches that are specific to SR images. There exists an assumption that the human visual system (HVS) is extremely adaptive to the statistics of the natural visual environment, and deviation from such statistics is an unnatural feature of the image. To better perform the objective QA of SR images, NSS methods are proposed on the basis of the assumption. With the fast advancement of deep learning in image recognition tasks, a large number of researchers have established many deep learning-based methods for evaluating SR images, especially convolutional neural networks (CNNs)-based methods [13]. Besides, in [14], Gao et al. presented a deep similarity (DeepSim) metric that utilizes different levels of feature maps extracted from pre-trained deep CNN models to calculate the similarity. In [15], Liang et al. established a dual-stream Siamese network for assessing the distorted image perceptual quality score. In [16], Kim et al. constructed a deep image quality assessment (DeepQA) model, which searches for the best visual weights according to the understanding of database information itself without prior knowledge. In [17], Ma et al. designed an NR image QA method for single-image SR with a two-stage regression model and constructed an SR image QA database. On the basis of this database, Fang et al. [18] and Bare et al. [19] presented different CNN models for NR image QA problem of single-image SR. For evaluating the performance of those QA models, we also compared them with state-of-the-art competitors using four extensive employed standards, i.e., Spearman rank correlation coefficient (SRCC), Kendall rank correlation coefficient (KRCC), Pearson linear correlation coefficient (PLCC), and root mean square error (RMSE).

The organization of this chapter is arranged below. Section 8.2 introduces in detail the modeling process of two types of SR image QA approaches, namely the deep learning-based SR image QA method and the natural statistics-based SR image QA method. Section 8.3 finally draws the conclusion and provides the future work.

8.2 Methodology

In this section, we focus on two QA methods based on deep learning and a QA method based on NSS of SR images presented recently. One of the deep learning-based QA methods of SR images is the method based on a cascade regression, which establishes the mapping relationship between multiple natural statistical features and visual perception scores by learning a two-layer regression model. The other deep learning-based QA method of SR images is the method based on the combination of SR image QA loss function and L_2 Norm, which can effectively assess the visual perceptual quality of SR images. The NSS-based QA method of SR images is the method that quantifies the degradation of image quality using deviations from statistical models of frequency energy falloff and spatial continuity of high-quality natural images.

8.2.1 Creation of the QA Database for SR Image

Visual QA of SR Image: Databases and Methods

The commonly used image QA database contains most of the noise, such as blur noise, JPEG, JPEG2000, and so on which basically do not appear in SR images. This section will introduce a public QA database called quality assessment database for super-resolution images (QADS), and a subjective assessment method for SR images. The QADS database is open and publicly available from [20]. In addition, it is considered that the artifacts of the distorted SR image often appear in the texture region, while the other artifacts appear in the structure region. Here, a selective structure-texture decomposition (STD)-based technique is used to divide the image into texture region and structure region with separate scores for the quality of the two regions [21].

QA Database for SR Images

The reference images in QADS can also be called source images, and in SR image they are also HR. To select clean and diversified images as reference images in QADS, 20 reference images are selected from the multiply distorted image database (MDID) [22]. The above images contain broader spatial information (SI) and color-fulness [23] than other image QA databases, while, in subsequent experiments, it is found that the SI values of the two reference images are small. It leads to different SR methods generating similar visual results, which makes the subjective score unreliable. Consequently, two reference images commonly used in SR tests are selected to replace the two source images with small SI values. The size of all source images is controlled to 504 × 384 without scaling or rotation.

SI plays a vital role in the background of SR, because the goal of SR is to improve spatial resolution. The range of SI and the type of image content in the database are positively correlated. As they increase, the utilization value of the image increases. The SI for measuring the applicability of the reference image can be given by

$$SI = \sqrt{mean(d) \cdot range(d)}, \tag{8.1}$$

where d is the SI value defined in [23]. $mean(\cdot)$ returns the mean value of reference images, and $range(\cdot)$ returns the value range of reference images' arguments.

In order to obtain an SR image, the size of reference images is first reduced by k times ($k \in \{2, 3, 4\}$) using bicubic downsampling. Then reduced images are restored to their original size by 21 SR methods, including 11 dictionary-based SR methods, 6 DNN-based SR methods, and 4 interpolation-based methods separately. In order to avoid the visual effects of image boundaries, the image is cut into blocks with the size of 500 × 380. Finally, 980 SR images were generated by repeating the above process.

Owing to the low sampling rate, aliasing occurs in the high-frequency region when generating images. The extraction of high-frequency information after aliasing is the key to obtaining SR images. If the high-frequency information in SR images cannot be restored, the image will become blurred. Another common artifact in SR images is jaggies. It is generated by the incorrect high-frequency component in the anti-aliasing operation of SR. In addition, some other types of artifacts are included in QDAS, which makes QDAS different from other image QA databases.

Subjective Evaluation

The most significant step in the process of constructing an image database is subjective assessment. A total of 100 subjects with normal vision are asked to complete their assessment in an indoor environment without any light. The display device is a 23.8-inch liquid crystal display monitor with a spatial resolution of 1440 × 900 and default values for the rest of the display configuration.

During the subjective evaluation, the display will show 4 windows at the same time. The first row is the SR image to be evaluated, and the lower right corner is the reference image. In the psycho-visual assessment, subjects are able to make decisions faster and more accurately by looking at different images in the same location. Subjects were asked to view images in a window in the lower left corner, which could be switched between two distorted images and a reference image. During the evaluation process, subjects can click ">", "<", and "=" to select. The pair comparison sorting (PCS) algorithm is adopted here [22]. After ranking each SR image score, we can get a number that represents its quality indicator. Since each reference image in QADS has 49 SR images, the numbers range from 1 to 49. The lower the number, the worse the image quality.

The reliability of the final score can be measured by the standard deviation (SD), while the applicability can be measured by the homogeneity of MOS values [23]. The SD value is negatively correlated with the consistency of different image perception quality, so a smaller SD value means a more reliable final score.

Image QA for SR Images Using Structure-Texture Decomposition

Some artifacts in SR images appear mainly in the texture part, followed by the structure part. Some artifacts have little effect on the structure during the construction of QADS, but can be easily observed in the visual psychological evaluation. Inspired by this, an FR image QA algorithm based on STD for SR images is proposed. It divides the image into structural regions and texture regions, and evaluates SR images, respectively, to test image QA scores of different artifact types.

If the textures of two areas belong to one category, it is difficult to detect the difference between them even if the difference between the fixed image position is large. In contrast, it is easy to detect large structural differences at fixed locations. The texture component and the structural component will then be grouped together separately, where the structural component will occur at a specific structural location. Since the HVS is more sensitive to structural changes than texture changes, most FR image QA methods concentrate on structural distortions. Nevertheless, it is vital for SR images to study the artifacts on the texture.

Textural Similarity

The HVS focuses on texture types. When two areas have completely different texture types, the difference between them is easily perceived. And when they have similar texture distribution, the visual perception is similar. So the texture distribution can be calculated by statistical descriptors. The scale-invariant feature transform (SIFT) descriptor [24] is applied to obtain a quality map with spatial variation for rendering the SI of artifacts. It can calculate the scale and rotation-free SIFT features for each pixel of the texture components. This is not only more efficient than considering both scale and rotation, but also satisfies the purpose of describing texture distribution. The dense SIFT feature is essentially a series of histograms that describe the gradient distribution of image regions. Using histogram-based features, the texture similarity measure of the ith pixel $S_t(i)$ is computed by

$$S_t(i) = \frac{\left\langle \frac{\mathbf{f}_r}{||\mathbf{f}_r(i)||_2}, \frac{\mathbf{f} f_u(i)}{||\mathbf{f}_u(i)||} \right\rangle + V_t(i)}{1 + V_t(i)}, \tag{8.2}$$

where $|| \cdot ||$ is L2-norm, and $< \cdot, \cdot >$ represents inner product. $\mathbf{f}_r(i)$ and $\mathbf{f}_u(i)$ are the histogram feature vectors of the ith pixel in the texture component of the pristine image and the SR image, separately. The adaptive variable V_t is defined as

$$K_t(i) = \frac{C_t}{m(v(t_r(i)), v(t(i)))}, \tag{8.3}$$

where $t_r(i)$ and $t_u(i)$ denote the patches and SR image centered on the ith pixel in the reference image texture component. C_t is a positive number used to constantly calibrate the range of V_t. The function of V_t is somewhat similar to the shielding parameter in [25]. $v(\cdot)$ and $m(\cdot)$ are variances in parameters and maximum values of parameters, respectively.

From the above two equations, it can be seen that texture similarity S_t has the following three characteristics. (1) S_t is between 0 and 1. The higher the correlation between normalized $\mathbf{f}_r$ and $\mathbf{f}_u$, the more similar the texture distribution, and the larger the value of S_t. (2) When the reference and SR patches are rich in texture, that is, when the variance is large, the effect of V_t on S_t is small. The value of S_t is determined only by $\mathbf{f}_r$ and $\mathbf{f}_u$. (3) If both the original image and SR patches have small textures, the V_t value will be very large, making S_t to 1. From a psychological point of view, a more reasonable approach is to perform frequency analysis and compare sensitivity functions to determine texture visibility. But the satisfactory results of Eq. (8.3) can already be achieved. After calculating each S_t, it is possible to get a texture similarity map.

Structural Similarity (SSIM)

In addition to the texture and checkerboard in the texture component, other artifacts, such as jaggies, mainly appear in the structural components of the image. Jaggies are a common artifact in SR images, which usually leads to directional distortion of the structure. In order to measure it, the dominant direction of gradient comparison in structural components is selected here. The semidefinite matrix J [26] can derive the dominant direction of plaque, which is defined as follows:

$$J(i) = \begin{bmatrix} \mathbf{g}_x^T(i)\mathbf{g}_x(i) & \mathbf{g}_x^T(i)\mathbf{g}_y(i) \\ \mathbf{g}_y^T(i)\mathbf{g}_x(i) & \mathbf{g}_y^T(i)\mathbf{g}_y(i) \end{bmatrix}, \tag{8.4}$$

where i represents the index of the patch center location. $\mathbf{g}_x$ and $\mathbf{g}_y$ represent the lexicographical gradient vectors along the x-coordinate and y-coordinate, respectively. The matrix J contains two eigenvalues, and the dominant direction can be represented by the eigenvector of the next eigenvalue. Similar to Eq. (8.2), the SSIM metric of the ith pixel $S_s(I)$ can be defined as

$$S_s(i) = \frac{|\langle \mathbf{n}_r(i), \mathbf{n}_u(i) \rangle| + V_s(i)}{1 + V_s(i)}, \tag{8.5}$$

where $|\cdot|$ is the absolute value symbol. $\mathbf{n}_r(i)$ and $\mathbf{n}_u(i)$ are normally feature vectors. The former represents the dominant direction at the ith pixel of the reference image structural component, while the latter is the dominant direction at the ith pixel of the SR image structural component. V_s is defined as

$$V_t(i) = \frac{C_s}{m(g_{mr}(i), g_{ms}(i))}, \tag{8.6}$$

where $gmr(i)$ and $gms(i)$ are the normalized gradient amplitudes at the ith pixel of the reference image and the SR image structure component, separately. C_s is the normal number to adjust the range of V_s. It should be noted that if n and $-n$ are the normalized eigenvectors corresponding to the given eigenvalues. In brief, the absolute value in Eq. (8.5) is very important.

Since Eqs. (8.2) and (8.5) have the same mathematical formula, S_s has similar characteristics to S_t. To be specific, if the reference image or SR image shows a strong structural gradient, the effect of V_s on Eq. (8.5) can be ignored. If they are structurally smooth, the estimation of the dominant direction will be affected by noise and become unreliable. In this case, V_s will play an important role so that S_s is 1 to get a reasonable result. The characteristics of V_s and S_t suggest that the design of texture and SSIM qualitatively conform to visual perception.

High-Frequency Similarity

SR images will become blurred when high frequency details are lost. Although the texture and structure of the image are blurred, the texture similarity defined by Eq. (8.2) can distinguish between blurred texture and sharp texture. The high-frequency similarity is used to calculate to distinguish Eq. (8.5) due to depend to the structural. The following equation is used to calculate the high-frequency energy of the ith pixel position:

$$h(i) = \frac{1}{N_D} \sum_{j \in D(i)} (s(j) - s_\sigma(j))^2, \tag{8.7}$$

where j represents the location index. $D(i)$ indicates the neighborhood of i and its number is represented by D_N. s is the structural component. In Eq. (8.7), s_σ represents the low-frequency part of s, which is obtained by convolution s of Gaussian filter with SD as σ. Comparing the reference image with the high-frequency energy in SR image, the high-frequency similarity of the ith pixel $S_h(i)$ is given by the following:

$$S_h(i) = \frac{2h_r(i)h_u(i) + C_h}{h_r^2(i) + h_u^2(i) + C_h}, \tag{8.8}$$

where h_r and h_u can be obtained from Eq. (8.7) in the original image and SR image, separately. C_h is the positive number set to prevent instability caused by too small denominators. In Eq. (8.8), it has been proved to be consistent with the masking effect in many previous studies [27–30].

Pooling

When calculating the final quality of SR images, the three quality maps are converted into three scores, and then they are fused into one score. The pooling of each map is achieved by a weighted average:

$$P_q = \frac{1}{N} \sum_i w_q(i)S_q(i), \tag{8.9}$$

where N refers to the pixel number in an image. q could be $t/s/h$, which is three similar indices. p_q is each similarity score, and w_q is the weight of each pixel. The weight in Eq. (8.9) is calculated by the content in each map:

$$w_i(i) = \frac{m(v(t_r(i)), v(t_u(i)))}{\sum_i m(v(t_r(i)), v(t_u(i)))}, \tag{8.10}$$

$$w_s(i) = \frac{m(g_{mr}(i), g_{mu}(i))}{\sum_i m(g_{mr}(i), g_{mu}(i))}, \tag{8.11}$$

$$w_h(i) = \frac{m(h_r(i), h_u(i))}{\sum_i m(h_r(i), h_u(i))}. \tag{8.12}$$

The denominators of Eqs. (8.10)–(8.12) are all used for normalization. If multiple quality maps are combined into a single map, the design of weights becomes more complex. By integrating the above three scores, the final single score P is obtained:

$$p = p_i^{\alpha} \cdot (p_s \cdot p_h)^{\beta}. \tag{8.13}$$

Both α and β are positive to adjust the influence of different similarity degrees. Since the structure and high-frequency similarity are both estimated in the structure component, their fractions use the parameter β with the same value. The structural information is more important in HVS generally, so β is greater than α. In keeping with this generality, α is set to 1. The value of β can be acquired by calculating the ratio between them:

$$\beta = \frac{\beta}{\alpha} = \frac{log(mean(|s|))}{log(mean(|t|))}, \tag{8.14}$$

where s is the intensity of image structure component, t represents the intensity of image texture component. In Eq. (8.14), the $log(\cdot)$ function is used to follow the Weber-Fechner law. Since the structural strength is generally greater than the texture strength, the β value is set to be greater than 1. In addition, the parameter β here is estimated from an external image, not from an image in QADS.

Subjective and Perceptual Evaluation of Single-Image SR Reconstruction

Twenty images of LR nature with diverse contents are selected, containing animals, natural landscapes, buildings, humans, and so on. The HR images with different distortions are generated by processing the LR images with two interpolation algorithms and six image enhancement algorithms. The above algorithms are separately nearest interpolation, bicubic interpolation iterative curvature-based interpolation, coupled dictionary training for image SR, Gaussian process regression for SR, and so on. When interpolating LR images, three different magnification factors are used, namely 2, 4, and 8. It has been experimentally proven that as the magnification factor increases, the MOS average value of the SR reconstructed image decreases accordingly. Finally, the produced HR images constitute a database.

The SR enhanced image is enhanced by bicubic interpolation, nearest interpolation, and fuzzy-rule-based approach for single-frame SR. As the magnification factor increases, the image quality after SR enhancement decreases. SR reconstructed images are often affected by a variety of distortions, including blurring, ringing, and unnatural local textures. Therefore, it is difficult to evaluate the perceptual quality of the SR reconstructed image with the image QA model designed for distortion.

To conduct a subjective QA method of SR image, twenty non-professional subjects are selected to attend the subjective experiment (all without visual impairment). They are between 20 and 30 years old. All SR-enhanced images displayed at the original resolution are shown to the candidates in a random order. At the commencement of the subjective experiment, a set of training examples is used to illustrate the range of quality levels. In order to obtain an accurate subjective score, the maximum and minimum values of each image are deleted. Then the MOS is calculated as the final image quality.

8.2.2 QA of SR Image Based on Deep Learning

The single-image SR reconstruction upsamples an LR image to produce a high-quality HR image with finer details, which cannot be directly captured by a physical imaging system. The HR image obtained by HR cameras will result in a lot of production costs and manpower. In order to solve this problem, researchers have carried out extensive research on the SISR algorithm. SR image quality assessment technique as one of the most important parts of the SR technique field can evaluate the quality of SR images and the superiority of SR algorithms. Researchers have designed many SR QA methods and introduced deep learning techniques to better achieve objective QA of SR images. In the following content, we will introduce two deep learning-based SR image QA methods based on learning cascade regression and specific loss functions.

Learning Cascaded Regression for NR SR Image QA

No-reference super-resolution image quality assessment (NR-SRIQA) is not dependent on any information from original images, which makes it more meaningful in practical application compared with the FR or RR methods. The NR-SRIQA extracts the statistical features of SR images and uses them to train models to estimate the quality scores of specific images. It is an effective method to assess the quality of SR images. By combining deep learning technology, the model can establish a more robust mapping relationship between the multiple natural statistical features and the visual perception scores. In this part, we will introduce a new cascaded regression model consisting of a two-layer regression model, which incorporates ridge regression and AdaBoost decision tree regression. The introduced method achieves a coarse-to-fine manner to obtain the predicted quality score of SR images by training on the multi-perceptual feature extracted from the SR images.

Multi-Perceptual Feature Modeling

The key problem is that the NR-SRIQA fails to extract effective visual perceptual features that can represent SR image degradation, while this part uses the following methods to acquire the features capable of representing the degradation mechanism of SR images.

Local Frequency Features In the local frequency, there are many methods that can be utilized to analyze the distribution of discrete cosine transform (DCT) coefficients. Among them, the generalized Gaussian distribution (GGD) is often utilized, and its expression is defined as follows:

$$f(z \mid \mu, \gamma) = \frac{1}{2\Gamma(1 + \gamma^{-1})} e^{-(|z-\mu|^{\gamma})}, \tag{8.15}$$

where z represents a random variable, μ denotes the average of z, γ indicates a shape parameter, and Γ is conventionally calculated by $\Gamma(u) = \int_0^\infty t^{u-1} e^{-t} dt$. The first part of local frequency is composed of γ values on different subbands. The DCT coefficients in each block are divided into 3 groups, and then the normalized deviation $\bar{\sigma} = \sigma/\mu$ is calculated. Next, the sum of the normalized deviation in each group is computed and these are used as part of the local frequency. The discriminative capacity of this model can be increased by using the top and bottom 10% after ranking, and those values are taken as another part of the local frequency features. The above three components can be assembled together to indicate the local frequency statistical feature x_1.

Global Frequency Features Generalized neighborhood wavelet coefficients can be obtained by an operable pyramid decomposition method considering global frequency. The shape parameters of different wavelet subbands can be calculated from six directions and two scales, which can be used as the first part of the global frequency features. In addition, the global degradation degree of the image can be predicted by measuring the structural correlation coefficient between the high-pass response and the corresponding bandpass response. The structure correlation coefficient can be defined as

$$\rho = (2\sigma_{ab} + c) / (\sigma_a^2 + \sigma_b^2), \tag{8.16}$$

where σ_{ab} represents the cross-covariance variance between the high-pass responses and the corresponding bandpass responses. σ_a is the variances of high-pass response and σ_b is the variances of the corresponding bandpass response, c is a constant coefficient. Same as the method used in local frequency features, the global frequency statistical features x_2 are composed of the aforementioned two statistical features.

Spatial Features In the spatial domain, singular values of local patches obtained by principal component analysis (PCA) can describe the spatial discontinuity of SR images. So, the singular values are regarded as spatial feature x_3 which measures the discontinuous artifacts of the SR images.

Cascade Regression

Evaluating Quality with AdaBoost Decision Tree

The AdaBoost decision tree regression algorithm adopts an addition model that combines the basis function in a linear way and a forward stage-wise algorithm. AdaBoost can be considered as an additive model with a decision tree as a basis function. The local frequency, global frequency, and spatial frequency models $\hat{q}_{M_j} \in R$ $(j = 1,\ 2,\ 3)$ that are independent of the others can be formulated as

$$\hat{q}_{M_j}(\mathbf{x}_j) = \sum_{m=1}^{M_j} \alpha_m T(\mathbf{x}_j \Phi_m), \tag{8.17}$$

where $T(\mathbf{x}_j;\ \Phi_m)$ denotes the special decision tree, and α_m represents the weight of the corresponding decision tree that is acquired by running the AdaBoost regression algorithm. x_j stands for the jth type of feature vectors and Φ_m is the corresponding parameter of mth decision tree. The parameter M_j represents the number of decision trees. The AdaBoost decision tree regression algorithm uses a forward stage-wise way to build the additive model. More specifically, the decision tree model obtained at the mth step can be formulated by

$$\hat{q}_m(\mathbf{x}_j) = \hat{q}_{m-1}(\mathbf{x}_j) + \alpha_m T(\mathbf{x}_j;\ \Phi_m), \tag{8.18}$$

where $\hat{q}_{m-1}(\mathbf{x}_j)$ represents the current decision tree model. Empirical risk minimization is used to determine the parameter Φ_m^* of the next decision tree model, which can be calculated by

$$\Phi_m^* = \arg\min_{\Phi_m} \sum_{i=1}^{n} L\left[Q_i, \hat{q}_{m-1}(\mathbf{x}_{ij}) + T(\mathbf{x}_{ij};\ \Phi_m)\right], \tag{8.19}$$

where Q_i denotes the subjective quality score of the ith SR image, and n represents the sum of training images. X_{ij} stands for the jth feature vectors of the ith SR image. $L(\cdot)$ refers to the squared error loss function; in the AdaBoost decision tree model, its representation can be described in the following form:

$$L\left[Q_i, \hat{q}_{m-1}(\mathbf{x}_{ij}) + T(\mathbf{x}_{ij};\ \Phi_m)\right] = \left[Q_i - \hat{q}_{m-1}(\mathbf{x}_{ij}) - T(\mathbf{x}_{ij};\ \Phi_m)\right]^2. \tag{8.20}$$

According to the constructing regression model described in Eq. (8.17), a rough image quality score estimation can be obtained by local frequency, global frequency, and spatial frequency models, respectively. With the above three models, we can obtain a vector $\hat{q} = \left[\hat{q}_{M_1}, \hat{q}_{M_2}, \hat{q}_{M_3}\right]^T \in R^3$, and the vector values $\hat{q}_{M_1}, \hat{q}_{M_2}, \hat{q}_{M_3}$ represent perceptual features of local frequency, global frequency, and spatial frequency, separately.

Improving Quality with Ridge Regression

The above three AdaBoost decision trees produce preliminary results for SR image quality scores. These vector values $\hat{q}_{M_1}, \hat{q}_{M_2}, \hat{q}_{M_3}$ can be further optimized to reduce the gap between the estimated value and the truth value and to make the assessment results more accurate. The linear regression can establish the mapping relationship between prediction quality and expected subjective quality score, which can be calculated with L2 Norm. The formula for L2 Norm is as follows:

$$b^* = \arg\min_b \left\{ \|\mathbf{Q} - b\hat{\mathbf{q}}\|_2^2 \right\}, \tag{8.21}$$

where $\mathbf{Q}$ is the subjective scores of all training images. The first level is the predicted score $\hat{\mathbf{q}}$ of the three AdaBoost decision trees for all images in the training set. b is the parameters to be learned by the model. Ridge regression is normalized by means of linear regression. Adding the regularization term $\beta\|b\|_2^2$ to the cost function makes the learning algorithm not only fit the data, but it also makes the model weight as small as possible. With the regularization term, the second level of ridge regression can be described in the following form:

$$b^* = \arg\min_b \left\{ \|\mathbf{Q} - b\hat{\mathbf{q}}\|_2^2 + \beta\|b\|_2^2 \right\}, \tag{8.22}$$

where β is a positive integer used to adjust the trade-off of reconstruction error and regularization term. The first item in Eq. (8.22) can be explained as the following. With the subjective evaluation score obtained by the AdaBoost decision tree regression, the second layer's prediction score should be consistent with the subjective scores. At the same time, the regularization term aims to acquire a more stable solution of the learnable parameter b. Equation (8.22) can be solved by calculating a closed-form equation, which can be represented as

$$b^* = \mathbf{Q}\hat{\mathbf{q}}^T \left(\hat{\mathbf{q}}\hat{\mathbf{q}}^T + \beta\mathbf{I} \right)^{-1}, \tag{8.23}$$

where $\mathbf{I}$ indicates a 3×3 identity matrix.

After getting the value of b, it is possible to acquire the final predicted quality score $\hat{Q}$ for the image. The following is the test procedure. First, local frequency, global frequency, and spatial features of the given SR image are extracted. Then, these features are put into the first stage of this model named the AdaBoost decision tree regression model. Finally, the vector values $\hat{q}_{M_1}, \hat{q}_{M_2}, \hat{q}_{M_3}$ obtained in the first stage are input into the second stage to acquire the final predicted quality score $\hat{Q}$, which is calculated by

$$\hat{Q} = \hat{\mathbf{q}}b^*. \tag{8.24}$$

Single-Image SR Driving Deep Target Quality Evaluation

In the area of image processing, single-image SR is a valuable research direction. By using this technique, an LR image can turn into an HR one. Recently, the proposed methods commonly use L2 Norm as the loss function, based on deep learning. These methods substantially improve the PSNR, but it has less effect on image per-

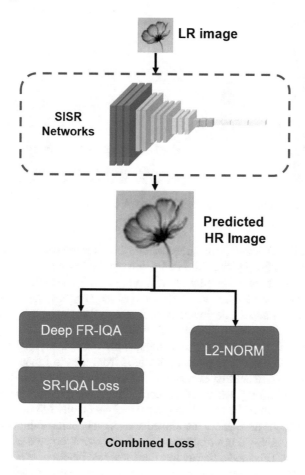

Fig. 8.1 The structure of the designed model

ceptual quality. In order to break through this limitation, an objective single-image SR QA method has been introduced.

Proposed FR Image QA Method

Figure 8.1 shows the structure of this method. It can be learned that the proposed single-image SR method utilizes an LR image as input and outputs the HR result. The HR image is generated by the guidance of the designed deep FR image QA method for SR images and L2 Norm.

In the training process of single-image SR method based on CNNs, the original images can be obtained. On this basis, an advanced SR image QA model based on deep learning [31] has been improved in three aspects. Firstly, this method's input is changed by the error map between the original image and the final results. Secondly, the normalization process utilized in [31] is elided. That is, the discrepancy

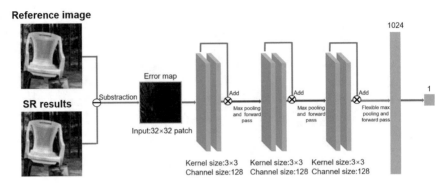

Fig. 8.2 The framework of the proposed FR image QA method

between the original image luminance map and the SR result becomes the input of the introduced FR image QA method. Finally, it fixed the flexible max pooling layer as the second layer after the first fully connected layer. The size of the flexible maximal pooling window can be found to be the same as the previous layer's output feature map size. It means that the flexible max pooling can alter the input's size into a fixed value and transmit it back to the first fully connected layer.

The framework of the FR image QA method is exhibited in Fig. 8.2. The input of this method is a 32×32 small patch, obtained from the error map. To be specific, this FR image QA model first extracts 32×32 patches without overlaps. Then, the method estimates each patch's quality score. Finally, all the patches' quality scores are utilized to compute the average score as the final quality score.

In addition to the differences mentioned above, other parts of this network are the same as Bare et al. So, a brief introduction of the overall process of this method is given as follows. This model first adopts three residual blocks to extract features. All the residual blocks are composed of two convolutional layers, in which the rectified linear unit (ReLU) as the activation function is utilized in the first layer. After residual blocks, max pooling is employed to expand the region of reception, which will lead to the convolutional layer's feature map size being shrunk by half. To better extract features, the channel size is expanded twice as large as before. After the two residual blocks, max pooling is added to expand the field of residual. Since the size of the pooling window is set to 2×2 with stride 2; the max pooling layer can fix the input size to better suit the training process of a variety of single-image SR methods.

Proposed Single-Image SR Method

To make a comparison of newly proposed methods with other advanced methods, the channel size of every convolutional layer is enlarged between 32 and 64. Based on previous studies [32], a novel designed loss function is adopted to guide the single-image SR network. It outperforms other SR methods in perceptual quality and the values of two metrics, i.e., PSNR and SSIM. In addition, the previous work's input is altered into the LR image, and transpose convolution is utilized to conduct upsampling in the final.

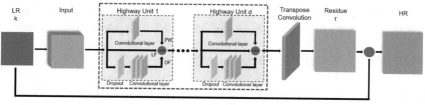

Bicubic interpolation

Fig. 8.3 The framework of the proposed single-image SR method

Network Framework

Figure 8.2 exhibits the model's structure. To converge faster, this method firstly preprocesses an LR image k, and produces a horizontal gradient map, vertical gradient map, and luminance map. Then these three maps are used together to generate a new signal. The new input signal passes cascaded architecture composed of n highway units and transposes the convolution layer to generate a residual map r. Finally, the bicubic upsampled version of k image and estimated residual image r are combined together to produce an HR image. This process can be defined as follows:

$$P = CL_{out}(HWU_n(HWU_{n-1}...(HWU_1(CL_{in}(Input))))), \qquad (8.25)$$

where HWU indicates the highway unit, and n is the sum of highway units. CL_{in} and CL_{out} represent the input and the output transpose convolutional layer, respectively. *Input* is the new signal obtained by combining three maps. The final HR image can be produced by

$$HR = Bicubic(LR) + P, \qquad (8.26)$$

where P represents the learned residual image, and $Bicubic(LR)$ is the upsampled version of LR image with bicubic interpolation.

The cascaded highway unit framework is the single-image SR network's main innovation. Since every pixel of the image has a different perception, a highway unit is designed to learn to signal each pixel's weight value, which is utilized to weightily increase both input and output signals. By transmitting the processed version of the LR image to the highway unit, an accurate residual image P can be obtained. The final HR image is visually pleasing and clear. From Fig. 8.3, it can be found that every highway unit composes of two branches. Three convolutional layers with 64 kernel sizes of 5×5 form the lower branch, which is adopted to transform the lower feature LF into the deeper feature DF. It is worth mentioning that the first two convolutional layers of the lower branch set the ReLU as an activation function, and the third convolutional layer is based on residual learning without nonlinear activation. To avoid overfitting, the dropout [33] is added at the beginning of the lower branch. The main function of the upper branch is to produce every pixel's weight value of PW. The upper branch only consists of a convolutional layer with 64 kernels of size 5×5 and a sigmoid layer. Since the weight value of each pixel is in the region of [0, 1], the sigmoid layer is considered as the nonlinear activation in the convolutional layer. The authors use the obtained weight values to combine LF and DF from the union layer. The process of combination can be expressed by

$$CO = PW \times DF + (1 - PW) \times LF, \qquad (8.27)$$

where CO indicates the final output of this combination process.

Novel Loss Function

The previous work about CNN-based algorithms [34, 35] takes L2 Norm as the loss function. With the decreasing of the L2 Norm, the perceived quality of the image decreases. To synchronously increase the measured PSNR value and perceived quality of the produced image, a novel loss function is constructed. This loss function is a weighted number of the L2 Norm and SR image QA loss, whose value is between zero and one. A value closer to 0 indicates a worse result and closer to 1 indicates a better result. Based on this, the $|1-SRIQA|$ is considered as an SR image QA loss. The three loss functions can be formulated as follows:

$$L_2 = ||G(LR : \omega) - GT||_2, \qquad (8.28)$$

$$L_{SRIQA} = ||1 - SRIQA(G(LR; \omega))||_2, \qquad (8.29)$$

$$Loss = L_{SRIQA} + \beta L_2, \qquad (8.30)$$

$$\omega = \arg\min Loss, \qquad (8.31)$$

where L_2, L_{SRIQA}, and L_{oss} denote the L2 Norm loss, SR image QA loss, and total loss function, respectively. $G(LR; \omega)$ represents the HR patch derived from the LR via the designed single-image SR network G with weight ω. GT is the ground value of HR patch, $SRIQA(\cdot)$ is the FR image QA model proposed for single-image SR, and β is the weight of L2 Norm. In the work, the β is set as 0.1 to make these two losses have unified magnitude order.

8.2.3 Natural Statistics-Based SR Image QA

Recently, a growing number of image SR methods have been developed to build better spatial resolution pictures from LR images. Although automatic or objective image QA techniques for image SR are very desirable, little progress has been made thus far. Due to the fact that a perfect quality HR image is unavailable to compare with, common image QA methods such as SSIM, PCNR are unreliable. This part will introduce two image QA algorithms based on the philosophy behind the NSS approach.

Image SR Quality Evaluation Based on Energy Change and Texture Variation

We introduce a new reduced-reference image quality assessment super-resolution (RRIQA-SR) based on LR image information in this part. The pixel correspondence between LR and HR pictures is first modeled using the Markov random field (MRF). The perceived similarity between picture patches of LR and HR images is predicted by two components based on the pixel correspondence, namely energy change and texture variation. The perceptual similarity between local image patches of LR and HR pictures is used to determine the overall quality of HR images.

Pixel Correspondence

The pixel connection between the LR and HR pictures is absent because of the large size of the HR image generated by the LR image pixels. To compute the local distortion in HR images, the MRF [36] in an energy minimization framework is used to represent the pixel correspondence between LR and HR images as follows [37]:

$$
E = \sum_p \min d\left(g(p), g\left(p'\right)\right) + \\
\omega \sum_{(p,q')\in\Phi} \min(|\mu(p) - \mu(q)| + |\nu(p) - \nu(q)|),
\tag{8.32}
$$

where $d(g(p), g(p'))$ denotes the distance between the features at pixel pair p and p', and $(\mu(p), \nu(p))$ is the vector at pixel p. Φ is the set including the spatial neighbors centering at pixel p, and ω is a parameter that determines the relative importance.

Energy Change and Texture Variation

In this part, the energy change and texture variation between image patches in LR and HR images are calculated. It can use IM_{LR} and IM_{HR} to represent an LR image and its corresponding HR image. Their sizes are represented as $M_{LR} \times N_{LR}$ and $M_{HR} \times N_{HR}$. Then the formula for calculating energy change and texture variation between LR and HR images is written. To calculate the energy change and texture variation, the authors extract one image patch pair based on the pixel correspondence of each image pixel p in the LR image:

$$
S_k\left(IM_{LR}, IM_{HR}\right) = \sum_{(b,b')} f_k\left(b, b'\right),
\tag{8.33}
$$

where k means the energy or texture feature, and f_k indicates the function controlling the energy change or texture variation. b and b' are the corresponding image patches centered on the pixel pair p and p' in LR and HR images, respectively.

Next, the DCT is introduced in this algorithm. The DC coefficient, which encompasses the majority of the image energy, indicates the image's energy, while the AC coefficient represents the frequency components in images [38]. The energy characteristic of each picture patch is represented by the DC coefficient, whereas the texture feature is taken from the AC coefficient.

Given any image patch pair b and b' from LR and HR images, the DC coefficient of b and b' is calculated by DCT as D and D', respectively. The mean energy change between the image patch pair can be calculated as

$$f_e\left(b, b'\right) = \frac{2im_D im_{D'} + C_1}{im_D^2 + im_{D'}^2 + C_1},$$

(8.34)

where C_1 is a constant, im_D and im'_D represent the mean energy values in image patches b and b', separately.

The AC coefficient is employed to express texture variation between picture patch pairs in LR and HR images. For any image patch b with size $N_b \times N_b$ in the LR image, it has $N_b^2 - 1$ AC coefficients: $A = \left\{A_1, A_2, A_3, \ldots, A_{N_b^2-1}\right\}$. For any image patch $N_{b'}$ in the HR image, there are $N_b^2 - 1$ AC coefficients: $A' = \left\{A'_1, A'_2, A'_3, \ldots, A'_{N_{b'}^2-1}\right\}$. Differences in the mean and standard deviation values of AC coefficients can be used to determine texture variation across picture patches in LR and HR images. The texture variation by the patch differences between image patches b and b' can be calculated as

$$f_t\left(b, b'\right) = \frac{(2m_A m_{A'} + C_2)(2d_A d_{A'} + C_3)}{(m_A^2 + m_{A'}^2 + C_2)(d_A^2 + d_{A'}^2 + C_3)},$$

(8.35)

where m_A and $m_{A'}$ are the values of the vectors $\mathbf{A}$ and $\mathbf{A}'$, separately. d_A and $d_{A'}$ denote the standard deviation of the vectors $\mathbf{A}$ and $\mathbf{A}'$. Thus, it is possible to estimate the energy change and texture variation of the HR image from the LR image.

Overall Quality Prediction

As mentioned earlier, the energy change in HR images degrades the image's overall visual information, whereas texture variation would produce the visual distortion in high-frequency regions. As a result, the visual quality of HR images can be evaluated by combining these two components with the following equation:

$$Q = F_e^\beta F_t^\gamma,$$

(8.36)

where F_e and F_t reflect the sum of predicted energy change and texture variation from all LR and HR patch pairs. β and γ are parameters used to adjust the relative importance of these two components and are set to 1.

Objective QA of Image SR: A Statistical Method for Natural Scenes

This part develops an objective image QA method for a given HR image using the available LR image as a reference. The NSS method is utilized. It is based on the idea that the HVS is well attuned to the statistics of the natural visual environment, and picture unnaturalness is defined by deviations from these statistics. The statistical models are created in both the spatial and frequency domains, then are integrated to get an overall HR image distortion metric.

Frequency Energy Falloff Statistics

The forehead study shows that the amplitude spectrum of natural images falls with the spatial frequency approximately following $1/f^p$. f is utilized to represent the spatial frequency, and p is used to denote image-dependent constant. This aids in the development of a statistical model based on frequency energy falloff. A steerable pyramid transform is utilized to break down both the HR and LR pictures into dyadic scales. The sum of squared transform coefficients in each scale is then computed, and the energy is observed as it decreases from rough to fine scales.

With this theory, we apply the aforementioned algorithm to high-quality LR and HR natural photo pairs, and then investigate how well the LR falloff curves predict the HR falloff curves. For HR and LR pictures, the slopes of the falloffs between the ith and $(i+1)$th scales are indicated as s_k^H and s_k^L. To predict s_k^H from s_k^L, the direct prediction is precise for the first two slopes, which can be represented as $\hat{s}_1^H = s_1^L$ and $\hat{s}_2^H = s_2^L$. The following linear models can accurately forecast the third and fourth slopes:

$$\begin{aligned} \hat{s}_3^H &= a_0 + a_1 s_3^L \\ \hat{s}_4^H &= b_0 + b_1 s_4^L \end{aligned} \tag{8.37}$$

The authors use genuine high-quality natural photos and a simple least square regression to generate the prediction coefficients a_0, a_1, b_0, and b. We then use $\hat{s}_3^H$ and $\hat{s}_4^H$ to predict the slope between the scales by

$$\hat{s}_5^H = c_0 + c_1 \hat{s}_3^H + c_2 \hat{s}_4^H. \tag{8.38}$$

After predicting all the slopes, we can reconstruct the predicted frequency energy decay curve of the HR image. The original HR image is inaccessible when working on the SR QA challenge. Depending on the picture and the SR or interpolation technique, the falloffs of obtained HR images might be rather varied. As a result, the normalized error in frequency energy falloff between the forecast and the slope of the HR image at the best scale is

$$e_f = \frac{\hat{s}_5^H - s_5^H}{\hat{s}_5^H}. \tag{8.39}$$

When the HR picture is a high-quality original image, e_f should be near zero. We test this using 1400 high-quality natural images and could fit it well using a GGD function:

$$p_{e_f}(e_f) = \frac{1}{Z_f} \exp\left[-\left(\frac{|e_f - \mu_f|}{\alpha_f}\right)^{\beta_f}\right], \tag{8.40}$$

where $Z_f = \frac{\beta_f}{2\alpha_f \Gamma(1/\beta_f)}$ is a normalization factor, μ_f is the center of the distribution, and αf and β_f are the width and shape parameters, separately. As β_f decreases, this density function becomes sharper at the center.

Spatial Continuity Statistics

This part studies the continuity-based statistical model in the spatial domain and relates it to the naturalness of images. Let $f(i)$, $i \in \{0, \ldots, N-1\}$ be one row (or column) of pixels extracted from the image, where N is the number of pixels in the row. Calculating an absolute different signal is a simple way to check for signal continuity:

$$g(i) = |f(i+1) - f(i)|, 0 \le i \le N - 2. \tag{8.41}$$

However, the even and odd samples in $f(i)$ may exhibit different degrees of continuity, which may result in patterns observed in $g(i)$ computed from high-quality natural images. To quantify this, we compute

$$e_s = \frac{1}{M} \sum_{i=0}^{M-1} [g(2i) - g(2i+1)], \tag{8.42}$$

where $M = N/2$. This spatial continuity measure is calculated for each row and column in the image. Then all rows and columns are averaged to obtain a single overall spatial continuity measure for the whole image. The histogram can be fitted with the following GGD model:

$$p_{e_s}(e_s) = \frac{1}{Z_s} \exp\left[-\left(\frac{|e_s - \mu_s|}{\alpha_s}\right)^{\beta_s}\right], \tag{8.43}$$

where Z_s is a normalization factor.

QA Model

According to the statistics, a high-quality HR natural picture obtains near-maximum values in both parameters with a high probability. The interpolated HR images may deviate from these statistics, resulting in lower readings. Assuming that the two probability models are independent, the normalized joint probability measure of naturalness is calculated by

$$p_n = \frac{1}{K} p_{e_f}(e_f) p_{e_s}(e_s). \tag{8.44}$$

It is straightforward to find that

$$K = \frac{1}{Z_f Z_s}. \tag{8.45}$$

This probability-based metric is converted to a "surprisal"-based distortion measure using a well-known approach in information theory:

$$D_n = -\log p_n. \tag{8.46}$$

Then it can finally get

$$D_n = \left(\frac{|e_f - \mu_f|}{\alpha_f}\right)^{\beta_f} + \left(\frac{|e_s - \mu_s|}{\alpha_s}\right)^{\beta_s} \equiv D_f + D_s, \tag{8.47}$$

where D_n is a straightforward and elegant measure that does not involve any training with corrupted pictures (all parameters are generated using just high-quality natural images). But it does not consider the differences in visual discomfort to different types of distortions. Giving various weights to different attributes is a natural extension of this strategy. As a consequence, a weighted distortion measure is calculated as follows:

$$D_w = (1 + w)D_f + (1 - w)D_s, \tag{8.48}$$

where the relative importance of D_f and D_s is determined by w.

8.3 Comparison and Analysis of Algorithm Performance

In this section, we introduce several state-of-the-art SR image QA methods. We focus on comparing and measuring the performance of the presented QA approaches in this chapter with these methods. The specific analysis will be illustrated in the following sections. It is worth mentioning that the analysis results show that the performance of these methods in this chapter perform quite well.

8.3.1 Performance Comparison and Analysis

In order to demonstrate the validity and superiority of the methods introduced in this chapter, we compare the proposed approaches with the state-of-the-art image QA methods. All methods are listed in Table 8.1. Among them, there are 17 FR methods, 1 RR method, and 12 NR methods, respectively.

Table 8.1 The proposed algorithms and modern developed QA models

Category	Abbreviation	Full Name	Refs.
FR	PSNR	Peak signal-to-noise ratio	[50]
FR	SSIM	Structural similarity	[27]
FR	MS-SSIM	Structural similarity	[39]
FR	IFC	Information fidelity criterion	[40]
FR	VIF	Visual information fidelity	[41]
FR	MAD	Most apparent distortion	[11]
FR	IW-SSIM	Information weighted SSIM	[39]
FR	FSIM	Feature similarity	[42]
FR	GSIM	Gradient similarity index	[25]
FR	IGM	Internal generative mechanism	[43]
FR	GMSD	Gradient magnitude similarity deviation	[7]
FR	SPSIM	Superpixel-based similarity	[30]
FR	NQM	Noise Quality Measure	[52]
FR	MAD	Most apparent distortion	[53]
FR	DASM	Directional anisotropic structure measurement	[54]
FR	SIS	STD-based image QA method for SRIs	[21]
FR	Yan et al.	–	[33]
RR	RRIQA-SR	Reduced-reference quality assessment metric for image super-resolution	[18]
NR	BRISQUE	Blind/referenceless image spatial quality evaluator	[44]
NR	NIQE	Natural image quality evaluator	[45]
NR	NFERM	No-reference free energy-based robust metric	[46]
NR	DIIVINE	Distortion identification-based image verity and integrity evaluation	[47]
NR	IL-NIQE	Integrated-local NIQE	[48]
NR	SISBLIM	Six-step blind metric	[49]
NR	BLIINDS-II	Blind image integrity notator using DCT statistics	[51]
NR	BIQI	Blind image quality index	[55]
NR	CORNIA	Codebook representation for no-reference image assessment	[56]
NR	DESIQUE	Derivative statistics-based image quality evaluator	[57]
NR	SSEQ	Spatial-spectral entropy-based quality	[58]
NR	Zhang et al.	-	[59]

We employ four commonly used metrics, namely PLCC, SRCC, KRCC, and RMSE to compare the above-mentioned QA methods of SR images. The evaluation accuracy can be measured by PLCC and RMSE, while the monotonicity of the prediction can be found by SRCC and KRCC. A higher value of PLCC, SRCC, and KRCC, and a lower value of RMSE represent the QA method with better performance. A logistic function is utilized to become linear, and the objective assessment scores are nonlinear by PLCC, SRCC, KRCC, and RMSE. We compute the image QA scores using these four criteria by the mapping including 5 parameters as follows:

$$f(x) = \beta_1 \left(\frac{1}{2} - \frac{1}{1 + \exp^{\beta_2(a - \beta_3)}} + \beta_4 x + \beta_5 \right), \tag{8.49}$$

where $f(a)$ and a are the subjective and objective scores, separately. $\beta_{i, i=1,2,3,4,5}$ represents the fitted parameter. It is apparent that the models introduced in this chapter have achieved encouraging results. We summarize the advantages of proposed models as follows.

(1) It can be found from the comparative experiments performed on the QADS database that the SIS metric not only has the highest PLCC, SRCC, and KRCC, but also has the lowest RMSE, outperforming the compared image QA approaches. In addition, the textural or high-frequency similarity of the SIS metric has already achieved similar performance as IFC, which has the highest correlation with the perceptual scores in the context of SR evaluation.

(2) The method proposed by Zhang et al. can achieve better consistency than other methods due to the effectiveness of integrating AdaBoost Decision Tree Regression and ridge regression for evaluating the visually perceived quality of SR images.

(3) Among the 17 FR QA methods, the approach presented by Yan et al. achieves the highest SRCC, which denotes there is a high correlation between it and the HVS. Besides, the approach presented by Yan et al. is significantly faster than other methods in terms of the running time of QA methods of SR images.

(4) The experiments carried out on the basis of the energy change and texture variation ingredients demonstrate that the visual distortion in high-frequency regions is more obvious than the overall degradation in HR images. Therefore, the RRIQA-SR method that combines the two ingredients can obtain better performance in the quality prediction of HR images than other existing ones. And it is able to predict the visual perceptual quality of all SR images consistently with the subjective data.

In general, the performance of SR image QA models introduced in this chapter is much better than the traditional models. Nevertheless, much effort is needed to develop efficient and accurate QA methods of SR images that are adapted to the complicated and dynamic environment.

8.4   Conclusion

More and more image SR algorithms have been designed recently to generate images with higher spatial resolution from LR images. In order to ensure high performance in subsequent image processing, image QA for SR images is required. This chapter introduces the QA methods of SR images based on deep learning and NSS, separately. Data-driven deep learning-based methods are mainly divided into two types, namely the learning cascaded regression-based methods and the specific loss function-based approaches. They have high accuracy, efficiency, and strong robustness in evaluating the SR image perceptual quality. The introduced NSS-based SR image QA methods depend on energy change and texture variation. They combine the statistical models in both frequency and spatial domains to produce the complete distortion measure of the HR image. Although the methods introduced in this chapter perform well, there still is an effort to be made to improve the effectiveness of these approaches. In the future, it is believed that through the joint efforts of researchers, better performing SR image QA methods can be proposed.

References

1. Shen M, Wang C, Xue P et al (2010) Performance of reconstruction-based super-resolution with regularization. J Vis Commun Image Represent 21(7):640–650
2. Wang C, Ping X, Lin W (2006) Improved super-resolution reconstruction from video. IEEE Trans Circuits Syst Video Technol 16(11):1411–1422
3. Keys RG (2003) Cubic convolution interpolation for digital image processing. IEEE Trans Acoust Speech Signal Process 29:1153–1160
4. Yang C, Ma C, Yang M (2014) Single-image super-resolution: a benchmark. In: Paper presented at European conference on computer vision 2014
5. Zhang Y, Liu J, Yang W et al (2015) Image super-resolution based on structure-modulated sparse representation. IEEE Trans Image Process 24(9):2797–2810
6. Ni KS, Nguyen TQ (2007) Image superresolution using support vector regression. IEEE Trans Image Process 16(6):1596–1610
7. Duchon C (1979) Lanczos filtering in one and two dimensions. J Appl Meteorol 18(8):1016–1022
8. Wu J, Lin W, Shi G et al (2013) Reduced-reference image quality assessment with visual information fidelity. IEEE Trans Multimedia 15(7):1700–1705
9. Liu Y, Zhai G, Gu K et al (2018) Reduced-reference image quality assessment in free-energy principle and sparse representation. IEEE Trans Multimedia 20(2):379–391
10. Chandler DM, Hemami SS (2007) VSNR: a wavelet-based visual signal-to-noise ratio for natural images. IEEE Trans Image Process 16(9):2284–2298
11. Larson EC, Chandler DM (2010) Most apparent distortion: full-reference image quality assessment and the role of strategy. J Electron Imaging 19(1):011006
12. Mittal A, Soundararajan R, Bovik AC (2012) Making a completely blind image quality analyzer. IEEE Signal Process Lett 20(3):209–212
13. Lecun Y, Boser B, Denker J et al (1989) Backpropagation applied to handwritten zip code recognition. Neural Comput 1(4):541–551
14. Gao F, Wang Y, Li P et al (2017) Deepsim: deep similarity for image quality assessment. Neurocomputing 257:104–114

15. Liang Y, Wang J, Wan X et al (2016) Image quality assessment using similar scene as reference. In: Paper presented at European conference on computer vision 3–18 Nov 2016
16. Kim J, Lee S (2017) Deep learning of human visual sensitivity in image quality assessment framework. In: Paper presented at IEEE conference on computer vision and pattern recognition 1969–1977, July 2017
17. Ma C, Yang C, Yang X et al (2017) Learning a no-reference quality metric for single-image super-resolution. Comput Vis Image Underst 158:1–16
18. Fang Y, Zhang C, Yang W et al (2018) Blind visual quality assessment for image super-resolution by convolutional neural network. Multimedia Tools Appl 1–18
19. Bare B, Li K, Yan B et al (2018) A deep learning based no-reference image quality assessment model for single-image super-resolution. In: Paper presented at IEEE international conference on acoustics, speech and signal processing, pp 1223–1227, April 2018
20. Zhou F, Yao R, Zhang B et al (2018) Quality assessment database for super-resolved images: QADS. http://www.vista.ac.cn/projects/vista-h/super-resolution/
21. Zhou F, Yao R, Liu B et al (2019) Visual quality assessment for super-resolved images: database and method. IEEE Trans Image Process 28(7):3528–3541
22. Sun W, Zhou F, Liao Q (2017) MDID: a multiply distorted image database for image quality assessment. Pattern Recognit 61:153–168
23. Winkler S (2012) Analysis of public image and video databases for quality assessment. IEEE J Sel Top Signal Process 6(6):616–625
24. Lowe DG (2004) Distinctive image features from scale-invariant keypoints. Int J Comput Vis 60(2):91–110
25. Liu A, Lin W, Narwaria M (2011) Image quality assessment based on gradient similarity. IEEE Trans Image Process 21(4):1500–1512
26. Aach T, Mota C, Stuke I et al (2006) Analysis of superimposed oriented patterns. IEEE Trans Image Process 15(12):3690–3700
27. Wang Z, Bovik AC, Sheikh HR et al (2004) Image quality assessment: from error visibility to structural similarity. IEEE Trans Image Process 13(4):600–612
28. Liu A, Lin W, Narwaria M (2011) Image quality assessment based on gradient similarity. IEEE Trans Image Process 21(4):1500–1512
29. Bae SH, Kim M (2016) A novel image quality assessment with globally and locally consilient visual quality perception. IEEE Trans Image Process 25(5):2392–2406
30. Sun W, Liao Q, Xue J et al (2018) SPSIM: a superpixel-based similarity index for full-reference image quality assessment. IEEE Trans Image Process 27(9):4232–4244
31. Bare B, Li K, Yan B et al (2018) A deep learning based no-reference image quality assessment model for single-image super resolution. In: Paper presented at IEEE international conference on acoustics, speechand signal processing, pp 1223–1227, April 2018
32. Li K, Bare B, Yan B et al (2018) HNSR: highway networks based deep convolutional neural networks model for single image super resolution. In: Paper presented at IEEE international conference on acoustics, speechand signal processing, pp 1478–1482, April 2018
33. Yan B, Bare B, Ma C et al (2019) Deep objective quality assessment driven single image super-resolution. IEEE Trans Multimedia 21(11):2957–2971
34. Dong C, Loy CC, He K et al (2016) Image super-resolution using deep convolutional networks. IEEE Trans Pattern Anal Mach Intell 38(2):295–307
35. Kim J, KwonLee J, MuLee K (2016) Accurate image super-resolution using very deep convolutional networks. In: Paper presented at IEEE conference on computer vision and pattern recognition, pp 1646–1654, June 2016
36. Li SZ (2001) Markov random field modeling in image analysis. Springer
37. Liu C, Yuen J, Torralba A (2011) SIFT flow: dense correspondence across different scenes and its applications. IEEE Trans Pattern Anal Mach Intell 33(5):978–994
38. Gonzalez RC, Woods RE (2008) Digital image processing, 3rd edn. Prentice Hall, USA
39. Wang Z, Simoncelli EP, Bovik AC (2003) Multi-scale structural similarity for image quality assessment. In: Paper presented at thrity-seventh asilomar conference on signals, systems and computers, pp 1398–1402, Nov 2003

40. Sheikh HR, Bovik AC, De Veciana G (2005) An information fidelity criterion for image quality assessment using natural scene statistics. IEEE Trans Image Process 14(12):2117–2128

41. Sheikh HR, Bovik AC (2006) Image information and visual quality. IEEE Trans Image Process 15(2):430–444

42. Zhang L, Zhang L, Mou X et al (2011) FSIM: a feature similarity index for image quality assessment. IEEE Trans Image Process 20(8):2378–2386

43. Wu J, Lin W, Shi G et al (2013) Perceptual quality metric with internal generative mechanism. IEEE Trans Image Process 22(1):43–54

44. Mittal A, Moorthy AK, Bovik AC (2012) No-reference image quality assessment in the spatial domain. IEEE Trans Image Process 21(12):4695–4708

45. Mittal A, Soundararajan R, Bovik AC (2013) Making a 'completely blind' image quality analyzer. IEEE Signal Process Lett 22(3):209–212

46. Gu K, Zhai G, Yang X et al (2015) Using free energy principle for blind image quality assessment. IEEE Trans Multimedia 17(1):50–63

47. Moorthy AK, Bovik AC (2011) Blind image quality assessment: from scene statistics to perceptual quality. IEEE Trans Image Process 20(12):3350–3364

48. Zhang L, Zhang L, Bovik AC (2015) A feature-enriched completely blind image quality evaluator. IEEE Trans Image Process 24(8):2579–2591

49. Gu K, Zhai G, Yang X et al (2014) Hybrid no-reference quality metric for singly and multiply distorted images. IEEE Trans Broadcast 60(3):555–567

50. Budrikis ZL (1972) Visual fidelity criterion and modeling. In: Proceedings of the IEEE, vol 60(7), pp 771–779

51. Saad MA, Bovik AC, Charrier C (2012) Blind image quality assessment: a natural scene statistics approach in the DCT domain. IEEE Trans Image Process 21(8):3339–3352

52. Damera-Venkata N, Kite TD, Geisler WS (2000) Image quality assessment based on a degradation model. IEEE Trans Image Process 9(4):636–650

53. Larson EC, Chandler DM (2010) Most apparent distortion: fullreference image quality assessment and the role of strategy. J Electron Imaging 19(1):011006

54. Ding L, Huang H, Zang Y (2017) Image quality assessment using directional anisotropy structure measurement. IEEE Trans Image Process 26(4):1799–1809

55. Moorthy AK, Bovik AC (2010) A two-step framework for constructing blind image quality indices. IEEE Signal Process Lett 17(5):513–516

56. Ye P, Kumar J, Kang L et al (2012) Unsupervised feature learning framework for no-reference image quality assessment. In: Paper presented at the 2012 IEEE conference on computer vision and pattern recognition, pp 1098–1105, June 2012

57. Zhang Y, Chandler DM (2013) No-reference image quality assessment based on log derivative statistics of natural scenes. J Electron Imaging 22(4):451–459

58. Liu L, Liu B, Huang H et al (2014) No-reference image quality assessment based on spatial and spectral entropies. Signal Process Image Commun 29(8):856–863

59. Zhang K, Zhu D, Jing J et al (2019) Learning a cascade regression for no-reference super-resolution image quality assessment. IEEE Int Conf Image Process 2019:450–453

Printed in the United States
by Baker & Taylor Publisher Services